LIBRARY OF NEW TESTAMENT STUDIES

438

Formerly the Journal for the Study of the New Testament Supplement series

Editor
Mark Goodacre

THE CONVERSION
OF THE NATIONS IN
REVELATION

ALLAN J. McNICOL

t&t clark

Published by T&T Clark International

A Continuum imprint

The Tower Building, 11 York Road, London SE1 7NX

80 Maiden Lane, Suite 704, New York, NY 10038

www.continuumbooks.com

All scriptural quotations are from the Revised Standard Version of the Bible unless otherwise noted. New Revised Standard Version Bible, copyright 1989, Division of Christian Education of the National Council of the Churches of Christ in the United States of America. Used by permission. All rights reserved.

British Library Cataloguing-in-Publication Data

A catalogue record for this book is available from the British Library

ISBN: HB: 978-0-567-02608-8

Typeset by Free Range Book Design & Production Ltd

Printed and bound in Great Britain

To Rhys and Braeden
ὁδηγήσει αὐτοὺς ἐπὶ ζωῆς πηγὰς ὑδάτων
Revelation 7:17b

CONTENTS

Acknowledgements

This book is dedicated to my two grandchildren. An attentive reader may pause briefly and perhaps wonder at the wisdom of an author who makes a choice to dedicate a book on Revelation to his grandchildren. This choice does not emerge out of a sense of sadomasochistic pleasure that some people seem to find in hurting those who are close to them. Despite the well-travelled view that John's Apocalypse is a book of gloom and doom, I believe the opposite. I contend that, at the bottom line, it is a book of hope. The downtrodden will triumph. The people of God will inherit the new Jerusalem. The nations will freely submit to the sovereignty of the God of Abraham, Isaac, Jacob, and Jesus of Nazareth. If one accepts the contours of this hope, one will not be afraid of the future world that the future generations will inherit.

This overall project has come to fruition in the context of my work as a professor in New Testament Studies at Austin Graduate School of Theology. I am thankful to the administration and board of trustees of the school that allowed a leave of absence from teaching in the Spring/Summer of 2010 to finish this work.

Besides my family who patiently tolerate the long hours of research for my writing projects there are several who have done special duty in assisting to bring this book to fruition. Todd Hall was always helpful in library services. Renee Kennell, Mark Luckstead, and Matt Porter developed special scribal skills as they sought to put various drafts of the manuscript into some order in the word processor. William Kjellstrand met the challenge to his professional copy-editor skills in making better sense of my technical arguments. Throughout the whole enterprise Cherise Person, my assistant, has continued to be a vital conversation partner with respect to my views about the Apocalypse.

Several years ago, when I was researching books on Revelation in one of the Austin libraries, I came upon a work exceeding five hundred pages. Essentially, it summarized the monographs and commentaries on Revelation coming from one section of Germany during an earlier century. Humbled, I had a moment of doubt. In the wider scheme of things I realized more than ever before that my work on exegesis of texts and analysis of the structure of Revelation is but a small tributary that feeds into a much wider stream when it comes to study of such a significant work. It will be left to others to judge whether this contribution will be seminal. Nevertheless, keeping in mind the image of the stream, without persistent research and reflection, these small tributaries will soon dry up. Without thoughtful theological conversation, maintaining the full body of knowledge that we have earlier accumulated will be diminished. I am thankful to the editors of T & T Clark for providing the opportunity for making this body of research available to a wider readership.

Finally, I am grateful to the many students who have patiently worked and wrestled with the text of John's Apocalypse in my classes during the past several decades. Their excitement in discovering that this is a work not to be feared but actually functions for the marginalized as a word of hope continues to encourage me to work with this text. I trust some of their enthusiasm finds its way into these pages which are intended to promote future readers to persist in pursuing disciplined study of its storehouse of treasures.

Abbreviations

AB	Anchor Bible
AnBib	Analecta biblica
BBR	Bulletin for Biblical Research
BETL	Bibliotheca ephemeridum theologicarum lovaniensium
BNTC	Black's New Testament Commentaries
BZNW	Beihefte zur Zeitschrift für die neutestamentliche Wissenschaft
CBET	Contributions to Biblical Exegesis and Theology
CBQ	Catholic Biblical Quarterly
ConBNT	Coniectanea biblica: New Testament Series
ECNT	Exegetical Commentary on the New Testament
EvQ	Evangelical Quarterly
HNTC	Harper's New Testament Commentaries
JBL	Journal of Biblical Literature
JSNT	Journal for the Study of the New Testament
JSNTSup	Journal for the Study of the New Testament: Supplement Series
JSOTSup	Journal for the Study of the Old Testament: Supplement Series
MNTC	Moffatt New Testament Commentary
NCB	New Century Bible
NIBCNT	New International Bible Commentary on the New Testament
NovT	Novum Testamentum
NSBT	New Studies in Biblical Theology
NTAbh	Neutestamentliche Abhandlungen
NTS	New Testament Studies
OTL	Old Testament Library
PSBSup	Princeton Seminary Bulletin: Supplement
PTMS	Princeton Theological Monograph Series
ResQ	Restoration Quarterly
SNTSMS	Society for New Testament Studies Monograph Series
SP	Sacra pagina
TynBul	Tyndale Bulletin
WBC	Word Biblical Commentary
WUNT	Wissenchaftliche Untersuchungen zum Neuen Testament
ZNW	Zeitschrift für die neutestamentliche Wissenschaft und die Kunde der älteren Kirche

Abbreviations of Biblical Texts

LXX	*Septuagint*
MT	*Masoretic Text*
NEB	*New English Bible*
NIV	*New International Version*
NRSV	*New Revised Standard Version*
OT	*Old Testament*
RSV	*Revised Standard Version*

INTRODUCTION

Almost three decades have gone by since, somewhat reluctantly, I consented to teach a graduate-level course on the book of Revelation. At that time, as they say in Texas, 'I knew enough to be dangerous.' My work with Nils Dahl, my teacher at Yale, had led me to see the importance of Jewish Christianity as a significant factor in the complicated ethos of the social world which we call 'early Christianity'. In this connection I had already developed a deep interest in the Gospel of Matthew which was cradled within the sphere of the Jewish world of Greater Syria. Why not also focus on the last book of the present order of our English New Testament which also bears a heavy imprint of a Christian-Jewish writer?

Written to be read among a circuit of small Christian assemblies in the Roman province of Asia (Western Turkey), as with Matthew, this book reflects deep concern about the ability of the Christian community to preserve its identity. As one of any number of small sectarian groups in the vast spectrum of the Greco-Roman world, the author viewed these small assemblies of believers in Jesus as the inheritor of the legacy of Israel. This created an added burden to the usual difficulty of survival in a predominantly pagan culture. In the heart of the Diaspora it was difficult enough for traditional Jewish communities to preserve their own historic identity. Now with the mother communities of Judaism considering them illegitimate, how much more difficult could it be for the Christian assemblies of Asia to have a sense of integrity?

Given the marginal status of the churches in the wider culture of the Greco-Roman world, I was interested in determining the approach the author would take in writing a word of encouragement to these communities. Broadly speaking, I could see quickly that he viewed his community, like Judah earlier, as having entered exile. Once again, historic Jerusalem lay in ruins. The new Babylon (Rome) was in control. What was needed was the formation of strong contrast-communities of the people of God in Asia. They, like the *maśkîlîm* in Daniel, must view themselves as light-bearers of an alternative vision of hope as they sought to survive among the religious systems operative in an increasing idolatrous setting. Only then could they expect the God of Abraham and Jesus to sustain and rescue them from their perilous situation.

Nevertheless, as with the book of Daniel, a number of puzzles about the nature of the argument of John's Apocalypse continued to concern me. These centred on gaining a clear grasp as to how the seer perceived the final outcome of things. Dahl had taught me that, most likely, the Christian-Jewish author of the Apocalypse shared the seething resentment of many oppressed communities toward the established order in the empire. There was no doubt that the prophet longed for Rome's destruction and for the world to return to something that approximated the biblical story of the idyllic existence at its beginnings. But why then did John envision the welcoming of the nations (Rev. 21.24-26; 22.2) into the new Jerusalem as the high-point bringing the book to closure? Why would he be open to welcoming the very people he resented? And how would an ending like this encourage readers who were struggling with the siren calls to submit to the enticements of Babylon?

It was with these questions in mind that I picked up Richard Bauckham's then recently published book, the *Climax of Prophecy*.[1] I devoured this collection of essays along with its more readable companion piece that emerged in the same year.[2] Here I discovered a coherent answer to some of my questions. The small struggling communities that John addressed, according to Bauckham, were exhorted to view themselves as the vanguard of a martyr-church. Their role was to continue the faithful witness of Jesus. By the strength of their witness, through the power of suffering-love, the nations would finally repent and submit to the sovereignty of God. To be sure, Babylon (Rome) would collapse. But, in the end, as a result of faithful witness by the followers of Christ, the nations would be submissive to divine sovereignty.

This was bracing stuff. Initially, I became favourably disposed toward the analysis. However, as I examined more carefully the fine print (the basis within the text of Revelation itself) I became convinced that Bauckham's thesis could not be fully validated. Yet, there is immense value in being led to wrestle with issues in this area. I was alerted to the considerable emphasis that the prophet John places on the nations. I became more aware of the deep tension in the narrative between the destructive defeat of the kings of the nations in Revelation 19.15-21 and the joyous welcome extended to them in 21.24-26. What accounts for this apparent incoherency? And how does defeat followed by conversion fit into John's strikingly influential construct of the last days and the role of the nations throughout the Apocalypse?

In seeking to answer these questions the project of this book began to fall in place. What I seek to show is that the views of the prophet John on the end-times were deeply formed by reading key passages of scripture on the pilgrimage of the nations, beginning with the period of the exile. From this foundation he began to formulate a coherent eschatological vision. Living within the ethos of early Christianity, John was convinced that it was the time of the last days. The people of God were again finding themselves confronting Babylon and her client nations. It remained for Babylon to be finally defeated and the people of God vindicated in the definitive sense that the prophets anticipated. For John, the time for these hopes to be realized was at hand.

---

1   Richard Bauckham, *The Climax of Prophesy: Studies on the Book of Revelation* (Edinburgh: T&T Clark, 1993).

2   Richard Bauckham, *The Theology of the Book of Revelation* (Cambridge, New York: Cambridge University Press, 1993).

Although a prophet, John was still a realist. He could see that in the ordinary communal life of witness operative among the small assemblies scattered across the empire Babylon would not be affected. It would take divine action to bring the change he envisioned. This divine action was finding expression in the wrath of God appearing in a series of ecological catastrophes across the created order. They would culminate in a divine theophany at the end of the age. John grounded the expectation of this theophany in a creative linkage between the early Christian doctrine of the parousia and the Jewish prophetic hope for a new creation. The result is that the nations which assault the people of God will be definitively routed. Sublimated, many among them would come to acknowledge the sovereignty of the God of Abraham, Moses and Jesus.

In the course of our analysis we venture to propose a description for this view concerning the destiny of the nations. We are calling it 'eschatological covenantal restitution'. After the final theophany, the people of God who now live in covenant with him will be vindicated by citizenship in the new Jerusalem. The sublimated nations will become participants in the benefits of the new creation through a restitution of the covenant with the nations. The thrust of the book is to establish in detail this outlined proposal.

Most of our discussion will involve analysis of texts that focus on the destiny of the nations. But in the course of our argument we will also be concerned to make an additional point. In our view, the prophet John did not set out to provide a lengthy treatise on the last days. He was concerned with a more immediate problem that he experienced close at hand. Within the churches of Asia there were forces and powers which, instead of appreciating the inherent danger of the new Babylon, sought to accommodate with it. I intend to show that the carefully organized narration of the prophetic visions was to express the conviction that the new Babylon will be destroyed. Those who ally with it will not participate in the vindication of the faithful as they share the fruits of covenantal blessings in the new creation. Those excluded from these benefits may well include a number within the churches who seek to accommodate to the prevailing civic culture of Rome. Deep down Revelation taps into pastoral concerns. The contrast-society needs reinforcement. By living in anticipation of the fulfilment of these prophetic hopes that the nations will be defeated and sublimated to God, the churches can maintain their integrity. Until that day the people of God are summoned not to deviate from their original calling.

When one ventures into a serious analysis of a particular issue in the Apocalypse there is always the temptation to stray into other related areas that have their own issues and concerns. In this study I have chosen to concentrate on the important issue of the conversion of the nations in the Apocalypse. I approach this study from my area of competency in compositional criticism of New Testament texts. Thus my selection of secondary literature involves detailed interchanges with those who have given particular attention to our topic from the perspective of critical exegesis. I regret not being able to interact with the growing body of excellent studies on the use of the Old Testament in Revelation[3] and the important recent developments in narrative criticism.[4] Greater attention to these areas would, no doubt, have sharpened and perhaps corrected some of my insights.

Readers will no doubt be interested as to where I stand on various traditional issues in the study of Revelation such as authorship, place and date of composition. I will respond briefly. Throughout this work I refer to the author as the prophet John. This is how the author refers to himself (1:3, 9; 22:7, 8). He does not refer to himself as an apostle or one of the Twelve. His understanding of the Twelve as an established body seems to indicate it is a precedent inherited from the past (21:14). It would be an unusual usage if the author viewed himself as one of the Twelve. Thus, I do not believe the author is the apostle John. Rather, I consider him to be a leader of a prophetic circle in the churches of Asia. Beyond that we cannot say much more. His understanding of the church as the reconstituted Israel under the lordship of Christ as well as his methodologies in using scripture almost certainly point to a lifelong heritage within Judaism. Despite the fact that many artists have pictured John as being in lone exile on the Aegean island of Patmos (1:9), it was highly unlikely that he was an ancient Robinson Crusoe. Many years ago, as a student intern, I was assigned to do some visitation in prisons. Repeatedly, I was amazed that the prisoners knew intricate details about everything they cared to know concerning what was happening on the outside. No doubt this was true with regard to John. We know there was regular traffic between Patmos and Miletus on the mainland. John would not be alone on the island. Almost certainly, at the time, Patmos had access to a version of a place of commerce, cultic centres and expressions of civic life similar to what was operative on the mainland. There is plenty of evidence that John was well informed about the situation in the churches of Asia. Finally, the issue of dating still remains a lively point of dispute without a clear consensus. Despite renewed interest in a date of the late sixties of the first century CE I am convinced that the emergence of the sea-beast in Revelation 13:1-10 refers to the rebirth of the Flavian dynasty. I cannot accept that this book was written in the Neronian era. I am open to a date coming from the early seventies to 96 CE.

For many years my family had a house in Australia not far from where the Brisbane River flowed into a large bay. Often I would sit on the beach nearby

---

3   Steve Moyise, *The Old Testament in the Book of Revelation* JSNTSup 115 (Sheffield: Sheffield Academic Press, 1995); also Paul B. Decock, 'The Scriptures in the Book of Revelation', *Neotesamentica* 33/2 (1999), pp.373–410 is a good place to start.

4   In the past decade the literature in this area is massive. Typical works are James L. Resseguie, *The Revelation of John: A Narrative Commentary* (Grand Rapids, Michigan: Baker Academic, 2009); David L. Barr, 'The Story John Told: Reading Revelation for Its Plot', in *Reading the Book of Revelation: A Resource for Students*, ed. David L. Barr, Resources for Biblical Study 44 (Atlanta: Society of Biblical Literature, 2003), pp.11–23.

and watch the great ocean freighters leave or enter the bay and the river. I marvelled at the size of those ships and the wealth of the commerce they carried. It must have been something similar for the prophet John. On Patmos he could watch the great vessels involved in trade with Rome go back and forth toward the East. For the prophet this wealth was under the control of demonic forces. We do not know the exact circumstances of his visions. But John began to perceive that one day it would be different. Even greater wealth and power would appear. It would be under the direction of different auspices and have a different form and content. We are still dealing with the impact of that creative burst of insight.

CHAPTER 1

THE PROBLEM OF THE CONVERSION
OF NATIONS IN REVELATION

Without question one of the most interesting if not bizarre discussions of the book of Revelation was D. H. Lawrence's *Apocalypse*.[1] The book was published posthumously. Lawrence, of course, hated Christianity. As a child he was taken regularly to the coal miners' chapels. There he not only discovered that Revelation was the favourite text of the coal miners (it nourished the hope that the establishment would be overthrown) but, as a literary person, he took great pleasure in the richness and strangeness of its images. Oddly, Lawrence considered that most of its images had an origin in paganism. Lawrence reckoned that John was in the business of attempting, somewhat unsuccessfully, to tame the images. But in the end Lawrence, as so many others, comes to the conclusion that the book of Revelation is all about vengeance.

> The Lion of Judah put on a fleece: but by their bite ye shall know them. John insists on a Lamb 'as it were slain:' but we shall never see it slain, we only see it slaying mankind by the millions. Even when it comes on in a victorious bloody shirt at the end, the blood is not its own blood; it is the blood of inimical kings.

> 'Wash me in the blood of my enemies and I shall be that I am,' says John of Patmos in effect.[2]

Even in our modern era with its massive preoccupation with violence, many of the images of the Apocalypse pull us up short. Lawrence wrote from the perspective of one who had exited the Christian community. But for many within the church Christopher Rowland aptly speaks on their behalf when he asserts that Christian humanitarian instincts cause believers to be repulsed at the apparent consigning of the majority of humanity to perdition.[3]

Yet the book of Revelation is part of the canonical legacy of Christianity. So perhaps not surprisingly, taking a second look, many have found a more inclusive strand in the book. As is well known, the visionary section of Revela-

---

1   D. H. Lawrence, *Apocalypse* (New York: The Viking Press, 1955 [original edition, 1931]).

2   Lawrence, *Apocalypse*, p.95.

3   Christopher Rowland, 'The Lamb and the Beast, the Sheep and the Goats: "the Mystery of Salvation" in Revelation', *A Vision for the Church: Studies in Early Christian Ecclesiology in Honour of J. P. M. Sweet* (eds. Markus Bockmuehl and Michael B. Thompson, Edinburgh: T&T Clark, 1997), p.181.

tion ends with the majestic vision of the new Jerusalem coming down from heaven and the kings of the earth bringing their glory into it (21.9-27, esp. vv.22-26). Then comes the return of paradise with the leaves of the tree of life facilitating the healing of the nations (22.1-2). Mathias Rissi sees in these passages hints that presage ultimate blessings for the human family. These blessings will not only benefit followers of the Lamb but will incorporate into the redemption of all creation those who presently do not believe.[4]

On the face of it this seems to be a venturesome interpretation. Throughout the Apocalypse a trinity of evil powers emerges (Satan, sea beast and earth beast or false prophet). After persecuting the righteous forces of the Lamb, these forces are thrown into the lake of fire which burns forever (19.20 and 20.10). Those deluded by the trinity of evil whose names are not found in the book of life are consigned to the lake of fire (20.15). The only exception seems to be the followers of the Lamb. All this comes only *after* the collapse of Babylon (the symbol of all earthly power) and her thorough desolation (17.1–18.24, esp. 17.16). After negotiating this thicket, brave is the exegete who would find thoroughgoing universalism in the Apocalypse.

More specifically, a major conceptual difficulty for understanding Revelation arises in the occurrence of contrasting accounts of the extermination and in-gathering of the nations. There are some amazing tensions here. On the one hand there is a series of warnings directed against the nations. These warnings function as calls to repentance. They end in accounts of the nations' failure to repent, their eclipse and apparent destruction (19.11-21; 20.3, 8-9). Further-more, the nations are clearly allied with the kings of the earth (βασιλεῖς τῆς γῆς) who play an important role in the Apocalypse (1.5; 6.15; 17.2, 18; 18.3, 9-10; 19.19; 21.24). As a result of their alliance with evil forces (17.2, 17; 18.3, 9), these kings also suffer destruction (19.19-21). Yet, on the other hand, in the last reference to these kings in Revelation, they are welcomed into the new Jerusalem bringing their offerings of glory (21.24). In their coming, the kings appear to function as templates for the conversion of all peoples or nations (21.3, 24-27; 22.2-3).[5] How can these contradictory narratives highlighting

---

4   M. Rissi, *The Future of the World: An Exegetical Study of Rev. 19:11–22:15* (London: SCM, 1972 [original publication in German, 1966]), p.82.

5   John Sweet, 'Revelation', *Early Christian Thought in its Jewish Context* (eds. John Barclay and John Sweet; Cambridge: Cambridge University Press, 1996), pp.160–73, points out that con-trasting features tend to be typical of the book. In the first verse the book claims to be an apocalypse; but in the third verse it refers to itself as a prophecy (Rev. 1.1, 3). It sets before its readership in the seven churches a detailed set of predictions of what would take place in the near future (Rev. 1.1, 19; 4.1; 22.6). But as in earlier Israelite prophecy one gets the impression that much of this may not happen if the hearers take heed, repent, and order their lives in new directions. We can add to these strong expressions of both monotheism and bi-theism (God and Christ) and determinism and free will standing side by side with one another. Surely the reader can sympathize with Sweet when he states that one may begin to wonder whether for this author the law of non-contradiction has been repealed. Yet, at the same time, anyone who has spent time with the book can appreciate the careful architectonic construction of its main lines of argumentation. The question is, 'Does tension on the

both the defeat of the nations and their redemption be explained? Is this a kind of poetic licence characteristic of a visionary? Is the author of the Apocalypse operating with a hermeneutical principle that can give coherence to these apparent contradictory statements? Can they in some Hegelian-like fashion be taken up and unified in some greater synthesis?

In this chapter, in order to give focus, we will examine the works of several responsible exegetes who have given close attention to these matters. They are representative of a considerable segment of modern scholarship. These exegetes are generally favourably disposed to the perspective that the literary world of Revelation ends with the hope of the conversion of the nations, although they get there by different routes. In their own way we will see that they lead us to ponder the exegetical conundrum of both the destruction and the salvation of the nations. This is such a critical feature of the argumentation of this book and is critical for the theological importance for Christian faith. As a result of this analysis we will note that, despite considerable attention, the juxtaposition of the judgment and conversion of the nations still remains an exegetical and theological issue to be resolved for interpreters of the book. We will conclude this chapter with a précis of our proposal which intends to argue that John's discussion of the destiny of the nations is coherent in light of his total eschatological vision of the coming of the Kingdom of God in its fullness.

J. P. M. Sweet on the Conversion of the Nations

John Sweet was well aware of the problem of thematic tensions in the Apocalypse.[6] He opines that for a western mind trained in rational and synthetic thinking the ingathering of the nations and their kings after their destruction is impossible.[7]

An alternate way to address this question is to consider that John's rhetoric is symbolic and doxological. It is more exhortation than prediction.[8] John is

---

destiny of the nations function as an essential part of the book's architectonic structure or is it just another one of its odd contrasting literary features?'

6   As well as the article cited in footnote 5, Sweet has two other critical studies that impinge on this issue. J. P. M. Sweet, *Revelation: Westminster Commentaries* (Philadelphia: Westminster Press, 1979); also *idem* the critical article 'Maintaining the Testimony of Jesus: the Suffering of Christians in the Revelation of John', in *Suffering and Martyrdom in the New Testament: Studies Presented to G. M. Styler by the Cambridge New Testament Seminar*, eds. William Horbury and Brian McNeil (Cambridge: Cambridge University Press, 1981), pp.101–17.

7   Sweet, 'Maintaining the Testimony', pp.110–11.

8   Sweet, *Revelation*, pp. 1–21; *idem*, 'Revelation', p.168. As an example, we read in Rev. 8.7 that 'all green grass was burnt up'. Yet, shortly after in the same sequence of trumpet visions we read of the locusts being told 'not to harm the grass of the earth' (Rev. 9.4). Apparently each vision has its own logic and rationale and does not always directly interconnect with other visions in a temporal or historical sequence.

painting a picture of the story of salvation with very broad strokes. Specifically he is concerned with making clear the impact of the testimony of the sufferings and victory of Jesus continuing to be manifested in the life of Christians. Ultimately this concludes with the defeat of their enemies. Regularly, this discourse is presented in symbols and images rather than in logical discourse.

According to Sweet, the confidence in victory for the Lamb and his martyred followers on the basis of the power of their faithful witness in suffering has often found expression in at least two mistaken views. In his 1981 article he notes, first, there is the Maccabean or punitive, destructive view.[9] Based on such passages as 2 Maccabees 7.9-13, 31-38; 4 Maccabees 6.27-29; and 17.20-22 this view affirms with strong assurance that the tables will be turned against the persecuted ones' enemies. God's glory will not only be shown by the merciful vindication of his righteous people, but by the harsh and final punishment of the persecutors. Satisfaction is established when justice is done. To be sure, elements of this perspective emerge in Revelation. There is a kind of vicious pleasure in the destruction of the harlot (Babylon) and her allies in Revelation 17–18 (cf. 14.9-11). This comes to light in the grisly banquet where the animals dine on the carcasses of the forces arraigned against the Lamb (19.17-18). But this is penultimate. The Maccabean view cannot do justice to anything like the conversion of the nations that emerges at the end of the book of Revelation. There is far more here than merely the expression of an opinion that God's enemies get their just deserts and their punishment will be followed by the restoration of a moral universe. The glories of the end-time seem to be of a different magnitude than the punishment of the wicked. Getting even is not a central theme of Revelation.

This brings Sweet to the second mistaken view. This centres on the claim that the Lamb and his followers are ultimately victorious because of the *moral* effect of their suffering as a testimony for the truth. Seeing the faithful witness of the martyrs, not only in word but in the confession of their lives, leads the nations to repent and embrace their testimony. But as powerful an image as that may be, Sweet will have none of it. Theologically this is no more than a pale imitation of the moral view of the atonement. More importantly, this seems to be in conflict with the thrust of the text. In Revelation chapters 11–16 the immediate effect of the suffering and martyrdom of the faithful is to increase the intensity of the opposition of the opponents of the Lamb.[10] To be sure, Sweet would not deny that the story of the cross has power. Proclamation of this story consistently results in a number of conversions to the way of the Lamb. But as far as the text of the Apocalypse is concerned these victories are only partial and proleptic.[11] In Revelation while the proclamation of the gospel is going on, most of fallen creation is

---

9   Sweet, 'Maintaining the Testimony', p.109; *idem*, 'Revelation', pp.169–71, 'Where Scripture is ambivalent, for example over the extermination of enemies, we must resist the temptation to go for one option [doxological over rational discursive thinking] instead of holding both in tension.'
10   Sweet, 'Maintaining the Testimony', pp.108, 114, 116.
11   Sweet, 'Maintaining the Testimony', p.116.

either indifferent or hostile to it. Is there any reason to believe that it will be ever any different no matter how many times the story is told?[12]

Nevertheless, the view that the suffering of the righteous has had a moral effect on opponents who are carrying out the persecution remains a popular option in both exegetical and theological circles.[13] It has been argued that in a key passage (11.3-13) the survivors of the earthquake which destroys the city, and who are ἔμφοβοι 'fearful' giving glory to God, were changed because of the power of suffering love exhibited in the martyrdom of the two witnesses.[14] But that is most unlikely. A plain reading of the text indicates that the death of the witnesses invokes mirth and glee among the nations (11.9-10). It is only *after* the exaltation of the witnesses and an earthquake that the survivors ('the rest' οἱ λοιποί), out of fear and awe, give glory to God. Thus it is hardly likely that the prophetic testimony of the martyrdom of the two witnesses, powerful as it may be, in itself is a catalyst for repentance.

Having disposed of these two misunderstandings of the text, Sweet falls back for his interpretation on a version of the *doxological* rhetoric of John for the explanation for the appearance of both the punishment and conversion of the nations.[15] For Sweet the underlying story line of Revelation is the problem of idolatry.[16] This is at the heart of the veneration of the evil trinity by the world. And it clearly lies behind many of the seductions to apostasy experienced by the believers in the seven churches. According to Sweet this idolatry is kept solidly in place by sheer power – albeit Satanic power. Ultimately it will be defeated. But this will be neither by moral effect nor human suffering love; only by a greater power. That greater power was expressed in the terrible cost of the death of the Son of God done out of divine love.

> The serpent's head is crushed not by divine *fiat* but by divine presence, and this presence conquers not by superhuman power and wisdom but by fidelity to itself, at the cost of itself. It is this incalculable cost to God, and to those who take his part, that the sacrifice story conveys.[17]

Sweet quotes T. S. Eliot:

> The wounded surgeon plies the steel
> That questions the distempered part;
> Beneath the bleeding hands we feel
> The sharp compassion of the healer's art...[18]

---

12   'Witness to the truth could go on forever and ever, attracting some and repelling others', Sweet, 'Maintaining the Testimony', p.116.

13   See below, for example, a version of this in the works of Richard Bauckham.

14   Despite the fact that in the NT ἔμφοβοι with a form of γίνομαι almost always means frightened in a sense of expression of terror – not repentance.

15   Sweet, 'Revelation', p.171.

16   Sweet, 'Maintaining the Testimony', p.115.

17   Sweet, 'Maintaining the Testimony', p.117.

18   Sweet, 'Maintaining the Testimony', p.117. The quote is from T. S. Eliot's *Four Quartets*, East Coker IV.

Thus the claim is that the testimony of Jesus, concretized first in the incarnation and his passion and then in his followers, will finally win out at the end of the day over evil. The truth of reality is that the sheer power of a (loving) God who invests his being in this creation will prove stronger than evil. And in this meta-story the juxtaposition of the contrasting features of the defeat of the nations and their conversion is taken up in a greater truth: the victory of truth over the lie of idolatry.

Despite the attractiveness of the view that, in the nature of things, truth defeats the lie, questions remain. Is Revelation essentially a great allegory on the defeat of deception by hard truth? What is the role of God's working in history in the thinly veiled attack on the spiritual destructiveness of the Roman imperial powers housed under the pseudonym of Babylon? If Revelation is primarily doxological, why does John go into lengthy detail to describe the rise and fall of contemporary Rome, often putting it in the context of 'what must soon take place?' Why is there so much eschatological fervor? And is it a point of encouragement to people who are about to face tribulation (6.10) only to be told that after much more suffering, in the total outcome of some great scheme of the course of human affairs, a mysterious divine power will vindicate their cause.

What is critical is the need to come to some resolution about the nature of the rhetoric of Revelation. Is it fair to read the Apocalypse as a work that presumes to house certain eschatological events that will unfold in history? For example, does the vision of Revelation 19.11-16 presume an actual parousia? And does Revelation 20.11-15, rich and filled with suggestive images as it may be, allude to an actual Last Judgment for evil doers, which is presumed to follow the parousia? Or are these verses proairetic? That is, we are invited to view Revelation 19 and 20 in the same way as we watch certain Hollywood movies where the emphasis is on action, not on coherence of plot. All sorts of inexplicable things happen. But at the end a number of enigmas remain unresolved.

Procedurally, it is our presupposition that the former of these two herme-neutical outcomes ought to be pursued first. Although Revelation is highly symbolic, the coin of its realm is traditional Christian-Jewish images of the end-times. Even though the order is not always consistent, certain things are going to happen. Going down this road means that the obvious contextual pos-sibilities on the destiny of the nations which operate internally within the book ought to be explored first to determine whether they have inner consistency and fit into a plausible scenario of an early Christian view of the end-times. In my view, Sweet did not pursue fully these possibilities. Only if this analysis proves unfruitful will it be necessary to explore the possibility that a different, more doxological form of rhetoric is at work.

It is generally accepted that Revelation is a very sophisticated literary compo-sition. It is the work of a very thoughtful author. Our expectation is that such an author would give attention to major themes and not allow them to dangle as inner contradictions in his literary magnum opus. Thus a thorough exegetical study on the overall function of the role of nations in the Apocalypse is needed.

As we pursue this study in the several chapters which follow, we will be called to go into more exegetical detail than that with which Sweet leaves us at the end of his very evocative essays.

Sweet hints that the diverse strands of both the punishment and conversion of the nations may be part of a wider story of the Bible. He never fully develops this theme.[19] This is a pity. Because just as Revelation attempts to narrate the completion of 'incomplete things' found in Ezekiel and Daniel, or some of the other prophets, so the author of the Apocalypse may view himself as creating a theological construct where the earlier accounts in scripture of the punishment and ingathering of the nations come to a final resolution. This intertextual usage often draws upon detailed scenarios in the prophets about the last days. If Revelation is attempting to accomplish something like this, it means that the book makes more than a generic claim that the truth of God will defeat idolatry. But this needs to be developed more.

Richard Bauckham on the Conversion of the Nations

No one has treated the issue of the destiny of the nations in Revelation more thoroughly than Richard Bauckham. His essay of about one hundred pages incorporated into a wider monograph represents a milestone on this subject. It is a masterful *tour de force* for which all commentators in the area have deep admiration.[20] We will interact critically with Bauckham's exegesis throughout this monograph since Bauckham's views can only be viewed fairly after an assessment of certain other interpretive presuppositions and exegetical decisions are made about the overall argument of the Apocalypse of John.

The idea is foundational for Bauckham that Revelation 1.1 declares itself to be an apocalypse (revelation) that has material content. Revelation's 'theme is the transfer of the sovereignty of the whole world to God from the dragon and the beast, who presently dominate it. It is the God of Abraham and Jesus whose universal kingdom is to come on earth.'[21] Central to this transfer of power is the appearance of the scroll in chapters 5 and 10, which Bauckham claims

19   Sweet, 'Revelation', p.169. For example, he notes that the story of the flood in Genesis certainly features an annihilation of the nations. And yet there remains a strand of grace in the rescue of Noah and the subsequent covenants with his descendants. Is this the appropriate analogy to facilitate understanding of Revelation's treatment of the fate of the nations? Sweet does refer to conversion of the nations as a minority strand that surfaces from time to time in the OT in such texts as Jonah 4.11; Isaiah 42.6; 49.6, 60.3; also Psalms 47, 67, 86, and 87. But he claims this must be balanced off against Isaiah 63.1-6.

20   Richard Bauckham, *The Climax of Prophecy: Studies on the Book of Revelation* (Edinburgh: T&T Clark, 1993) pp.238-337; *idem, The Theology of the Book of Revelation* (Cambridge: Cambridge University Press, 1993) pp.84-107. The latter summarizes and attempts to give theological coherence to the more detailed work of the former volume.

21   Bauckham, *Climax of Prophecy*, p.242.

contains the secret purposes (i.e. the revelation) of how the establishment of God's kingdom will take place.

Already in Revelation 1.1-2, Bauckham argues, a chain is established where we learn that the revelation will follow a path from God to Jesus Christ, then to John via the angel, and finally to his servants (believers in the churches). In 5.1 the Lamb (Jesus) takes the scroll from the right hand of God. With the opening of the seven seals and the blasts of the seven trumpets a series of anticipations of the central message of the scroll begin to appear. Two of these anticipations are worthy of mention. First, in such passages as 7.1-3 and 9.4-5 the followers of the Lamb are sealed against ultimate destruction. Although they will undergo a spiritual journey that may end in martyrdom they will be vindicated at the Last Judgment.[22] Second, a series of woes are let loose on the created order to encourage people of the empire to renounce their idolatry and come to repentance. The latter process is an abject failure (9.20-21).[23] Mere judgments alone will not produce repentance. Finally, in chapter 10 the scroll (according to Bauckham, the same as the one in 5.1) reappears. The angel gives it to John. After internalizing its message by consuming it, John is ready to set forth its claim. Then in 10.11 he begins to utter its message.[24]

A précis of the revelation of Revelation is found in Revelation 11.1-13 in the images of the measuring of the sanctuary (11.1-2) and the two witnesses (11.3-13). It consists of bringing to light the secret about the process for the establishment of the kingdom. God's kingdom already appears in an anticipatory form with the exaltation of the Lamb and the institution of the Church. Bauckham argues that the full emergence of the kingdom will be neither by a dramatic rescue of the Lamb snatching his followers from Satan and his allies nor through a crushing judgment of the rebellious peoples of the earth. Rather it will emerge with the eventual repentance of the nations whose obedience to the Lamb is crucial to the triumph of the kingdom.[25] The nations are to be led to repentance in two stages: first through the sacrificial death of the Lamb (5.6) and second through the divine power of that sacrifice rendered through faithful prophetic proclamation and martyrdom on the part of the followers of the Lamb. Formally this occurs under the transparency of the work of the Two Witnesses (11.3-13). Bauckham makes much out of the fact that the Two Witnesses have the characteristics of Moses and Elijah.[26] By this he means that the Two Witnesses embody the truth of earlier prophetic proclamation among the people of God. But, if we follow the flow of the narrative, prophetic witness – always characterized by judgment in and of itself – never brings about

---

22   Bauckham, *Theology of Revelation*, p.79.

23   Bauckham, *Climax of Prophecy*, p.259.

24   Bauckham, *Climax of Prophecy*, pp.265–6.

25   Bauckham, *Climax of Prophecy*, p.258.

26   Bauckham, *Climax of Prophecy*, pp.279–80. In Jewish tradition Elijah does not die and Moses' body is taken up into heaven. Thus, interestingly enough, in contrast to the message of Revelation, Moses and Elijah are as far away from martyrdom as any prophetic figure can be.

the conversion of the nations. In the prophetic witness of the church, words of judgment alone will fail to produce repentance (cf. 9.20-21). Repentance, putatively, comes after faithful witness (11.13).[27] Thus the process for drawing the nations' allegiance away from the demonic powers is a combination of prophetic proclamation reinforced by committed servant life that culminates in martyrdom. The kingdom will not come through the slaughter of the enemies of God (as with Elijah at Mount Carmel) but by the power of embodying the testimony of Jesus in not resisting being slaughtered by the enemies. The revelation of Revelation is that the power of the testimony to the Lamb unto martyrdom, incarnated in his followers, is the instrument for the conversion of the nations of the world.[28]

This set of presuppositions thus provides the matrix for Bauckham's inter-pretation of the last half of the book. In Revelation 12.1–14.5 the followers of the Lamb engage fully the forces of the dragon. For Bauckham this is not a chapter in church history (the confrontation of the church with Rome in the early centuries) but is parabolic. The 144,000 in Revelation 14.1-5, as the Lamb, triumph by means of their sacrificial death.[29] As the tide turns and the trinity of evil begins to self-destruct indicators of the conversion of the nations begin to become stronger. The vision of the grain harvest (14.14-16) is an intima-tion of the coming ingathering of converted nations. The Song of Moses and the Lamb is reinterpreted as a new exodus after a witness that culminates with martyrdom. It becomes a paean of praise wherein the nations (anticipating the eschaton) now give praise to the Lamb (15.2-4).[30] The victory of the martyrs is not their own deliverance but consists of an 'effect on the nations in bringing them to worship God'.[31] In the end the trinity of evil and other followers of the dragon are punished in universal judgment.[32] But final judgment is only one image of the end. It does not have to be 'logically compatible' to say that side-by-side with the image of universal judgment will also be the universal worship of God. This comes with the establishment of the new Jerusalem and the conversion of the nations already anticipated in Isaiah 60.3, 5, 11 (cf. Rev. 21.1–22.5).

At the outset one may be pardoned for standing in awe at the sheer audacity of the exegetical artifact that Bauckham has attributed to the prophet John. The most far-reaching of the expectations of Israel's prophets for the recognition of

27   Bauckham, *Theology of Revelation*, p.84.

28   Bauckham, *Climax of Prophecy*, p.230.

29   Bauckham, *Climax of Prophecy*, p.230.

30   Bauckham, *Climax of Prophecy*, pp.296–307.

31   Bauckham, *Climax of Prophecy*, p.306, also *Theology of Revelation*, p.104, 'John takes up the most universalistic form of the hope of the Old Testament. It will not be Israel alone that will be God's people with whom he dwells. It will not even be the eschatological Israel, redeemed from every people. Rather, as a result of the witness of the special people, all the peoples will be God's peoples (21.24-26).

32   Bauckham, *Climax of Prophecy*, p.309.

Yahweh's glory by the nations are brought to fulfilment through the sacrificial martyrdom of the followers of the Lamb.

But questions may be asked. Is this reading of the *Apocalypse* plausible either exegetically or theologically? We will only attempt to stake out cursorily a response. As noted, more detailed interaction with Bauckham will come throughout the book.

First, there is the matter of exegesis. Central to Bauckham's analysis of Revelation is his view that the faithful witness and martyrdom of the followers of the Lamb will be the instrument that will bring about the conversion of the nations. Upon the arrival of the new Jerusalem after his parousia, Christ will receive the glory and honour of the converted nations. They will have unhindered access to the holy city (21.24-27; 22.2-3). There are four key texts that appear to function as anticipatory of this outcome. They are Revelation 1.7, 11.13, 14.14-16, and 15.2-4.

Yet in all four instances, although more detailed analysis will have to wait for now, such conclusions are open to dispute. First, with respect to the coming of Christ in Revelation 1.7, Bauckham argues for a controversial reading. He understands the text to say that Christ's coming will not be to punish the nations but to receive 'repentant acknowledgment of God's rule over them'.[33] Yet an alternative reading such as the NEB that has the nations at this time 'lament in remorse' seems to be equally plausible as a plain reading of the text.[34] Second, we have already noted that an ordinary reading of Revelation 11.13 would lead the reader to conclude that the offering of glory to God by the people in the city was precipitated by plain old fear. The sources of this fear were the exaltation of the witnesses to heaven after their death, followed by an earthquake, not the faithful suffering witness unto death by believers. Short-lived repentance is a characteristic of some opponents in prophetic books (e.g. the veneration of Yahweh by the king of Babylon after some of the feats of Daniel). After the crisis is over, the Gentiles go back to their old ways. The conduct of the nations under the power of a Satanic triad in Revelation 12–13 hardly seems to intimate that they respected the witness of the martyrs. In similar fashion Revelation 14.14-16 can easily be viewed as an account of judgment in tandem with the following vintage scene of the winepress of wrath in Rev. 14.17-20, not as the Son of Man reaping the harvest of his kingdom won from the dominion of the beast.[35] And an ordinary reading of Revelation 15.2-4 leads one to conclude that what is being celebrated is a fairly standard articulation of God's eschatological victory over the nations based on the model of the Exodus. Thus Bauckham's claim that the burden of these texts articulates that the suffering witness of the church results in the conversion of the nations is open to considerable question. In each instance, Bauckham's interpretation of a conversion of the

33   Bauckham, *Climax of Prophecy*, p.322.
34   Cf. Matt 24.30. Note Robert H. Mounce, *The Book of Revelation* (revised edition), NIBCNT (Grand Rapids, Michigan: Eerdmans, 1998), p.51.
35   Bauckham, *Climax of Prophecy*, p.295.

nations through the suffering witness of the church appears to be read into the text. Revelation 11–19 is about many things. But a great success in conversions does not seem to be one of them.

Second, there still remains the wider theological problem as to the plausibility for either John or his readers to view the submissive sacrifice of the martyrs as the divine strategy that leads to conversion of the nations. The slaughter of the Lamb and the witness of the primitive church (already in the past) had so little effect on their rebellious world. Here we are left with Sweet's observation that this kind of witness may well go on forever 'attracting some and repelling others!' Given the pathos of the death and resurrection of the Son of God, would continued witness by the followers of the Lamb make such a qualitative difference to a rebellious world? In recent decades millions in Africa and China, often in staggering anonymity, have died simply because of adherence to the name of Christ. What difference has this made in the total order of things? The visions of the seals, trumpets and bowls of wrath indicate that John was capable of viewing this in a similar light. To sum up, one may well ask whether Bauckham's proposal really accounts for the conversion of the nations. Indeed the text seems to go out of its way to say just the opposite. The idolatrous nations refuse to repent (9.20-21; 16.9, 11, 21). Thus, with this proposal we seem to be no closer to solving the problem of the apparent inner contradiction of the nations and their kings being punished absolutely in Revelation 19 yet being full participants in the new Jerusalem in chapter 21.

In his writings, Bauckham eschews a thoroughgoing universalism.[36] Using the proclamation of Revelation 14.6-11 as a call to choose between the destiny of Babylon and the new Jerusalem, Bauckham claims that the text balances not on the reality of actual descriptions of the respective responses, including approximate numbers, but on the priority of the decision of whom to follow.[37] This begs the question of how one arrives at a reading that the nations, now so firmly under the spell of idolatrous evil, will ultimately turn and be set free by the suffering testimony of the church. And what are the ultimate consequences for all those who submitted to Babylon? This is not meant to be over-critical of Bauckham for his insightful work. It is only to point out that questions remain. These two recent works featuring discussion on the conversion of the nations, which we have noted (Sweet and Bauckham), thus leave us with the impression that the Apocalypse of John is still an enigma with regard to its teachings about the course and destiny of the nations. Under the template of the destiny of the nations and their kings we find both expressions of their destruction and full acceptance into the new Jerusalem. Which is it to be? How is all this supposed to unfold?

Sweet and Bauckham have left some with the impression of veering toward a version of universalism. But, in my reading, this seems to go a little too far.

36   Bauckham, *Theology of Revelation*, pp.102–103.
37   Bauckham, *Theology of Revelation*, pp.102–103.

Others are more emphatic in their tilt toward universalism.[38] This seems to be a major thrust in much recent exegesis. But do such exegetical moves do justice to the thrust of the entire argument of the book?

Other Recent Studies

In this chapter we have focused upon the writings of J. P. M. Sweet and Richard Bauckham as significant representatives of those who recently wrestled creatively with the function of the Conversion of the Nations in Revelation. Both scholars highlight the tension between texts on the destruction of the nations and their salvation. As a way of resolving the tension, both view it as inherently rhetorical. Sweet viewed the function of the destruction/salvation texts as a vision of 'two opposing courses' from which the reader is invited to choose.[39] These texts are not meant to be a panorama of the actual future course of history, but an exhortation to the original readers in the seven churches to ponder the consequences of compromises in their allegiance to the Lamb. Those who cast their lot with the Roman imperial powers will suffer destruction. Those who live in a way congruent with the testimony of Jesus will ultimately emerge as the winners. This applies not only to the church but is applicable to the nations. Bauckham adopts a similar posture toward this tension between the texts on destruction and salvation. He also does not view Revelation as a predictive description of future events. Nevertheless, because of his interpretation that the open scroll (10.8) reveals ultimately the process of how the suffering witness of the church will lead to the conversion of the nations, priority in outcome is given to such texts as Revelation 21.24-26 and 22.2. A tone of cautious universalism intrudes. God will be 'all in all' through the recognition of his glory by the nations. For Bauckham, the question is not so much the outcome as it is his unique interpretation of what leads to the outcome.

---

38   Walter E. Pilgrim, 'Universalism in the Apocalypse', *Word & World* 9/3 (1989), pp.235–43. Also, W. J. Harrington, *Revelation*, Sacra Pagina 16 (Collegeville, Minn.: Liturgical Press, 1993), pp. 229–35; *ibid.*, 'Positive Eschaton Only: Revelation and Universal Salvation', *Proceedings of the Irish Biblical Association* 15, pp.42–59; Vernard Eller, 'How the Kings of the Earth Land in the new Jerusalem, "The World" in the Book of Revelation', *Katallagete* 5 (Summer, 1975), pp.21–7; M. Eugene Boring, 'Revelation 19–21: End Without Closure', *PSB* Sup 3 (1994), pp.56–84; *idem*, *Revelation: Interpretation Commentary Series* (Louisville: John Knox Press, 1989), pp.226–31. In these studies there is a constant emphasis on the tensions of the text between total destruction of the enemies and full vindication of the faithful. This is often interpreted as giving permission that allows later interpreters to open up new possibilities of meaning that usually drift towards a version of universalism.

39   As noted by David Mathewson, *A New Heaven and New Earth: The Meaning and Function of the Old Testament in Revelation 21:1–22:5*, JSNTSup 238 (London: Sheffield Academic Press, 2003), p.172. Also, *idem*, 'The Destiny of the Nations in Revelation 21:1–22:5: A Reconsideration', *TynBul* 53.1 (2002), pp.121–42.

Since the late twentieth century several major studies have given special attention to this issue. Two authors, David Mathewson[40] and Ronald Herms,[41] are important because their monographs address directly this issue. Mathewson follows in the stream of Sweet and Bauckham. He stresses that the tension in the fate of the nations between destruction and salvation is mainly rhetorical.[42] Mathewson is concerned to view this tension as being held by John in a delicate balance. He conveniently summarises his conclusions:

> I would suggest that the effect of this tension in John's vision is primarily rhetorical: by juxta-posing pictures of absolute judgment and salvation the writer contrasts the opposing options that confront the nations–judgment and destruction for those who persist in rebellion, and salvation and a share in the new Jerusalem for those who repent and give glory. However, the author depicts the end without quantifying the outcome. Rhetorically, then, the tension functions in a hortatory manner.[43]

Given the fact that these visions function rhetorically rather than as an actual description of how the end-time events may actually take place, Mathewson considers that Bauckham goes too far in giving priority to the concluding narrative of the salvation of the nations over their judgment.[44] This seems to be the major thrust of his critique. The rhetoric of destruction/salvation needs to be kept in a more appropriate balance.

In many ways Ronald Herms' project overlaps with my own. In his opening page Herms states deliciously an interesting question.

> Will the full realization of God's kingdom be characterized by the destruction of all earth's peoples, save the faithful, or will the nations finally acknowledge God as Creator and King in a comprehensive moment of repentance and conversion?[45]

Herms examines carefully comparative Jewish Apocalypses of roughly the same era as Revelation. He notes saliently that these apocalypses have a wide range of perspectives on the fate of the nations.[46] Several interesting texts are evaluated, including 1 Enoch 90.16-38 which incorporates an account of both the destruc-tion of the nations and final restoration that places them in a position of divine acceptance.[47]

---

40   The works of Mathewson are noted above in footnote 39.

41   Ronald Herms, *An Apocalypse for the Church and for the World: The Narrative Function of Universal Language in the Book of Revelation*, BZNW 143 (Berlin: de Gruyter, 2006).

42   Mathewson, *A New Heaven and a New Earth*, p.174.

43   Mathewson, *A New Heaven and a New Earth*, pp.174–5.

44   Mathewson, *A New Heaven and a New Earth*, p.175.

45   Herms, *An Apocalypse for the Church*, p.1.

46   Herms, *An Apocalypse for the Church*, pp.50–137.

47   Herms, *An Apocalypse for the Church*, pp.130–35.

After a discussion of the appropriate texts in Revelation, often in close conversation with Richard Bauckham, Herms comes to his conclusion:

...this tension in Revelation is less real than apparent.[48]

Of course, Herms is referring to the tension between the destruction of the nations and their conversion. He seems to mean that Revelation follows the general pattern of the treatment of the nations he found in apocalyptic literature of the same era as Revelation. He notes there is a tendency in this literature to universalize. But its essential function is to promote a form of rhetoric serving as a vehicle to vindicate the faithful by suggesting that in a future eschatological time the current enemies of Yahweh will come to recognize the sovereignty of the messianic king and his kingdom.[49] Whatever this may mean, Herms does not consider that the prophet John is arguing for universal destruction or salvation. That is simply not the nature of the narrative. Rather it is rhetorical and hortatory. It is not a purported account of objective reality. As a source of encouragement it represents a call to its hearers to choose a particular course of action because its eventual destination will be that of the winners. What is critical is that the readers choose to take careful note of the images that suggest the consequences of pursuing different routes in their ultimate allegiances.

Summary and Précis of our Argument

Elizabeth Schüssler Fiorenza has come up with an insightful image to describe the compositional strategy of the author of Revelation. Referring to the climactic end-time events of the book, she states that they are inserted like 'pieces of mosaic stones arranged in a certain design'.[50] Without question, the entire action of the book culminates in a total rout and eventual destruction of the forces of Satan. This is followed by vindication of the people of the Kingdom of God and their full recognition by the nations. What is difficult to determine is the principle that the arranger of the mosaic utilizes to construct the final artifact. Clearly the author is working within the framework of early Christian eschatology, which sits within the wider framework of Jewish apocalyptic discourse, but it is unclear why some aspects of it play a major role while others are left out.[51] She takes a strong position that the author of the Apocalypse is not intent on narrating an unfolding series of sequential historical events that

48   Herms, *An Apocalypse for the Church*, p.257.
49   Herms, *An Apocalypse for the Church*, p.260.
50   Elizabeth Schüssler Fiorenza, *The Book of Revelation: Justice and Judgment* (Philadelphia: Fortress, 1985), p.47.
51   For example, although the parousia of Christ was a capstone of early Christian eschatology it is only echoed directly in 1.7 and the concluding chapters of the book (19.11-16).

supposedly will take place in keeping with a pre-determined end-time plan.[52] Rather, the focus is elsewhere. I propose that it is anchored in John's comprehensive vision of the fortunes and destiny of the Kingdom of God.

It is relatively clear that for John the kingdom was established with the redemptive death and exaltation of Christ (1.5-6; 5.9-10). But even as Christ attained his victory only after suffering and horrors, so the people of the kingdom must undergo a similar journey. Understandably they ask, 'How long?' (6.9-11); and ultimately they wish to know 'What is the outcome?' The description of that struggle and outcome constitutes the basic theme of the major second vision of the book (4.1–22.9). A major feature of this struggle is the matter of allegiances of the nations. For John of Patmos at first they enter into disastrous alliances with the dragon and allied evil forces. But a time is coming when these nations will acknowledge the universal lordship of the Lamb (21.3, 24-26; 22.5). This still leaves us with major questions. If it is not by some pre-determined time in history, what initiates the change in the allegiance of the nations? We see the final outcome in the arrival of the new Jerusalem where that change is presupposed. But what was the process of interpretation and theological thinking that led John to this conclusion? No consensus has emerged among modern commentators.

I intend to argue that John's narrative discourse on the end-times goes beyond the purposes of offering, rhetorically, a set of options for future moral and religious conduct. He is speaking about an actual Day of the Lord which, long delayed, he believes will take place. Through careful compositional analysis of the structuring of the discourse in conjunction with the use of scripture, we believe that the discrimen of John's theological argumentation emerges. It is grounded in prophetic models of what will take place in the last days. These models, found in the Psalms and major prophets, moulded and nourished John to seek fervently their fulfilment. On the basis of the Christ-event, this expectation was deepened. The language has been reformulated. Yet the basic patterns of earlier eschatological thinking remain in place.

With respect to the nations the prophets speak about their assembling against the holy city and the Lord's anointed. But they are defeated by the Lord (the Divine Warrior) in a theophanic confrontation. The survivors of this defeat, joined by the purged faithful people of Judah, return to renewed Zion to acknowledge and serve the God of Israel. This is the underlying archetype of John's eschatological thinking. It is precisely the eschatological model for the description for what the prophet argues is about to take place in the Apocalypse. I have created the term 'eschatological covenantal restitution' to describe the pattern.

As a means of fortifying and encouraging the faithful in the small Christian assemblies in the Roman province of Asia, John presents what he calls an ἀποκάλυψις 'revelation' of what must take place (1.1). In true esoteric fashion he represents himself as being given a preliminary glimpse of these realities

---

52 Fiorenza, *Justice and Judgment*, pp.47, 49.

which are already established in the heavenly places. Our focus is in determining what he has to say about the destiny of the nations. The whole pattern of argumentation is not merely rhetorical but pastoral in scope. He argues that the ultimate defeat and conversion of the nations will take place in the context of the awesome presence of the Divine Warrior. The reader is left to ponder the implications with respect to the manner of life of the people in the churches? We will explore these matters as the monograph unfolds.

Procedurally, in the next chapter, we will move directly into the text and examine carefully what it has to say about the course and destiny of the nations before the culminating events of the Day of the Lord. This will set the scene for additional discussion about their ultimate destiny.

Some years ago Nils Dahl noted that John's work may not only be motivated by a plea to underwrite the vindication of the followers of the Lamb but may also reflect 'the hatred latent in many minority groups in the empire; in their attitudes to Rome'.[53] This insight from social-history needs to be probed. Additional examinations of the social world in which the Apocalypse emerged are providing additional clues that need to be pursued in teasing out why the destiny of the nations is important for the Apocalypse. In other words D. H. Lawrence's chapel preachers who railed against the establishment did have precursors in Early Christianity. They may not have been that far from some of the motivations propelling the production of this prophecy and closer to the truth of the matter than Lawrence. The issue of the social world of the Apocalypse is now beginning to receive well-deserved discussion.[54] Revelation may be truly the most monumental first-century minority report on the worth of the Roman Empire. These insights and others that will emerge in our analysis of key texts on the nations in the Apocalypse will now be taken up for consideration.

---

53   Nils A. Dahl, 'Nations in the New Testament', in *New Testament Christianity for Africa and the World: Essays in Honor of Harry Sawyerr* (eds. M. Glaswell and F. Fasholé-Luke, London: SPCK, 1979), p.68.
54   A good example of this voluminous discussion is the work of Leonard L. Thompson, *The Book of Revelation: Apocalypse and Empire* (New York: Oxford University Press, 1990).

CHAPTER 2

THE ROLE OF THE NATIONS IN REVELATION

In the previous chapter we were confronted with contradictory evidence about the destiny of the nations. In Revelation 19.11-21 the Lamb and his armies confront the kings who have power over the nations. The Lamb defeats them decisively. Their bodies are strewn across the battlefield. Yet in Revelation 21.24 the kings of the earth become full participants in the new Jerusalem. How are we to assess these contradictory conclusions? Will the nations be tolerated or converted? Or is there something in the rhetoric of the Apocalypse and the extravagant visualization of its imagery which will allow us to accommodate these opposites? In short, is it the case that John's rhetoric differs in terms of our visual perception of a logical and objective discourse in favour of a more impressionistic mode of argumentation?

The Context

Before we proceed with our analysis of the role of the nations in the Apocalypse, it is important to note briefly the context in which they enter significantly into the drama of the unfolding narrative.[1] This involves an initial glance at structure. In the first half of the book action centres around the appearance of a sealed scroll which 'the one seated upon the throne' (God) has in his right hand (5.1-5). After a cosmic search the Lamb (Christ) is the only one judged worthy to open it (5.6-9). The content of the mysterious message of the scroll becomes a major focus of the book. Already in the book's opening lines the author establishes a chain of messengers (God → Christ → Angel → John) who bring word to the readers of 'what must soon take place' (1.1-2). By chapter 5 this word, embedded in the scroll, has moved to the Lamb (Christ); and in 10.1-7, after Christ has broken its seals, a mighty angel brings the open scroll to earth and announces that the mystery of God announced to the prophets is about to be fulfilled.[2] As Richard Bauckham points out, the burden of this mystery is not

---

1   A wider discussion of the biblical theme of the pilgrimage of the nations, particularly as it applies to other biblical writings, will unfold in Chapter 4.

2   Some have questioned whether this is the same scroll as the one in 5:1-9. John uses the Greek diminutive βιβλαρίδιον 'little scroll' (Rev. 10.2, 9, 10) rather than the normal βιβλίον of

conceived as fresh revelation *per se* but information which supplements and clarifies what the OT prophets saw but remained obscure to them.[3]

After John internalizes the message of the scroll (10.8-10), he is told, 'you must again prophesy against many peoples and nations and tongues and kings' (10.11).[4] In Revelation 11.1-13 John begins to unfold the divine prophetic message. Central to it is the word that during the coming crisis (1260 days) the nations under demonic leadership will assault the people of God (11.2, 9; 13.7). It is at this point that the nations and their destiny become significant factors in the message of the book. Throughout this chapter we will attempt to show how the destiny of the nations becomes an important issue as the narrative of the message of the book unfolds. Before we begin to frame our argument, we will note the terminology and references to the nations in Revelation, which provide the data for our analysis.

The Greek word ἔθνος 'nation' occurs 23 times in the book of Revelation.[5] The terminology is not entirely limited to one particular part of the book. Several key references come in the first half (2.26; 5.9; 7.9). However, the bulk of the references occur in the latter section, from chapter 11 to the end, after the scroll is opened.

Besides the references to the 'nations' a key feature of the terminology is that a number of crucial synonyms occur in what appears to be a deliberate formulation. A fourfold formula based on four nouns: φυλή 'tribe', γλῶσσα 'tongue', λαός 'people', and ἔθνος 'nation' occurs first in 5.9 and then (with slight variants 'kings' in 10.11 and 'crowds' in 17.15) six other times throughout the book.[6] The context of Revelation 5.9 clearly indicates that this formulation

---

chapter 5. However, use of the diminutive is characteristic of John, and the two Greek words are used interchangeably in 10.8 and 9. This seems to indicate that the scroll in chapter 10 has a connection with the one introduced in 5.1. The essential difference is that in chapter 10 it is open thus indicating that the time for the exposition of the message has come.

3   Especially Daniel 12.8-9 where, according to Bauckham, *Climax of Prophecy*, p.252, this does not refer to the book of Daniel itself, but implicitly to a heavenly scroll 'containing the divine purpose' which Daniel saw but did not yet understand. Now, in keeping with the eschatological world in which he lives, John considers that he is able to make the appropriate interpretive connections with respect to the end-times.

4   Habitually most translators of this verse translate the Greek word ἐπί as 'concerning' or 'about' instead of the stronger 'against'. Our preference for the terminology 'prophesy against' is supported by two reasons: (1) because this is the first reference of a number of special passages that deal with the struggle to free the nations from the rule of the beast, which will be a central feature of the drama in the last half of the book (cf. 11.2, 9, etc.); (2) the phrase προφητεύειν ἐπί 'to prophesy against' occurs over twenty times in the LXX, mainly in Ezekiel – a book from which John draws much of his inspiration.

5   2.26; 5.9; 7.9; 10.11; 11.2, 9, 18; 12.5; 13.7; 14.6, 8; 15.3-4; 16.19; 17.15; 18.3, 23; 19.15; 20.3, 8; 21.24, 26; 22.2.

6   5.9; 7.9; 10.11; 11.9; 13.7; 14.6; 17.15.

is a recognition that the impact of the Lamb encompasses a universal constituency. The use of the fourfold expression as a technical grouping for comprehensiveness is a feature of all seven references.[7]

The Basic Perspective

The initial focus of the fourfold grouping is to assert that people from all tribes and cultures have a place in the praise of the Lamb and his triumph (cf. 5.9; 7.9). In 5.9 and 7.9 the emphasis is on the people of God as a constituency drawn from all the nations. But from 10.11, 11.9, and especially 13.7, 14.6, and 17.15 the emphasis shifts. The focus moves to the allegiance and control of the nations by the forces of the beast. This is a matter of deep significance. Toward the end of the book the narrative leads the reader to anticipate a time when the nation's allegiance to the trinity of evil will be broken. For John this will be a time that is correlated with the full emergence of the kingdom of God. The nations are liberated from the evil power of the beast which lured them into idolatry. As a result they will have unlimited access to the new Jerusalem (21.24, 26; 22.2-3).

In many ways this important movement beginning with the formulation of the community of the Lamb drawn from the nations, moving on to the conflict over the object of their allegiance, ending with their entry into the new Jerusalem, correlates with a major theological focus of the book: the transfer of power in the created order from the hands of the dragon (beast) and his allies to the rule of the saints of the most High. In a general sense this seems to be the message of the open scroll. This transfer comes in three stages. First, the process has already been inaugurated with the death and resurrection of the Lamb. The death and resurrection of Jesus is a pledge that God's sovereign rule over the creation is once-and-for-all assured as an accomplished fact. This comes to light in Revelation 1.6, 5.9, and 7.9-10. Second, in the present, as a result of the resurrection of Christ, Satan has been dethroned as the believers' accuser before God. However, heaven's gain is earth's problem. Satan becomes more active on earth by raising up agents and rulers who enthrall and control the peoples and the nations through allegiance to Babylon (13.7). This situation inaugurates a crisis. The nations under the thrall of Babylon prosper. However, all is not well and ultimately some rebel. Among the people of God a tone of anxiety, deep concern, and even depression pervades during this period. The counter-cultural community of the Lamb becomes involved in a life-and-death struggle with the dragon and his minions (12.7-17). Only the Creator and the

---

7   This is yet another example of the author utilizing a set of sevens for his compositional usage (seven seals, trumpets, macarisms, etc.). In this particular instance one could not agree more with Bauckham, *Climax of Prophecy*, p.326, 'In the symbolic world of Revelation, there could hardly be a more emphatic indication of universalism.'

Lamb can ultimately rectify the situation through a coming holy war, which will have cosmic implications. Eventually the time comes when the beast and his allies among the nations are destroyed (19.11–20.15). The nations are freed from the power of Satan. God's purposes are accomplished in his new world in the same manner as he rules heaven (21.1–22.5).

The entire panorama of the rule of God, past, present, and future, in the world of the Apocalypse, vitally involves the destiny of the peoples or nations. Understanding what is involved in the transfer of their allegiance from idolatrous devotion of the beast and his allies to giving glory and praise to the Lamb is central to understanding its message. Not only will close analysis allow us to determine what the author perceives to be the ultimate role and destiny of the nations, but also it can serve as a vital clue for determining the overall thrust of John's eschatological perspective. John is a member of a small contrast-society living among a vast sea of tribes, peoples, and ethnic communities which constitute the Roman Empire. He is not at all enthralled by Rome. He is in the business of developing a minority report against what he considers to be a demonic regime. The leaders of this vast constituency, the 'kings of the earth', appropriately give allegiance to Rome. Some, 'the earth-dwellers', enforce allegiance with ideological zeal. John's community, the followers of the Lamb, itself a small multi-ethnic constituency, encounters growing division within its ranks with respect to how it should relate to the Roman imperium. It is out of this perspective that the prophet describes symbolically the present crisis and begins to envision its resolution.

For purposes of analysis, John's understanding of the role of the nations may be organized into five categories. These categories can conveniently be grouped into sets of texts:

A   Acknowledgement that the constituency of the Lamb is drawn from all nations and peoples (5.9-10; 7.9).
B   Characterizing the struggle between the people of God and the nations during the time the nations are under the sway of the rule of the beast (10.11; 11.2, 9; 13.7; 14.6, 8; 16.19; 17.15; 18.3, 23).
C   The promise that the Lord and his agents will subdue the nations based on Psalm 2 (2.26; 12.5; 19.15; 11.18).
D   The description of the Lamb and his allies destroying the beast and his allies and exercising dominion over the nations (20.3, 8-9).
E   Echoing Isaiah 60 and 63 and other key prophetic texts, the covenant with the nations is renewed and they are incorporated into God's new world (21.24, 26; 22.2).

Analysis and Procedure

In this chapter we will examine the first three categories of the morphology. We will begin by discussing those texts that describe the people of God who worshipped the Lamb in small communities drawn from the vast number of tribes and peoples in the Eastern Mediterranean areas of that day. Of course, they were insignificant and powerless compared to the vast constituencies (nations) which gave allegiance to the Roman power structure. The impact of this power structure upon the people of God will be a central focus of this chapter. I will argue that John views the nations as entrenched in their demonic ways and bent on a course that will eventuate in their ultimate destruction. They are not prepared to heed the call to repentance which is inherent in the witness and proclamation of the followers of the Lamb. That is the burden of our analysis of the first three categories of John's treatment of the nations. It is the argument of this chapter. It will be followed by analysis of the last two categories in the next chapter. It will show how John envisions changes in the allegiance of the nations which are contingent upon the coming of Christ as a Divine Warrior. Procedurally, we will examine each text in context. Special attention will be given to any evidence where compositional features of the author emerge. For example, we will be interested in which Old Testament texts he chooses to use and what we can determine about the principle of selection. Our objective is to discover evidence that the author is utilizing a basic theological typology in his composition and what it is. This will be pursued in the last three chapters of this work.

The Lamb's Constituency

In his intriguing article 'Nations in the New Testament', Nils Dahl notes that for the New Testament, unlike the situation in the Old Testament, the nations are not separate countries such as Edom, Moab, Israel, or Ammon, but tribal areas and provinces within the Roman empire.[8] Indeed these are usually lumped together by translators and referred to as τὰ ἔθνη 'the Gentiles' as opposed to the Jewish people, God's elect nation.[9] Yet, as Dahl notes, the book of Revelation with its references to 'tribes', 'tongues', and 'peoples' underscores a vivid awareness of the existence of a great diversity of ethnic and tribal groups both in the Eastern Roman Empire and beyond the Euphrates;[10] and as already noted, perhaps, this terminology also subtly veils a seething resentment among some that they were under the control of Rome and they did not like it. Thus τὰ ἔθνη in the Apocalypse almost invariably refers to a plurality of tribes and ethnic groups and has come to be translated in English 'the nations' rather than 'Gentiles'.

This is the essential linguistic background to the reference to 'nation' in Revelation 5.9. In 5.1-7 the Lamb (Christ) receives the scroll containing God's plans for the future. This takes place in the sanctuary of heaven. This action precedes a burst of praise to the Lamb as worthy from the heavenly council which is ap-

---

8   Dahl, 'Nations in the New Testament', p.56.
9   Dahl, 'Nations in the New Testament', p. 57.
10   Dahl, 'Nations in the New Testament', pp.66–8.

propriately labelled 'a new song' (5.9-10). Essentially the 'new song' celebrates the redemptive activity of the Lamb. On the basis of his death he has purchased a new universal community from every nation and tribe.

The poetic reference to a deliverance ἐκ 'out of' other nations into a new contrast-society echoes the book of Exodus in several places. The terminology is dependent especially upon Exodus 19.5 where Israel learns that from all peoples she is the elect; and in the next verse (19.6) she is destined to be a kingdom of priests. This promise of the election of Israel from all the people of the earth is a feature of the Torah (cf. Exod. 23.22 [LXX]; Deut. 7.6; 14.2; 26.18-19). With this biblical warrant it then can be easily appropriated to John's understanding of the church as the reconstituted Israel in 5.9-10.

After the Exodus Moses and Miriam sing the song of triumph (Exod. 15.1-21). This is paralleled in Revelation 6.9-10 when the heavenly retinue sings 'a new song' of the triumph of the Lamb. Israel has learned to celebrate its ransom from Egyptian bondage in the death of the paschal lamb (Exod. 12.21-28). Likewise, evoking similar imagery based on the sacrifice of the paschal lamb, the violent death of Jesus as a ransom is considered the source of Christian redemption (cf. 1 Cor. 5.7; 1 Pet. 1.18). This is the underlying motif in Revelation 5.9-10. Following the deliverance at the sea God calls Israel as a priestly kingdom (Exod. 19.6). Likewise, the account in Revelation of the Lamb's redemption creates a kingdom and priests (cf. 1.5-6). But unlike Israel, which was constituted as a separate ethnic nation, *apart* from the other tribes and peoples of the ancient Near East, the Lamb's kingdom has a constituency *drawn from many peoples*.[11]

The fourfold terminology of tribe, tongue, people, and nation clearly echoes a Greek translation of the Bible (cf. LXX Dan. 3.4, 7, 96; 5.19; 6.26; 7.14). The terminology is now used to refer to those who acknowledge the lordship of the Lamb. They no longer owe their allegiance to their ancestral people. As a counter-cultural community drawn from many tribes and groups including the Jews, they constitute a kind of anti-empire over against Rome.[12] Astonishingly, given the context in which they live, they receive a promise to reign as kings and priests with the Lamb on earth. This seems to be an anticipation of Revelation 20.4-5 where the faithful are invested with the vocation of judging and ruling in the millennium. In any case, the text is a clear expression of the

11   Bauckham, *Climax of Prophecy*, pp.326-37. Elizabeth Schüssler Fiorenza, 'Redemption as Liberation: Rev. 1:5-6 and 5:9-10', CBQ 36 (1974), pp.220-32, reprinted in *Justice and Judgment*. Notice also the reference to 'people/s' in Rev. 21.3. As a kingdom and priesthood, the Christians in the province of Asia can already claim an incipient victory. Probably the strongly contested reading of βασιλεύειν 'to rule' in Rev. 5.10b is a future tense. But the decisive point is that believers in the Lamb are already part of a privileged community. There remains a strong tension between what they perceive themselves to be and their actual situation.

12   Elizabeth Schüssler Fiorenza, *Revelation: Vision of a Just World*, Proclamation Commentaries, Gerhard Krodel, ed. (Minneapolis: Fortress Press, 1991), pp.61-2.

strength of the vision of mission in early Christianity. It links John's view of the ultimate outcome of Christian mission with an anticipation of the submission of the allegiance of the 'nations' to the lordship of Christ.

Much the same point is made in Revelation 7.9. In this verse, using similar terminology to 5.9, but in a different order, John envisions the triumph of a 'great multitude which no one is able to number'. Again the scene is in heaven. Clothed in white robes and waving palm branches, the multitude is honoured because its members have emerged as victors from 'the great tribulation' (cf. 7.13-14).[13] A key exegetical issue involves the precise identity of the great multitude, especially since in the immediately preceding verses of 7.1-8 there is a very careful delineation of the group which numbers 144,000.

As a prelude to determining the referent to 'the great multitude' it is important to note that Revelation 7.9 occurs in the interlude between the sixth and the seventh seal. The interlude covers the text of 7.1-17. It is of equal importance to observe that there are two identifiable pericopes in the interlude (7.1-8; 7.9-17). The former pericope connects directly with the sixth seal (6.12-17). The latter consists of an anticipatory description of what takes place at the culmination of the end-time. The pericope dealing with the call of the 144,000 in 7.1-8 is a response to the question of Revelation 6.17 as to who can survive the wrath of the coming Day of the Lord narrated in the sixth seal. The answer is provided in 7.2-3: only those who are sealed as a sign of God's protection and ownership will survive. As in the practice of holy war, before the battle a census of the warriors is taken (Numbers 1.26). Here the δοῦλοι 'servant-warriors' (7.3), who are linked linguistically to the σύνδουλοι of 6.11, constitute a select community which watches the astonishing effect of the eschatological plagues of the last days. They learn that their survival depends on God's seal. The census arrives at the number 144,000. The number itself is 'a "square number" of perfection',[14] symbolically reflecting the totality of all the warriors of the Lamb who will endure through the coming horrors. On the grounds of God's protection they will ultimately triumph by being vindicated at the last day (cf. 6.11).

This brings us to the second pericope (7.9-17), wherein we find the reference to the nations (7.9). Whereas in 7.1-8 we see the faithful at the beginning of the time of horrors, 7.9-17 portrays the victory of the sealed at the end of the time of tribulation (cf. 7.14). It is crucial to note that this group, now delineated in 7.9 'a great multitude', is a description of the eschatological people of God in their entirety. As the people of God washed their garments to purify their approach

---

13   This is the only use of this phrase in Revelation. Matthew 24.21 has the same technical usage and is probably dependent on Daniel 12.1. Revelation is notoriously vague with respect to its references to time, but one would not go far wrong if he or she associates this reference as a time of horrors immediately preceding the eschaton. It is marked by the symbolic short period of 42 months or 1260 days (11.2, 3; 12.6).

14   Bauckham, *Climax of Prophecy*, p.218, citing A. Farrer, *The Revelation of St. John the Divine* (Oxford: Clarendon Press, 1964), p.106.

to God at Sinai (Exod. 19.10), so the eschatological people of God triumph and gain access to God because of the victory of the Lamb. The 144,000 sealed Israel of God described in 7.1-8 are numbered from a different perspective.[15] It is the final and ultimate celebration of victory. To summarise, Revelation 7.1-8 depicts the people of God at the outset of the horrors. Revelation 7.9-17 is a description of a heavenly scene at the end of the course after all the horrors are over. Reflecting the growing success of the early Christian mission in considerable portions of the Roman empire people from different ethnic groups and languages join in praise to the Lamb (7.9-12). In their white robes (7.9) John links them with the witness of earlier martyrs (6.9-11) as the total complement of 'warrior servants' is brought to completion. The Abrahamic promises of Genesis 15.5 and 22.17 are reckoned to find their true fulfilment in this number that no one is able to count (7.9).[16]

Thus in 7.9, as in 5.9, the emphasis is on the constituency of a universal people of God and their triumph. They constitute a contrast-society over against their earlier family and heritage within the wider tribes and nations. As the narrative of Revelation unfolds, however, the basic allegiances of the various peoples of the empire are raised as a crucial concern. The fact is that many peoples, tribes, and nations within the empire are not neutral with respect to the followers of the Lamb. Under the power of the beast they will oppose those who have left them to become part of the contrast-society of the people of God (1 Pet. 4.12–5.10). The precise form that the captivity of these nations to other powers (the beast) takes will be traced in the next section of this chapter.

15   Facile discussions such as the first group are Jewish Christians and the second Gentile believers are not convincing. In John's view the innumerable number of the second group (7.9) comes ἐκ 'out of' or 'from' every nation, tribe, *et al.* The use of ἐκ simply functions prepositionally to 'help out' the genitive to delineate a special group (the church) who are called out of the nations. Surely this would include Jewish believers, who comprised a considerable segment of the early church, as well as groups of Gentiles from innumerable ethnic groups.

16   The issue as to whether 'the great multitude' consists totally of martyrs is one that should be nuanced carefully. One may certainly get that impression from the clear linguistic connections already noticed between 'those slain for the word of God' in 6.9-11 and 7.9-14. Furthermore, as commentators frequently point out the terminology of the 'great tribulation' of 7.14 is a clear echo of not only Daniel 12.1 but of the total Danielic unit from 11.33-12.10 where the *maśkîlîm* 'wise' are subdued and made white by their martyrdom (cf. Bauckham, *Climax of Prophecy*, pp.226–9). Since a good case can be made that the sealed followers of the Lamb, facing the coming crisis, constitute the Danielic antitype of the *maśkîlîm*, it appears to follow that the latter have also 'washed their robes' in martyrdom. But, as noted, 'washing one's robes' may be a metaphor for doing what is right in preparing for access to God. Thus the idea the multitude are all martyrs needs to be nuanced. To say the least, it would be ironic for the faithful to escape God's wrath against the rebellious creation in the coming days of testing only for all to end up martyred. Some protection! During the coming crisis those redeemed by the Lamb's blood (1.5) may suffer persecution and even (for some) martyrdom. Nevertheless, they will ultimately be judged to be victors on the last day. That is a crucial message of the book (cf. Mounce, *Revelation*, pp.164–5). The victory celebration of the Lamb is a song of triumph after this terrible battle.

The Nations Under the Sway of the Beast

The Commission to speak against the nations (Revelation 10.11)
After John internalizes the message of the scroll he proceeds to deliver a word against 'the peoples, nations, tongues, and many kings' (10.11).[17] This verse clearly echoes Ezekiel 3.4. Ezekiel 3.4 is directly preceded by the prophet consuming a scroll (Ezek. 2.8–3.3). Something similar occurs in Revelation 10.8-9. As is often observed, even though the fourfold formulary is similar to 5.9 and 7.9 the context is different. In the former the fourfold formulary featuring the people(s) or nations centres on the separateness of the church from the vast spectrum of the population of the empire. The emphasis there was on the results of mission in calling into existence a counter-cultural community whose allegiance is to the Lamb. In this pericope the centre of attention is the nations themselves. It anticipates much of the central action of the latter half of the book which features the fortunes and destiny of the nations after they submit to the dragon and his allies.

The consequences of the nations' rebelliousness through maintaining allegiance to the empire and its gods are highlighted especially. The reference to βασιλεῦσιν πολλοῖς 'many kings' is especially striking.[18] The nations, especially their rulers, conduct their affairs under the panoply of the beast (11.7-9; 13.7; 17.12-13).[19] Here John begins to deliver a prophetic word, announcing in considerable detail what will ensue in the coming days if the nations continue giving their allegiance to Rome.

Revelation 10.11 is part of a significant interlude between the sixth and the seventh trumpet (10.1–11.14). As with the first interlude in 7.1-17 there is concern about the situation of the elect during the time the plagues are hurled against a rebellious world. The message that John brings is both sweet as honey

---

17   See footnote 4 for the rationale that ἐπί means 'against'. The RSV translates freely λέγουσιν μοι ordinarily 'they say to me' as 'I was told'. This, however, covers over who is authorizing John to speak. Contextually, both a mighty angel (10.1-3, 5-7) and a 'heavenly voice', i.e. God (10.4, 8; 11.3), speak in the pericope. The plural is used to emphasise that John is speaking with the whole authority of heaven. The use of πάλιν 'again' echoes the earlier commission to announce the earthly vision. John now unfolds the meaning of the scroll which came from heaven.

18   The 'many' may ultimately be derived from John's reading of Dan. 7.24, which he reinterprets in 17.12-13, 16-17 as ten kings, earlier allied with Rome, who now cast their lot with the mysterious leader from the East who seeks to usurp Rome's power. On this reading the focus is on the number of client kings who join this alliance. In any case *kings* can be a general term for the local rulers of major ethnic groups and constituencies within the empire. Grammatically, the use of πολλοῖς 'many' qualifies kings only and not the other substantives in the verse. This may be an anticipation of the narrative in the last half of the book.

19   At the opening of the book Jesus is identified as the ruler of the kings of the earth (1.5). Yet, as far as the narrative is concerned, this is not the reality on earth. The kings of the earth, earthly rulers and elites exercise their power under the aegis of the emperor to whom they give their allegiance. They are mostly viewed in the narrative in a negative sense. It is not until the end of the book that things change (cf. 21.24).

in his mouth, but turning sour upon entering his stomach (10.9). It is sweet because God's people will ultimately be sustained. It is sour because God's people must go through a coming ordeal at the hands of the nations. The nature of that ordeal is previewed in the latter part of the interlude (11.1-14).

The nations trample over the people of God (Revelation 11.2, 9)
The unit elaborating the word of the open scroll in 11.1-14 follows directly John's commission in 10.11 to prophesy against the nations. It is a précis of what will take place when God's prophetic messengers encounter the power of the nations in alliance with evil powers. The analogue in chapter 11 to John's commission to speak in Revelation 10 is the proclamation of two witnesses. These witnesses are prophets symbolizing the counter-cultural message of the church to the Roman world. Just as Moses and Elijah confronted idolatrous power structures of their day so the witnesses manifest similar characteristics as they confront the nations (11.3-6, 9). In John's world the time frame in which this takes place is circumscribed by a symbolic period of 42 months – the antitype of the crisis that initially was perceived by Daniel (Dan. 7.25; cf. 8.14 and esp. 12.7, 11, 12). The content of the message of the witnesses is not directly divulged. But the alert reader of Revelation 9.20-21 would readily presume that the focus is a call to renounce any alliance with the dominant idolatrous culture of the emperor cult so evident in the major cities of Western Asia when John was writing. The presence of the cult is symbolized by the initial appearance of the beast who responds to the prophetic witnesses by making war against them (11.7). When the witnesses are killed, the earth-dwellers, under the spell of the beast, express delight and in joy exchange gifts over what has taken place.[20] It is in this context that the two references to nations in this chapter (11.2, 9) should be analysed. In both instances the nations function as an expression of human hostility to the Lamb and his people.

Revelation 11.1-2 describes a temple whose sanctuary is measured and marked off as a place of holiness. The image of the sanctuary is a reminder that God has a presence in the world. It finds expression in the prophetic witness of the faithful church. The announcement is that this witness will continue to abide. But from another perspective, symbolized in the court outside the

---

20   The reference to κατοικοῦντες ἐπὶ τῆς γῆς 'those who dwell upon the face of the earth' in 11.10 comes in the same context as the reference to the nations in 11.9. Yet, in Revelation a distinction must be drawn between the two groups. On the one hand the earth dwellers, the quintessential persecutors of God's people, are always characterized as evil, and under the sway of malicious forces (6.10; 8.13; 11.10; 13.8, 12, 14; 17.2, 8); cf. Schuyler Brown, 'The Hour of Trial' (Rev. 3:10) JBL 85 (1966), p.309; and Bauckham, *Climax of Prophecy*, pp.239–41. In short, they act as 'storm troopers'. They work ceaselessly on behalf of the idolatrous powers. On the other hand, the nations only give honour to the beast temporarily. Finally their allegiances will be transferred elsewhere (21.26). Also worthy of note is Bauckham's observation, *Climax of Prophecy*, p.281, that Rev. 11.10 represents a bizarre reversal of Purim (Esther 9.19, 22). Instead of the people of God celebrating their deliverance from persecution by exchanging gifts, the earth dwellers, deliriously rejoicing over the demise of the witnesses, are the ones who exchange gifts.

sanctuary and the holy city that houses the sanctuary (11.2), God's world is currently under assault by the beast and his minions: the nations bent on idolatry (11.2). As when the faithful *maśkîlîm* suffered in Daniel's time, so the implication of the account of the trampling of the temple courts is that a purging will take place during this circumscribed time of crisis. This purging may involve the people of God. Nevertheless, the final word is not defeat but hope. Despite harassment and persecution God knows his elect and will vindicate them (11.11-12).

Revelation 11.1-13, in which the references occur, is a unit that bristles with exegetical questions and issues. To enter into a full-scale analysis of the unit would take us too far away from our central focus: the nature of the reference to the nations in 11.2, 9. Nevertheless, precision does demand that several particular exegetical issues in the pericope be addressed.

At the outset, as already noted, the references to the nations in both Revelation 11.2 and 9 refer to their collective hostility toward the people of God. But the particular contexts of the respective texts demand different emphases.

First, Revelation 11.2 appears in a brief unit (11.1-2) that may be titled 'The Measuring of the Sanctuary'. John is given a measuring rod. He is told to measure the ναός 'inner sanctuary' of the temple, presumably as a sign of its protection and preservation.[21] Here we encounter immediately two key exegetical issues: (1) What is the point of the measurement of the inner sanctuary for protection and preservation? (2) What is the scope and function of the reference to the part of the sanctuary that is not measured and will be given over to the trampling of the nations? (11.1b-2).

With respect to the former, most commentators consider that the measurement of the inner sanctuary symbolizes a promise of *spiritual* protection for the followers of the Lamb through the impending crisis of the 42 months of tribulation. This reading is often linked with the fate of the outer court which is thought to symbolize the vulnerability of the faithful to *physical* suffering or martyrdom during the same period.[22] But would the paradox of spiritual protection while one suffers physically make sense to an ancient reader – especially in the seven churches of Asia? The immediate danger that faced small struggling churches, especially in light of potential persecution, is whether one considers the commitment to be worthwhile. In other words, this doesn't seem to be much of an offer. Is this all there is?

Numerous asides throughout the narrative of the Apocalypse deal with the potential danger and implications of apostasy.[23] The real goal of spiritual protection is to protect against apostasy and the divine judgment which follows.

---

21   Fiorenza, *Justice and Judgment*, p.48; Grant R. Osborne, *Revelation*, ECNT (Grand Rapids: Baker Academic, 2002), p.409, and most modern commentators.

22   David Aune, *Revelation 6–16* WBC 52b (Nashville: Thomas Nelson 1998), pp.597–8, lists copious commentators holding this view. He also notes other positions fairly.

23   Note especially the seven beatitudes (Rev. 1.3; 14.13; 16.15; 19.9; 20.6; 22.7, 14; 24) as well as the constant warnings to the seven churches (cf. 2.6, 16, 22; 3.3, 16).

Persecutions and tribulation are givens for the reader. But the measuring for protection against apostasy is a word of hope. The interlude of testing will not be long (Rev. 11.2). Divine protection for those who maintain the faith is assured – now and at the final judgment.[24]

This then takes us to our second question: the identification of that part of the sanctuary that John is told not to measure because it is given over to the nations or Gentiles. The text is somewhat loose and straggly since it is held together by a series of usages of the Greek conjunction καί which not only can function as a connective, but can also be used adversatively and epexegetically. This allows a wide range of possibilities for translation. Progress in understanding can be made if we note that the current text of Revelation 11.1b-2 also has multiple echoes of Ezekiel 8.16. The latter text speaks of idolatrous worshippers occupying the temple courtyard adjacent to the sanctuary bent on worshipping the sun. Of course, Ezekiel is horrified. There follows immediately his word of judgment against the temple and the people of the holy city (Ezek. 8.17–9.11). With this in mind, it is our view that we should read Revelation 11.1a as a command to John to measure for purposes of sealing and protection of the true people of God as an assurance against total apostasy. The text then should be followed by a colon. The rest of Revelation 11.1b starting with καί τὸ θυσιαστήριον 'but the altar' and all of 11.2 is a second sentence. The point of the sentence is to draw an analogy with Ezekiel 8–9. Just as with the corrupt temple in Ezekiel's time, the worshippers in the outside courtyard of John's vision are destined for judgment. The suggestion that the worshippers by the altar in the courtyard refers to those in the churches of Asia who are partial to accommodation with the emperor cult commends itself.[25] Thus the central thrust of the unit emerges. The inner sanctuary is a symbol of the people of God holding the faith steadfast. But the outer court has become profaned and subject to judgment (Ezek. 8.1–11.25; Dan. 8.9-14). The worshippers are cast out. But just as the prophets believed a remnant in Judah would be preserved, so the faithful (measured) church will be preserved from God's judgment both in the coming 42 months and in the final judgment at the last day.[26] On the other hand, the followers of the beast and those (even in the churches) who ally with his idolatrous practices will suffer sure and certain retribution.

24   Marko Jauhiainen, 'The Measuring of the Sanctuary Reconsidered (Rev. 11.1-2)', *Biblica* 83/4 (2002), p.522, sees, among the many echoes to scripture here, a strong reference to Ezek. 8–9. Especially, Jauhiainen draws attention to Ezek. 9.4 where the faithful receive a mark to separate them from the idolaters who are destined for destruction. This seems to correspond with the sealing of the 144,000 in Rev. 7.2-3 (cf. 9:4). In short, the sealing or protection is the sign that the faithful will not undergo God's judgment either in the present evil age or the age to come. But it is no promise of protection with respect to the temporary onslaughts of the evil powers and their allies as is evident in 11.3-13 and 12.1-13.18.
25   Jauhiainen, 'Measuring of the Sanctuary', pp.522-3. He also notes M. Kiddle, *The Revelation of St. John*, MNTC (London: Hodder and Stoughton, 1947), p.189.
26   This is similar to the conclusion of Jauhiainen, 'Measuring of the Sanctuary', pp.525-6.

Finally, this brings us directly to the reference to the nations in Revelation 11.2b. Here there is an interesting play on the Greek word ἐδόθη 'it is given'. The word introduces the unit in Revelation 11.1 where John receives the rod to measure the inner sanctuary. The same word reappears in Revelation 11.2b as part of the divine verdict that those in the outer court and the holy city will be trampled by the Gentiles or nations. The nations fill a traditional role as vehicles of God's punishment. Here the echoes of numerous earlier texts that speak about God's use of the nations as a rod of his judgment against his house and his holy city are invoked (Ezek. 40.3; 41.1; Isa. 63.18; 64.10; Zech. 12.3; Dan. 8.10-14; 1 Macc. 3.45, 51; 4.60; Pss. Sol. 2.19 17.22).[27] John's point seems to be that these texts are a metaphor for God's judgment against the compromisers: those who acted like those in Judah in earlier times and amalgamate the people of God with idolatrous practices. In the end the Nicolatians (2.6, 15) and those who advocate the teaching of Balaam and Jezebel (2.14, 20-23) will suffer a similar fate. The reference to the holy city is an echo of the earlier words of judgment against Jerusalem in the Old Testament. When John wrote, he knew about the physical situation of Jerusalem. But that would not be the last word. In contrast to its present shabby situation with respect to God's sanctuary, God's presence will emerge again in the new Jerusalem (21.1–22.5).

Turning to Revelation 11.9 we see that the nations are again represented as playing a role of opposition to the people of God. Here they are not trampling over the premises, but have control over the city that is implacably hostile to the mission of the two witnesses and was responsible for the death of the Lord (11.8).[28] This is another one of the seven instances of the fourfold formula that is used to describe the universality of the nations. Bauckham views it as close

---

27   Also, the use of Lk. 21.24 must be noted. In an earlier article, 'Revelation 11:1-14 and the Structure of the Apocalypse', *ResQ* 22 (1979), pp.198–202, I argued that at one level the reference to the holy city in Revelation 11.2 reflected early Christian polemic against some Jews in a post-70 context (cf. Rev. 11.8). The gospel traditions narrate that Jewish leaders in Jerusalem handed over one of their own to a Gentile to be put to death. Lk. 21.24 represents a similar polemic based on Dan. 8.13-14 and especially 9.26-27. For a fuller analysis see Allan J. McNicol, *Jesus' Directions for the Future: A Source and Redaction-History Study of the Use of the Eschatological Traditions in Paul and the Synoptic Accounts of Jesus' Last Eschatological Discourse*, New Gospel Studies 9 (Macon, Georgia: Mercer University Press, 1996), pp.136–9. It is not possible to say whether the prophet John had access to Luke's composition. But given the tension between some early Christian prophets and the Jewish community in Asia that did not accept Jesus as Messiah (Rev. 2.9; 3.9), it is not out of the question that John would view these people as subject to a similar judgment as the aberrant prophets within his own community.

28   The origin of the gloss of Rev. 11.8 ὅπου καὶ ὁ κύριος αὐτῶν ἐσταυρώθη 'where their Lord was crucified' remains an unsolved puzzle in the study of the Apocalypse. If it is not genuine in the early Johannine text the reference to 'the great city' would be an anticipation of the role of Babylon which becomes significant later in the book. As the text stands now it seems to represent old Jerusalem as being in collusion with the same demonic forces as will emerge in Rome.

to Revelation 17.15 in form and meaning.[29] John creatively correlates the three and a half years of the defilement of the sanctuary in Daniel (cf. Rev. 11.2) with the death of Jesus in three days. He is saying that for a limited period the nations under the spell of the beast will battle strongly against God's elect. As they seemed to triumph with Jesus' death so it will appear they are gaining an upper hand in the last days of the coming time of crisis or tribulation.[30] Despite the trampling under the feet of the nations, this state of affairs will be brought to an end. There is a time for the 'rage of the nations' (11.18). But it is limited. Jesus of Nazareth, the Lord of the witnesses, was vindicated. Likewise, the faithful witnesses will be validated by the resurrection of the last day.[31] Nevertheless, in both texts it is clear that the nations are pictured as a hostile force.

The compliance of the nations with the emperor cult (Revelation 13.7; 14.6)
After two successive panoramic series of plagues sketching the details of a coming crisis which will precede the coming of the new age (6.1-8.1; 8.2-11.18), in 11.19–16.21 John expands further his exposition of a sequence of events he visualizes immediately preceding the climactic events heralding the parousia. Both of the previous series of the seven seals and seven trumpets featured an interlude. Likewise, this final series of plagues (the seven bowls of wrath) also features an 'interlude'. But, in this case, the interlude (11.19–15.4) *precedes* the seven bowls of wrath instead of following the sixth episode as in the visions of the seals and trumpets.

The placement of this 'short aside' provides the basic clue to its major thrust. In chapter 11 it emerges that the reference to 42 months is the duration for the time of crisis (11.2, 3).[32] This is a symbol for a short period. The horrors

---

29   Bauckham, *Climax of Prophecy*, pp.326-7.
30   The failure to allow burial is, of course, the absolute insult. Christ died in abject humiliation outside the gates of the holy city but at least was given a tomb. The rebellious nations in control of the city do not even allow this minimal act of decency (Ps. 79.1-4).
31   Ezek. 37.1-10 is clearly in the background. Notably Elijah and Moses (in tradition) did not suffer death. However, the ultimate fate of the witnesses who preach with the power of Moses and Elijah is bound up in the destiny of Jesus. Thus, even though the witnesses' destiny will have parallels to Moses and Elijah, they must pass through death, as did their Lord. Moreover, it is not without interest that in the OT narrative of the lives of the two prophets (Moses and Elijah), selected as templates for the proclamation of the church, there were encounters with Balaam (Numbers 23–25) by Moses and Jezebel (1 Kings 18–19, 21) by Elijah. See Stephen Pattemore, *The People of God in the Apocalypse: Discourse, Structure, and Exegesis*, SNTSMS 128 (Cambridge/New York: Cambridge University Press, 2004), pp.162-3. Minimally, this seems to be another signal from John that the prophetic assessment applies not only to the earth dwellers and nations that support the emperor cult. Even those within the churches who advocate and allow a coalescence of the way of the Lamb with the dominant culture no longer stand under the seal of God's covenantal protection.
32   The 42 months occurs in Rev. 11.2 and 13.5; the variant 1260 days is in 11.3 and 12.6; and the Danielic terminology 'time, times, and half a time' for the 42 months (Dan. 7.25; cf. 12.7) is found only once in Rev. 12.14. Essentially this is another instance where John is echoing the time

will be limited in their duration. Chapters 12–13, in particular, engage the reader in an extended discourse on both the economic impact and the religious implications of the idolatrous claims of the resonant imperial power. These forces were spreading through the sponsorship of cults where the emperors and their supposed divine sponsors were worshiped. According to John, they would become ubiquitous during the period of 42 months (13.5; cf. 12.6, 14). Afterward, commencing with the seven bowls of wrath, the whole system comes crashing down. Thus the logic is clear. This unit commences with an extended elaboration of the nature of emperor worship and its impact upon the people of God alluded to in 11.1-13. The three references to 'nations' in Revelation 13.7, 14.6, 8 simply assert that the tribes, nations and ethnic groups of the empire are in compliance with this perceived idolatry. These references illustrate the total pervasiveness of the emperor cult. The fact that in both 13.7 and 14.6 the fourfold formula for humanity (tribe, tongue, people, nation) is used is illustrative of its ubiquity.

In 13.1-3 the dragon (Satan) enlists as an ally the sea beast recently recovered from a mortal wound. It is generally understood that this is a reference to the recovery of the Roman empire under the Flavian dynasty after it unravelled with the 'death' of Nero and subsequent civil war.[33] The beast has absolute power for a restricted period of time (13.5). The worship of this beast and its investiture of absolute authority is reckoned by John as blasphemy (13.4-6). The emergence of the sea beast in 13.1-10 is replete with echoes of Daniel 7 since John views the situation of the rise of the Flavians as its true fulfilment. Thus 13.7a, an echo of Daniel 7.21 (the little horn), refers to the revived emperor making war against the saints (the people of God) in the coming day. There also seems to be a literary connection with Revelation 11.7 where the beast makes war against the two witnesses – who function as a transparency of the prophetic mission of the church.[34]

It is in this context that Revelation 13.7b-8 should be analysed. Two perspectives are set forth. First, the sea-beast is allowed (ἐδόθη) to have universal authority. John echoes the familiar fourfold refrain of tribe, people, tongue, and nation to describe this universal authority. This will be an established reality. During the 42 months, viewed from this perspective, the human tribes and

---

period for the crisis or what he calls the great tribulation that comes to the fore in Daniel 7-12. John views his prediction as part of the fulfilment of what Daniel was told to seal up until the end (Dan. 12.4).

33   Hans-Josef Klauck, 'Do They Never Come Back? Nero Redivivus and the Apocalypse of John', *CBQ* 63 (2001), pp.683–98.

34   Revelation 13.5-7 uses the Greek aorist passive ἐδόθη 'he was given' four times in 13.5-7. Clearly the beast was given its power directly from the dragon. But John is surely saying something more. Even though the beast can do terrible things there are limitations set by God, the ultimate Giver. God gives the sea beast latitude to persecute; but he will not allow him to utterly destroy God's elect.

nations have little choice in the matter. They simply acquiesce. I believe a distinction can be made between the earth dwellers and the nations. The dwellers
on the earth choose enthusiastically to worship the beast. It is no 'given' for
them. This is their *raison d'être*. Here I would argue that the καί 'and' that introduces 13.8 is not epexegetical. It does not function merely as an additional
explanation to 13.7. Rather, in John's world of the coming tribulation, the earth
dwellers will embrace and celebrate the worship of the sea beast (i.e. emperor
worship). They become active partisans of the new regime. Because they are
flagrant idolaters and persecutors of the people of God, John asserts flatly that
these earth dwellers will have no place in the book of life.[35] Such is not the case
with the peoples and nations. They are quiescent in what they probably view as
an inevitable reality. These may ultimately change their allegiance. Nevertheless, there is strong irony here. In 5.9 the Lamb ransomed his people from the
tribes and nations; now in 13.7 the saints (priests and kings) are subject to the
demonic leadership of the nations.[36]

The consequences of the allegiance of the nations to the imperial powers
also form the subject matter of the warning of the three angels in 14.6-11:
a later section of the 'interlude' before the seven bowls of wrath. In 14.6-7
the first angel issues a general call for both 'those who live on the earth' and
'every nation and tribe and tongue and people' to abandon their idolatry. At
first glance it may appear that this is a clear case of the earth dwellers and the
nations being directly linked together. But on closer observation we note that
the Greek phrase in 14.6 τοὺς καθημένους ἐπὶ τῆς γῆς 'those who live upon
the earth' is different from the usual phraseology for earth dwellers, who, in
the Apocalypse are the unqualified enemies of the people of God.[37] Richard
Bauckham has argued that the text of Revelation 14.6-7 echoes phraseology of
Psalm 96 (LXX Psalm 95) and 98:7 (LXX Psalm 97), affirming the proclamation
of God's triumph over the nations.[38] Since 14.6-11 is also an announcement of
the pending judgment of God the use of Isaiah 52.7 may also be considered
one of John's sources for this announcement. Revelation 14.6-7 takes Isaiah's

---

35   The easiest reading of 13.8b, 'from the foundation of the world', in the Greek order would
refer this to the death of the Lamb (cf. NIV and Mounce, *Revelation*, p.252). The idea appears to
be that the death of the messiah was decreed from the foundation of the world, thus echoing the
message of Ephesians 1.4. The RSV gives the wrong impression that John is saying that one's name
is in the book of life before the foundation of the world. In the world of the Apocalypse one's name
is in the book of life by becoming part of the people of God. According to Rev. 3.5 one can lose this
inheritance by being unfaithful.

36   Bauckham, *The Climax of Prophecy*, p.330 and p.333.

37   Invariably John uses forms of the Greek verb κατοικέω 'to dwell' with a form of γῆ 'earth'
to get his word 'earthdweller'. Other linguistic equivalents are οἰκουμένη ὅλη the 'whole world of
habitation' understood as those who are against the people of God (Rev. 3.10; 12.9; 16.14). It is
significant that this terminology in 3.10 is used in apposition with 'those who dwell upon the earth'.
Note also ὅλη ἡ γῆ in 13.3.

38   Bauckham, *Climax of Prophecy*, pp.286–9, cf. p.240.

good news of the defeat of Babylon by Cyrus as the declaration that God is coming to vindicate the righteous and to judge evil-doers in the new Babylon (cf. 14.8). The text is emphatic on the matter of final accountability. But, unlike 13.8, where the earth dwellers are flatly excluded from the book of life, Revelation 14.6-7 functions as a final warning to the totality of the whole earth, that it is time to shift allegiance from idolatry to the one Creator God.

This is reinforced by the message of the second angel, where, for the first time, Rome is introduced under the template of Babylon, the traditional enemy of the people of God (14.8). Babylon has intoxicated πάντα τὰ ἔθνη 'all of the nations' with irresistible offers of power. But she is already introduced as fallen (cf. Isa. 21.9; Jer. 51.7). Therefore all of the nations are warned against placing their hope in her.[39] It is to this text we will turn shortly as we begin to note the consequences of the allegiance of the nations to Babylon.

The Fall of Babylon the Enticer of Client Kings and the Nations (Revelation 14.8; 16.19; 18.3, 23; 17.15)

The third series of unfolding visions (11.19–16.21) that detail an impending crisis as a coming time of tribulation for the people of God ends with the account of the full fury of the seven bowls of wrath poured out upon their enemies (15.5–16.21). In a critical verse that highlights the end of the drama of this time of great tribulation a loud voice comes from the throne announcing, 'It is done' (16.17).[40] As already noted in Revelation 14.8 there is a preliminary announcement of the fall of Babylon.[41] But in the narrative flow of the Greek text of that unit in 14.9, 10 the tenses (future in 14.10) are used to create for the

---

39   Indeed, this warning becomes explicit in the message of the third angel (14.9-11). Echoing the terminology of chapter 13 a stern warning is given to those who embrace the emperor cult. They will receive the same punishment as Babylon. Those in the churches, especially those labelled as the followers of Balaam and Jezebel (cf. Rev. 14.12-13), should take note and heed the call to patient endurance and obedience to God's commandments (cf. Rev. 14.12-13). Jan Fekkes, *Isaiah and Prophetic Traditions in the Book of Revelation: Visionary Antecedents and their Development*, JSNTSup 93 (Sheffield; JSOT Press, 1994), p.88 and p.204, notes that the announcement of the fall of Babylon (Greek Aorist) is an example of a prophetic perfect. It anticipates the actual narrative fulfilment in Revelation 16.19. In addition, Fekkes finds that the echoes of OT texts in Rev. 16.8-11 function as anticipations of a fuller explication of the narration on Babylon's fall in 16.19-19.5.

40   Its importance is highlighted by the only other occurrence of this phraseology 21.6, which immediately precedes the coming of the new Jerusalem (Rev. 21.9-22.5).

41   Babylon is mentioned six times in Revelation (14.8; 16.19; 17.5; 18.2, 10, 21). This is a direct echo of Daniel 4.30 (cf. Sib. Or. 4.93). In Scripture, Babylon is the traditional enemy of the people of God because of its destruction of Jerusalem in 588–586 BCE. Especially after Rome destroyed Jerusalem in CE 70 throughout esoteric circles touched by Judaism, the eternal city is encoded as Babylon (4 Ezra 11–12; Sib. Or. 5.162-78, cf. 1 Pet. 5.13). The author of the Apocalypse adopts a similar convention.

reader a sense of anticipation of Babylon's ultimate demise. That demise occurs during the seventh bowl of wrath (16.17-21). It is underscored by additional commentary on its fall in 17.1–19.10. Indeed, the author leaves the reader in little doubt that his glee at the fall of Babylon is scarcely concealed. Rome, with its massive economic and military might, seemed invincible to an ancient. It incorporated vast numbers of peoples, tribes, and nations. These various ethnic groups and entities had their own leaders (kings) who acted as clients either of the emperor or someone who aspired to that role. John weaves this social reality into the Apocalypse by drawing upon similar terminology used in Jeremiah, Ezekiel, and Daniel to describe the constituency of the imperial powers of the Ancient Near East – especially ancient Babylon (Dan. 3.4-7, 29; 5.19; 6.25; 7.14). Thus, it is easy for the reader to draw the conclusion that the true antitype of the Danielic visions of a great imperial power incorporating many peoples and nations was Rome: the modern Babylon of his time.

Revelation 14.8 is part of a unit of three announcements of judgments upon the inhabitants of the world (14.6-13). Each announcement comes from an angel. The theme of the first announcement (14.6) is that since God is victor, it is time to fear and give him glory for he is about to avenge the righteous. The second announcement focuses upon the source of their problem – it is their subjection to Babylon. There is an announcement that Babylon is fallen (Isa. 21.9). Although, in the flow of the narrative, this is preliminary and anticipatory (cf. 16.17-20, 18.3), it is certain. What is highlighted is that Babylon is the controlling power of all the nations. Every possible ethnic, tribal, or national unit is subject to Rome.[42] Yet this subjection came about through nefarious means. John introduces the metaphor of Babylon as seducer. She gives an intoxicating cup that casts a spell over the nations (cf. Jer. 51.7). But as the narrative unfolds she will pay the price (18.3).[43]

By the time the reader reaches Revelation 16.18-19, the narrative has arrived at a crucial point. The crisis of the great tribulation is now over. 'It is done' (16.17). Rome ('the great city', Babylon), the actual embodiment of all things evil, lies in ruins.[44] The description of its destruction, beginning in Revelation 16.18, echoes language drawn from the theophany at Sinai (Exod. 19.16-19). At Sinai God appears in the power of theophany as a prelude for covenant. Here his appearance is in judgment. The reader has been prepared for something like this in the vision of the seven trumpets (8.2-9.21) where there are clear

---

42   Dahl, 'Nations in the New Testament', p.66. Note the phraseology πάντα τὰ ἔθνη 'all nations' (cf. Rev. 12.5; 14.8; 15.4; 18.3, 23).

43   Aune, *Revelation 6-16*, pp.831-2 conveniently lays out the close verbal parallels between 14.8 and 18.2-3 where the latter launches the famous dirge over Babylon.

44   The precipitating political factors behind Rome's demise and John's perception of the actual process of its defeat is retrospectively chronicled in the vision of the seven kings and the beast in 17.9-18.

echoes of Joshua 6.[45] As the falling of huge hailstones assisted Joshua in holy war now huge hailstones pelt down from the heavens (16.21; cf. Joshua 10.11; Exod. 9.22-26). The city disintegrates into three parts. The cities of the *nations* under its control collapse. This is a sign that Rome can function no longer as a worldwide power (cf. Rev. 14.8). It loses the client nations over which it earlier exercised hegemony.

Revelation 16.18-19 occurs within the structure of the seventh bowl of wrath (16.17-21). Before we take up the reference to 'the nations' in 16.19 it is important to comment briefly on the function of this pericope in the narrative flow of the Apocalypse. In response to the question of the martyrs (6.10) under the altar who cry for vindication the drama of Revelation 6.12–15.8 centres around an intensifying struggle between the forces of the Lamb who contest the hegemony of the dragon and his allies. The martyrs are told this struggle will be for 'a little while' (6.11). The visions of the seals, trumpets, and interlude to the bowls of wrath chronicle what is to take place during this 'little while'. At Revelation 16.1 the time has come for accounts to be settled. In its fullness, God's wrath pours down on the forces of the opponents of the Lamb. In Revelation 16 the focus of the wrath seems to be on a major earthly city which holds in its control the reins of earthly power. It is, and remains, implacably hostile to the forces of the Lamb. That power, of course, is Babylon (16.19). John draws upon both the motif of the Exodus (featuring the plague tradition designed to let the people of God go) and Old Testament prophetic terminology directed against Babylon to furnish the content of the description of God's judging wrath (16.1-20).[46]

In terms of what follows, Revelation 17.1–19:10 is an appendix chronicling the fall of Babylon. Then in 19.11-21, as generally accepted, John highlights the central early Christian feature of the events involving the coming in full force of the Day of the Lord: the parousia of Christ. This pericope narrates the rout of the earth and sea beast (false prophet) and all of their captains, cohorts, and devoted allies. Thus the action initiated in 16.1-21 culminates with what takes place in 19.11-21.[47]

---

45   In Joshua 6 the Israelites march around Jericho one time each day blowing trumpets. But on the seventh day, they march around the city seven times, then shout, and the city walls collapse. Although, perhaps a little of a stretch, the drying up of the Euphrates in Rev. 16.12 seems to have an eerie parallel with the holding back of the Jordan prior to Joshua's crossing into the land (Joshua 3.1-17).

46   Fekkes, *Isaiah and the Prophetic Traditions*, pp.86–91, has a series of handy tables and references that show clearly that John has studied carefully and utilized in a massive way the prophetic judgment oracles against Babylon in Jeremiah, Isaiah, Ezekiel, and Daniel in the service of his polemic against Rome.

47   Indeed, the action bringing the wrath of the Lamb at the parousia to its point of completion is not finished until 20.15. This comes with the consigning of Satan and Death and Hades to the lake of fire. The well-travelled comment that the defeat of the enemies of the Lamb (Babylon, sea beast, earth beast, and dragon) comes in reverse to the order in which they were introduced is worthy of recall. This is another indication of John's careful compositional strategy.

In view of our concern to explicate the role of the 'nations' in Revelation 16.18-19, we must first return briefly to note the relevant features about the sixth bowl of wrath (16.12-16). The unit opens with the announcement that the Euphrates is dried up as a prelude to allow the kings of the East to pour west across the Roman Empire (16.12). Then some 'kings from the East' or 'kings of the whole world' (16.14) appear. They will emerge as a significant part of the full power (ten horns) of the beast in 17.12.[48] Following a common procedure of the OT prophets where God, as Universal Sovereign, causes one nation to go up against another (cf. Isa. 43.3; 45.1) to fulfil his ultimate purposes, the narrative of the sixth bowl of wrath prepares the reader for the destruction of Babylon (Rome). This takes place in 16.17-20 (the seventh bowl). The whole point is that the kings of the East (forces from beyond the Euphrates), after subduing Rome (17.16-17), will join the remnants of the empire for a final assault against divine power which John understands as being within the province of the Lamb (cf. 17.13-14; 19.11-21).[49] The sixth bowl is preparatory for the defeat of Babylon and the seventh bowl announces it as taking place. Revelation 17.16-17 deals with it retrospectively.

This brings us to our second observation: the dispute over the site of the battle (16.14, 16). It is well known that strictly in terms of etymology Armageddon (a combination of the Hebrew word for mountain and the northern plain and fortification site of Megiddo) makes little sense. Although Megiddo was a major route for invading armies across the Fertile Crescent from time immemorial, there is no mountain nearby at the building site. Given this incontrovertible point it seems reasonable to interpret the reference here to Armageddon as a symbol. Major recent articles cover a range of possibilities.[50] Viewed as a symbol, the mountain image seems to be the key. We propose that it function as an image for the place of violence counterbalancing Mount Zion (14.1-5), which symbolizes God's place of protection of his people.[51] Given the violent terminology that is used to describe

---

48   Marko Jauhiainen, 'The OT Background to Armageddon (Rev. 16.16) Revisited', *NovT* 47/4 (2005), p.388.

49   John is drawing upon the motif of the Return of Nero, which had a number of manifestations in various circles of the empire in the latter half of the first century. Richard Bauckham, *Climax of Prophecy*, pp.429-31, suggests John's version of it may be elaborated in the fifth Sibylline Oracle, or, at the very least, in similar traditions. Bauckham makes a convincing case for both John's dependence on this tradition and the need to differentiate it from other texts behind Revelation in a wide range of mainly apocalyptic sources. We would add modestly that this is further evidence for John's contact and sympathy with various circles that are in strong opposition to the Roman imperium.

50   Jauhiainen, 'OT Background to Armageddon', pp.381-93; John Day, 'The Origin of Armageddon: Revelation 16:16 as an Interpretation of Zechariah 12.11', in S. Porter and P. Joyce (eds.), *Crossing the Boundaries: Essays in Biblical Interpretation in Honour of Michael D. Goulder* (Leiden: Brill, 1994), pp.315-26; M. Oberweis, 'Erwägungen zur apokalyptischen Ortsbezeichnung "Harmagedon"', *Biblica* 76 (1995), pp.305-24.

51   Jauhiainen, 'OT Background to Armageddon', p.392, offers for consideration one lexical reading of the Hebrew 'mountain of slaughter' or 'mountain of the cut down'. In any case, the important factor is that it represents the opposite to Mount Zion.

the end of the harlot (Rome) in Revelation 17.6 we propose that Armageddon represents synecdoche for the destruction of Babylon (Rome). God uses the forces from the East as the vehicle for his judgment. The seventh bowl of wrath confirms this with its soaring announcement of Babylon's destruction (16.19).

After the announcement of the seventh bowl of wrath in 16.17 the pericope can be divided into an ABA'B' format (16.18-19a with 16.20-21a the storm theophany, and God's judgment in 16.19b and 21b).[52] Yet this division is somewhat artificial. On an ordinary reading the unit is remarkably compact. It features a compact account of the divine theophany in judgment and its impact. It concludes with the refrain of 16.9, 11 that the recipients cursed God on account of what had happened. The description of the theophany features thunder, lightning, storm and earthquake. Particular attention is drawn to the earthquake which is noted as coming last in the list of natural phenomena associated with the theophany. Bauckham has no difficulty chronicling a lengthy exegetical tradition on theophany which concludes with the function of the earthquake as the beginning of God's final judgment.[53] Revelation 16.18 represents the last of a series of four stereotyped linguistic expressions of theophany in Revelation (4.5; 8.5; 11.19; 16.18-21).[54] Revelation 4:5 introduces this pattern as part of its description of the heavenly throne. Then in 8.5 in response to the prayers of the righteous, further expressions of theophany accompany the censer filled with fire thrown down upon the earth. This action introduces the vision of the seven trumpets. For the first time there is a reference to the earthquake in these theophanic episodes. Theophanic activity frames the vision of the seven trumpets which concludes at 11.19. This latter verse marks both the end of the vision of the seventh trumpet and the beginning of the vision of the seven bowls of wrath. It has not only the reference to the earthquake, but also a reference to great hail. Thus 11.19, in turn, frames 16.18-21. Not only that, but it is very clear that each theophany signals growing tempo and greater intensity in expression. This development is an anticipation of the fullness and comprehensiveness of God's judgment that now is strongly unleashed in 16.18-21.

Revelation 16.19a opens with the statement that 'the great city was in three parts', presumably as a result of the earthquake referred to in 16.18b. Then there is the reference to the fall of the cities of the nations – our particular focus in this study. Finally, in 16.19c we are told that God remembered 'Babylon the great' forcing her to drain the cup of his wrath. There is an exegetical issue as to whether the first city (16.19a) is the same as Babylon (16.19c) or is it a separate city? The matter cannot

---

52   Osborne, *Revelation*, p.598. The reference to the seventh angel anticipates 17.1 and 21.9 which serve as inclusios for description of what is considered to take place to bring about the fulfilment of the coming climactic eschatological events. As noted earlier, the use of the perfects for γίνομαι 'it is finished' in 16.17 and 21.6 fortifies this inclusio. In 16.17 the end of the period of the plagues has come with the destruction of Babylon. In 21.6 it is the end of the eschatological events of the Day of the Lord and the beginning of the new heaven and earth.

53   Bauckham, *The Climax of Prophecy*, pp.199–209.

54   Bauckham, *The Climax of Prophecy*, p.202 gives a helpful Greek table highlighting the points of comparison.

be decided simply on grammatical grounds because all of Revelation 16.19-21a is a series of paratactic clauses linked together by the coordinating conjunction καί 'and'. Some of these uses of καί may well be epexegetical. So a resolution will have to come on other exegetical grounds.

The major alternative to the view that the city in 16.19a is Babylon (Rome) is that it refers to Jerusalem.[55] The basic argument for that position is that the phraseology of 16.19c that God remembered 'Babylon the great' differentiates this reference from 'the great city' of 16.19a; and since Jerusalem is the immediate referent to the phraseology 'the great city', in Revelation 11.8, Jerusalem is the city of 16.19a. This position has been supplemented in recent times by arguments from both Barker and Jauhiainen. Barker returns to an earlier perspective that the reference to 'the great city' dividing into three parts alludes to various factions in Jerusalem that led to its weakening and final conquest in the struggle against the Romans in 67-70 CE.[56] However, it is doubtful what relevance this would have for mainly Gentile believers in Asia. Jauhiainen takes the division of the city into three parts as being positive. This is because he reads the text as reflecting dependence in some sense upon the splitting of the Mount of Olives in Zechariah 14.4-5.[57] Among some Jews the splitting of the Mount of Olives was a sign of the dawn of the new age and resurrection. Jauhiainen views this as John's anticipation of the vindication of the followers of the Lamb and the parousia in Rev. 19.11-16. However, the theme and thrust of the seventh bowl is not vindication but judgment. The splitting of the city is because of an earthquake. Clearly, the entire thrust of Revelation 16.19 is a description of the onslaught of terrifying judgment.

Thus we take the position that the reference to 'the great city' in Revelation 16.19a is to Babylon (Rome). Revelation 17.1-19.10 then follows as an appendix to this description of the beginning of eschatological judgment. This analysis is strengthened through consideration of the common use of various forms of the adjective μέγας 'great' (16.19; 17.1, 5, 18; 18.2, 10, 16, 18, 19, 21). Especially important is the reference in 17.18 to the woman sitting on the scarlet beast being identified as 'the great city' which is sovereign over the kings of the earth. [58] This echoes Revelation 16.12, 14 which, as noted, prepares in summary form the reader for the action elaborated in the appendix on the fall of Babylon. In Revelation 17.17-18 the great city exercises control over the provincial leaders of different groups in the empire.

---

55   Alan James Beagley, *The 'Sitz im Leben' of the Apocalypse with Particular Reference to the Role of the Church's Enemies*, BZNW 50 (Berlin/New York: Walter de Gruyter, 1987), pp.90-91. Aune, *Revelation 6-16*, p.900, lists Bernhard Weiss, Lohmeyer and Schlatter in favour of this view, although he accepts that the reference is to Babylon.

56   Margaret Barker, *The Revelation of Jesus Christ* (Edinburgh: T&T Clark, 2000), p.278.

57   Jauhiainen, *The Use of Zechariah in Revelation*, p.120, arrives at the three parts through the splitting of the Mount of Olives (Zech. 14.4) plus the temple mount. This explanation is forced.

58   This terminology deals a fatal blow to the view of the minority of interpreters who, on the basis of Jerusalem being identified as 'the great city' in 11.8, insist that all references to the 'great

In Revelation 16.19b, the *cities of the nations* that collapse when the great city falls represent the dependence of the myriad of cities on Rome's imperial power.[59]

Thus the conjunction καί that precedes the reference to Babylon in Revelation 16.19c functions epexegetically. ('The great city…and her imperial clients…that is the great Babylon.') For John, Babylon is destined to drain the cup of God's wrath (cf. 6.16-17; 11.8; 14.10; 18.6). The language of the first anticipation of the eschatological judgment that first surfaces in the sixth seal comes to full fruition in 16.20 (cf. 6.14). The nations that already are in turmoil have now lost the dynamic city that furnishes the core energy of their power. Consequently, the nations languish. This point is solidified in the references to nations in the Babylon appendix of 17.1–19.10.

In the last unit we noted that what we are calling the appendix details the destruction of Babylon in 17.1–19.10. The appendix falls into three parts. First, in chapter 17, the destiny of Babylon (Rome) is sketched under the image of both apostate woman and a scarlet beast. Second, in chapter 18 John incorporates into his narrative a dirge over the fall of Babylon. Finally, in 19.1-10 the counterpoint of the marriage feast of the Lamb is highlighted.

We pick up our discussion first with two texts that refer to the nations in the dirge over Babylon. This is because there is a connection between 16.19, which we discussed immediately above, and 18.3. As in 16.19, it is announced that Babylon, the great city, is fallen (cf. 18.2). The grounds for her destruction are stated clearly. Under the umbrella of her invincibility she has seduced all the nations, kings, and merchants to drink the intoxicating wine of her terrible adulteries.[60] Of course, the strong metaphorical language refers to Rome's offer of a share in her power in exchange for engaging in the idolatrous actions of emperor worship. The image of the cup/wine of wrath can also be linked with 16.19. In 18.3 the nations drink Rome's cup of enticements to enter into an adulterous relationship with her (cf. 14.8; 17.2, 4).[61] But this exchange has consequences. The nations, as a result of their perverted relationship with Rome, will receive another cup, along with the kings of the earth and the merchants: the wine of God's wrath.[62] The dirge of Revelation 18 functions as a taunt to these groups for making the wrong choice.

---

city' should be interpreted consistently throughout as Jerusalem. Jerusalem in the first century can be accused of many things; but no one can say it was an empire that had in its control various client kings and nations. Fekkes, *Isaiah and the Prophetic Traditions*, p.212, notes that 4 Ezra 15.46-49 has a reference to a province which entered into a sycophantic relationship with Rome. Given the terminology of Revelation, this province may be viewed as a nation. In 4 Ezra 15 that nation is Asia.

59   Mounce, *The Book of Revelation*, p.303.

60   This assumes that the appropriate textual reading is πεπότικεν 'have drunk', the perfect form of ποτίζειν 'to drink'. This reading is scarce in the textual tradition but it is understandable that the more usual variant forms of πίπτειν 'to fall' came into the text by scribal errors due to attraction to the use of the same verb in 14.8, 16.19 and 18.2 to describe Babylon as 'fallen'. It clearly echoes OT texts such as Jeremiah 25.15-17 and 51.7.

61   Fekkes, *Isaiah and the Prophetic Traditions*, p.205.

62   The use of θυμός usually translated 'wrath' in 18.3 is worthy of note. Rev. 18.3a echoes

Similarly, in Revelation 18.23, which serves to create an inclusio with 18.3, at the end of the dirges the merchants and the nations are again closely linked.[63] As a point of emphasis, it is now stated that the grounds of Babylon's destruction were because she deceived the nations by her φαρμακεία 'sorceries'.[64] Rome's offer of economic security and political power was far too tempting for her client kings and merchants to reject. They are devastated at what has happened.

Finally, the reference to nations in Revelation 17.15 is the last of the seven instances of the use of four similes for humankind (5.9; 7.9; 10.11; 11.9; 13.7; 14.6; 17.15). This passage serves as part of John's explanation of the mystery of the woman on the scarlet beast (17.1-7). The scarlet beast is Rome. Likewise, from a different perspective, the woman, through her enticing power, is also Rome. By her splendour she co-opts the gullible 'earthdwellers' and client kings into idolatrous allegiance. The woman sits upon many waters (17.1, 15).[65] This is allegorized in 17.15 along with John's formulaic construction ('peoples, crowds, nations and tongues') to refer to the entire population of the empire.[66] Prostitute (Rome) and

Jeremiah 51.7-8 (MT). But this text does not refer directly to the wrath of God. W. Bauer, W. F. Arndt, F. W. Gingrich, and F. W. Danker, *Greek-English Lexicon of the New Testament and Other Early Christian Literature*, 3rd edn (Chicago: University of Chicago Press, 2000), p.461, lists as a translation of the two genitives of apposition in Rev. 14.8 and 18.3a the wine 'of her passionate immorality'. But then the entry goes on to say that the metaphors may be mixed. The wine of Babylon's harlotry functions as the wine in God's judging anger against both the nations (14.8; 18.3a) and Babylon (16.19). This seems to be in keeping with the seer's basic usage (cf. 12.12). Thus we prefer to translate 18.3a 'Babylon has fallen ... on the grounds that all that drink from the wine of her immorality drink God's judging anger.'

63   The terminology for Rev. 18.23 is probably drawn from oracles in Isa. 23. Isa. 23.3 refers to the nations while Isa. 23.8 refers to the merchant and rulers beguiled by Satan. For a definitive statement on wealth in the Apocalypse see J. Nelson Kraybill, *Imperial Cult and Commerce in John's Apocalypse*, JSNTSup 132 (Sheffield: Sheffield Academic Press, 1996); also note Christopher Rowland, *Revelation: Epworth Commentaries* (London: Epworth Press, 1993).

64   Fekkes, *Isaiah and The Prophetic Traditions*, claims that the reference to 'sorcery' echoes Isa. 47.9, 12. The spell, primarily in Revelation, is not that of wizards but of wealth.

65   This is another instance where John returns to Jeremiah 50–51 to use material from the oracle against Babylon. There is a strong echo of Jer. 51.13 (MT). There, Jeremiah is referring to Babylon as a city built on a mass of land served by many canals. The OT descriptions for Babylon in the Apocalypse is close enough to be transferrable to Rome.

66   Bauckham, *The Climax of Prophecy*, pp.326–37, has an intricate evaluation and set of conclusions with respect to John's fourfold use of terminology for the nations that is difficult to assess. The argument ranges from detailed analyses of stereotyped phrases found in biblical texts to major conclusions built on numerical symbolism. On p.336 there is an example of the latter. He takes seven (the number for completeness) and multiplies it with four (the symbol for the world) so that the seven instances of the fourfold formula for the nations come to 28 (the number of instances of the use of ἀρνίον 'Lamb' in the Apocalypse). In my judgment this represents a level of confidence in the Nestle-Aland reconstructed text that is open to substantial question. So, although we are not prepared to grant that a clue to John's 'prophetic conviction' about the conversion of the nations is inherent in the terminology of this formula, we concede that there are exegetical observations that Bauckham makes along the way which are worthy of note. Still there are issues. With respect to 17.15 there

empire (the four peoples) appear invincible. But in several following verses the unfolding of the mystery (17.5) indicates a very different future for Rome. Ten kings from the East, allied with a 'returning Nero' figure, destroy the city (17.16-18). Rome is destined to collapse.

Yet what is noticeable in all these texts on the fall of Babylon is the clear distinction drawn between Rome and the client peoples of her empire. Rome as the source of terrifying idolatry is destroyed. Smoke rises from her burning ruins (18.18). She must pay the price for her wantonness. But while she may be devastated the peoples and nations still stand. In the dirge of Revelation 18 the client kings, sailors, and merchants mourn because they have lost the source of their power and benefits. But, at least, they are alive to mourn. The real issue is to whom will Rome's former vassals now give their allegiance. This becomes a crucial question as the concluding chapters of the Apocalypse unfold.

The Promise that the Lord and His Saints will Subdue the Nations Based on Psalm 2 (Revelation 2.26-27; 12.5; 19.15; 11.18)

At this stage in our discussion of the role of the nations in the Apocalypse we have learned that in John's view their allegiance with Babylon will turn out to be a failed enterprise. But what will be their ultimate destiny? Now it is time to take up another crucial theme in the Apocalypse: the announcement that the nations are destined to be forced to change their allegiance and become subject to another sovereign – a ruler from the family of David and his kings and priests. Before we turn to an analysis of what John says about this, we will give a brief overview of the crucial importance of Psalm 2 for the development of John's theological strategy.

In many ways Psalm 2 functions as a plot outline. When glossed and supplemented with linguistic and thematic connections to other texts, it serves as a template for the foundation of the scroll's message in Revelation. The following cursory table of major themes found in both Psalm 2 and Revelation gives a broad overview as to how suggestive this psalm was for the author of the Apoca-

---

is a need to account for the sole appearance of ὄχλοι 'multitudes' in the seven instances of the fourfold terminology for the nations. Bauckham notes that elsewhere in the appendix on Babylon the use of ὄχλος refers to the multitudes in heaven (19.1, 6; cf. 7.9). He even draws attention to an interesting parallel to the 'waters' (Rev. 19.6 and 17.15; cf. 14.2). But again, to say that the first two synonyms (λαοί and ὄχλοι) of the fourfold formula refer to followers of the Lamb, while the latter two ('nations and tongues') refer to those who serve Babylon, and John is drawing a contrast between the two, stretches the evidence. The use of λαοί 'peoples' is vitally connected in other texts in Revelation with the terminology for 'tongues' and 'nations' (5.9; 7.9; 10.11; 13.7; 14.6). Why is 17.15 any different? We are happy enough to say the use of multitudes in 17.15 is an ironic contrast to its use in 19.1, 6.

lypse. After we set forth our table we will begin to address our major concern 'the promise to subdue the nations', found in Psalm 2.8-9.

Psalm 2		Revelation
Verses in Ps. 2	Themes in Psalm 2	References in Revelation
1-2	The Kings of the earth/rulers and nations prepare for war against the Lord's anointed	3.7; 5.5; 6.15; 11.18; 19.19; 22.16
4-5	The Lord derides this challenge and vows to bring wrath upon these opponents	6.16-17; 11.18; 14.10; 16.19; 19.15
6-8	The Lord sets his son as king on Mt Zion and gives the nations as an inheritance to him and his people	1.5; 1.13; 2.26; 11.15; 12.5; 14.14; 15.1-4; 17.14; 19.16; 20.4
9	The Son will break the nations with an iron rod	2.27; 11.18; 12.5; 19.15
10-11	Given the certainty of defeat of the rulers and the allies, now is the time to repent	11.18

Promise to subdue the nations in Psalm 2.8-9
In the initial verses of the Apocalypse we learn that Jesus Christ is the ruler of the kings of the earth (Rev. 1.5). In parallelism we are told that he has made his followers a kingdom and priests (1.6). Then, in Revelation 2.26-28 the church at Thyatira receives from the prophet John a twofold promise. If they keep the words of the Lord until the end they will have 'power (authority) over the nations' and will be given 'the morning star'. It is concerning the promise of power over the nations based on Psalm 2 that we wish to focus our attention in this section.[67]

The promise of having power over the nations is formulated in language that echoes Ps. 2.8-9.[68] Psalm 2 is a polemic against peoples and nations who resist the power of the Lord's anointed. It is generally agreed that in its original setting

---

67   With respect to the latter we are inclined to follow Richard Bauckham's interpretation that the 'morning star' is a symbol for the parousia of Christ at which time the nations will be subject to him (Rev. 22.16; 2 Peter 1.19). Cf. R. Bauckham, *Jude, 2 Peter*, WBC 50 (Waco, Texas: Word Books, 1983), pp.225–6; *idem, The Climax of Prophecy*, pp.323–6.

68   See David E. Aune, *Revelation 1–5*, p.209, for a helpful chart illustrating linguistic connections between Rev. 2.26b-27 and Ps. 2.8-9 LXX.

it functioned liturgically in connection with the coronation of the Davidic kings. Rhetorically, in the investiture ceremony the king, as Yahweh's representative, becomes sovereign not only over Israel but also over the nations. The psalm celebrates the ideal that all peoples will some day recognize and acknowledge Yahweh's sovereignty through the prism of accepting the Davidic king as the Lord's anointed. Verses 7-9 of the psalm describe a decree given to the anointed one (perhaps during the coronation ceremony itself) wherein the king is acknowledged as God's son (representative). The decree states that he is the beneficiary of supreme power over the nations and, as such, is empowered to subdue them. The psalm concludes in verses 10-11 with a warning to other Near-Eastern powers to accept the sovereignty of Yahweh.

Given the fortunes of the Davidic dynasty throughout both the first and second temple eras there is no doubt that this psalm had a chequered reception history. In the pre-exilic era, when it appears to be composed, there must have been occasions when the psalm would be recited with a note of triumphalism. But in the second temple era the reality of the absence of a Davidic ruler would surely mean that any plausible hearing of its claims could only function in the context of eschatological anticipation. With the coming new world the anticipation would be of a Davidic king being restored to his appropriate status. It is in such a context that a very striking use of Psalm 2.7-9 occurs in Psalms of Solomon 17 which, interestingly enough, also has considerable significance for the study of the Apocalypse of John.

Psalms of Solomon 17 and the subjection of the nations
The Psalms of Solomon were composed in the vicinity of Jerusalem in the first century BCE. Throughout this collection there are a number of echoes and allusions to Pompey's plunder of Jerusalem in 63 BCE followed by his death in Egypt in 48 BCE. It would seem reasonable to conclude that these psalms were composed shortly after this time.[69] This was an era when the Gentiles reigned supreme and trampled over Jerusalem. The parallels with the time of the Apocalypse are all too clear. In chapter 17 the author views this terrible situation as God's just punishment for the sins of Israel (Pss. Sol. 17.5-20).[70]

---

69   *The Apocryphal Old Testament*, ed. H. F. D. Sparks (Oxford: Clarendon Press, 1984), pp.650–51. The Psalms of Solomon were probably first composed in Hebrew but are now only available to us in a Greek recension and a later Syriac translation from the Greek. Citations are drawn from A. Rahlfs, *Septuaginta II* (Stuttgart: Württembergische Bibelanstalt, 1962), pp.486–8.

70   According to Sam Janse, '*You Are My Son*': *The Reception History of Psalm 2 in Early Judaism and the Early Church*, CBET 51 (Leuven: Peters, 2009), pp.55–66, the Psalms of Solomon represents a sweeping interpretation of the situation of Judaism in about the last century of the Second Temple Era. Through a helpful table (57–60) he shows that the author of Pss. Sol. 17 'mined' not only major themes of Psalm 2, but supplemented it in 'midrashic' fashion with 2 Sam. 7.1-17; Ps. 89; Isa. 11.1-10 and 49.1-6 to give a detailed picture of the eschatological hope for the emergence of a new David characteristic of much of the Judaism of this time. Echoing a pattern appearing frequently in the latter chapters of Zechariah, Janse notes that Pss. Sol. 17 focuses on such key

Here the claim is made that God will recompense the Romans for their ἔργα 'works' (Pss. Sol. 17.8).[71] After the allusion to Pompey's conquest of Jerusalem taking captives from Jerusalem back to the West (Pss. Sol. 17.11-15) the author speaks of χριστὸς κυρίου, an 'anointed one of the Lord' (17.32), who will bring freedom to Israel (Pss. Sol. 17.21-46; cf. the heading of chapter 18;[72] 18.7). He is referring to an anticipated resumption of the Davidic monarchy.

Throughout Psalm 17 a clear distinction is made between Israel and the nations. At the time of writing Israel is dispirited and defeated (Pss. Sol. 17.6-7, 13-14, 20, 45). With the coming of the anointed one and the restoration of the kingdom of David the scattered tribes of earthly Israel will be re-gathered (Pss. Sol. 17.44). They will no longer suffer the indignity of being ruled by a ἀλλότριον γένους 'foreigner to the race' (Pss. Sol. 17.7; cf. 17.15). This strong, almost contemptible dismissal of the Gentiles is a feature of the psalm (cf. Pss. Sol. 17.20, 27).

In keeping with one reading of the OT texts on the pilgrimage of the nations, at an appropriate time the Gentiles will come to Jerusalem and give glory to God (Isa. 60.2-3; cf. Pss. Sol. 17.30-31); but they will be under the yoke of the Lord's anointed and will fear him (Pss. Sol. 17.30, 34). This also seems to be the main thrust of the psalm. The reader of the psalm is informed that 'our Kingdom of God' stands eternally in judgment over the Gentiles (Pss. Sol. 17.3-7). The constant refrain is for the God of Israel to free God's elect people from the filth of unclean enemies (Pss. Sol. 17.3, 45). This strong ethnic differentiation between Israel and the Gentiles is clearly a central feature of Psalms of Solomon 17. The nations who took the people of the land into exile will be the agents to restore them to their homeland (Pss. Sol. 17.31). The underlying tone of a desire to get even follows what was identified in chapter 1 as the punitive model of suffering.

As part of the description of the rout of the nations the author of Psalms of Solomon 17 uses Psalm 2.8-9. The structure of the two psalms is similar. The people of God have suffered under the cruel punitive aggression of the nations. The holy city is overrun by the Gentiles. But God has not forgotten His anointed and will launch a holy war against the nations; and they will be defeated (Pss. Sol. 17.21-25, 35).

In Psalms of Solomon 17.23b the author picks up the terminology of Psalm 2.9 with his use of the metaphor of a potter smashing his (defective) pots to

---

themes as the restoration of the kingship of David, purging of the Jewish people in Jerusalem and the Gentiles returning to the city to see its glory. As we note below, Pss. Sol. 17.23-24 frequently uses Ps. 2.8-9 as a key text in his argumentation.

71   This is the first distant linguistic hint of a connection with Rev. 2.26-28. Given that this is a different usage in Revelation. The one in the church at Thyatira who is faithful to the end in his works (ἔργα) is the recipient of the promise to rule in God's new world.

72   It is possible, as suggested in the textual apparatus, that this phraseology may be an emendation of Christian scribes. Nevertheless, the idea of the restoration of a Davidite is very clear.

describe the defeat of the enemies of the Lord's anointed. Then he follows immediately with the reference to the ῥάβδῳ σιδηρᾷ 'iron rod' also in Psalm 2.9, as the preferred method of destruction.[73]

But interestingly enough the close web of linguistic and literary connections between Psalm 2.8-9 and Psalms of Solomon 17 with respect to the defeat of the nations does not end there. In Psalm 2.8 (LXX) there is the decreed promise that the Davidic king will receive honour from the nations as his κληρονομίαν 'inheritance'. Similar terminology with respect to the ideal Davidite occurs in Psalms of Solomon 17.23 when it is stated that he will strip the sinners of the 'inheritance'.[74] Furthermore, the use of ποιμαίνειν 'to shepherd' or 'rule' in Psalm 2.8 to describe the power of the Davidic king over the nations has an analogue in Psalms of Solomon 17.40 where similar terminology refers to the Davidic king re-gathering Israel in the land.

In drawing attention to these linguistic and thematic connections between Psalm 2.8-9 and Psalms of Solomon 17 we are attempting to substantiate the existence of an exegetical tradition, utilizing Psalm 2, on the promise of the victory of the Lord's anointed over the Gentiles. It especially comes to the fore in the threat that the Lord would banish the sinners like a potter destroys a defective jar. He will punish with an iron rod (Ps. 2.9/Pss. Sol. 17.23-24). These traditions abound in post-exilic interpretation in Israel (Tobit 13.11-13; 14.5-7; T. Zeb. 9.8; T. Benj. 9.2; and especially Sib. Or. 3.767-795). With their own set of mutations they appear to resurface in the Apocalypse. The common thread is the claim that at the end of the age the Lord's anointed will ultimately subdue and smash the rebellious machinations of the nations. Both the Davidic king and his people will share sovereign rule over them. In Psalms of Solomon 17 it is clear that the rule and exercise of power over the nations entails the re-establishment of the Davidic rule in Jerusalem, the navel of the earth, and their compulsive recognition of the sheer power of his sovereignty by the nations.

The use of Psalm 2.8-9 in Revelation 2.26-27

It is often noted that the author of Revelation never formally quotes a passage of scripture directly but relies upon allusions.[75] In some cases this can be a distant echo. But in this instance there are three strong allusions in Revelation 2.26-27 to Psalm 2.8-9 (LXX).

---

73   The order of iron rod and potter's vessel in Pss. Sol. 17.23b-24a is in the reverse of the order in Ps. 2.9, but the literary dependence is incontestable.

74   Rev. 21.7 also uses similar terminology, ὁ νικῶν κληρονομήσει ταῦτα 'the one conquering will inherit these things'. This is immediately followed by an echo of Ps. 2.7, 'I will be his God and he will be my son', echoing the promise of 2 Sam. 7.14 in one of the earliest scriptural arguments for the special sonship of Jesus that early Christians articulated. See Barnabas Lindars, *New Testament Apologetic* (London: SCM Press, 1961), pp.139–44. In Rev. 21.7 the promise is democratized to apply also to the followers of Jesus (cf. 2 Cor. 6.18).

75   G. K. Beale, *The Book of Revelation* NICNT (William B. Eerdmans/Paternoster: Grand Rapids, MI/ Cambridge, UK, 1999), pp.76–99, who gives a helpful overview of the issue. J. Lambrecht, 'The People of God in the Book of Revelation', *Collected Studies on Pauline Literature*

At the outset, however, it is worth reiteration that at the beginning of the book the prophet John declares that 'Jesus Christ, the faithful witness, the first born of the dead ones', is also said to be 'the one who rules over all earthly kings' (Rev. 1.5). This is a fundamental presupposition that stands at the heart of the Apocalypse. When Jesus comes in the final battle he has on his cloak the inscription 'King of kings and Lord of lords' (Rev. 19.16). It is also worth repeating that followers of Jesus Christ are promised a share in this rule. Revelation 1.6 asserts boldly that he (Jesus Christ) 'has made for us (believers) a kingdom...' . Revelation 1.9 paradoxically asserts that while believers now must exhibit 'patient endurance' during the present testing and in the coming days, they are to comfort themselves with the full realization that they constitute a kingdom.[76] Thus it is no great surprise that the first promise to the faithful believers at Thyatira is that they will receive authority over the nations. Thus the ruling capacity attributed to Jesus in 12.5 and 19.15 goes to the believers in 2.26. The wording, with a major difference in person, reflects direct dependence upon Psalm 2.8 as the following parallel wording drawn from Aune indicates.

Ps. 2.8b	Rev. 2.26b
Καὶ δώσω σοι	δώσω αὐτῷ
and I will give to you	I will give to him
ἔθνη τὴν κληρονομίαν σου	ἐξουσίαν ἐπὶ τῶν ἐθνῶν
nations as your inheritance	Authority over the nations
καὶ τὴν κατασχέσιν σου	
and as your possession	
τὰ πέρατα τῆς γῆς	
the ends of the earth[77]	

The allusions in Revelation 2.26 to Ps. 2.8b are clear, although the extension of the promise to the Davidic king of the inheritance of both the nations and the ends of the earth as his possessions does not occur directly in the text. Toward the end of the narrative of Revelation the rebellious nations, ultimately to be overthrown in 20.9, come from 'the four corners of the earth'. Psalm 2 centres on the actual exercise of power over the nations by a Davidite on the throne in

and on the Book of Revelation AnBib 147 (Rome: Pontifical Biblical Institute, 2001), p.389; Paul B. Decock, 'The Scriptures in the Book of Revelation', pp.373–406.

76   The classical verse of Rev. 5.10 adds the promise of ruling on earth. The textual issue (βασιλεύουσιν or βασιλεύσουσιν), as noted earlier, is important. It is helpful to survey a fair discussion on the issue given by Håkan Ulfgard, *Feast and Future: Revelation 7:9-17 and the Feast of Tabernacles*, ConBNT 22 (Lund: Almqvist & Wiksell, 1989), pp.41–7, who approaches it from the perspective of realized eschatology.

77   Aune, *Revelation 1-5*, p.209.

Jerusalem. Revelation's omission of any specific reference to the nations as an inheritance, and the ends of the earth as their (believers') possession, indicates that the prophet John visualizes the exercise of power as being of an order different from a political reign over the nations on earth with its trappings of wealth and prestige.[78]

Yet one should be careful here. Just because John does not say that believers will actually rule over the nations in the manner that the Israelites idealized an eschatological Davidite, one should not embrace the other extreme and spiritualize the passage so that it becomes merely a metaphor for the idealized Christian life.[79] The prophet John is far too involved in the contemporary realities of his time to take that route. He is in full expectation that an impending conflict that has cosmic implications is on the horizon. Relief to his fellow oppressed believers from idolatrous power symbolized by Rome will only come when that *mode* of power is broken. The whole progression of the series of visions in Revelation, although primarily literary in its movement, points to an actual reversal and renovation of the order of things at the end of the age. And just as in Psalm 2 the thought is that the messianic rule will bring an ideal order possibly similar to Isaiah 11.1-9, so also John's contemplation of the new order of things will entail an even more radical cosmic change with the arrival of a messianic age of peace. Then the messiah will reign and the ethos of his people of peace will permeate everything (cf. Rev. 21.1–22.5). A contemplation of the replacement of the Roman political order seems to be the thrust of the other copious references to authority in the Apocalypse whether it is the coming rule of the beast or its overthrow by the Christ (6.8; 9.3; 13.2, 4, 5, 7, 12; 12.10; 17.13). But it is fair to observe that John is not interested in stating that this great reversal will merely put the people of God in the same situation as their present oppressors. John is far too subtle for that.

The second allusion in Revelation 2.26b-27 to Psalm 2.8-9 involves the extension of the promise of Psalm 2. Not only will the people of God have authority over the nations but they will have the capacity to ποιμαίνειν

---

78   This does not mean that the author of the Apocalypse had no interest in the references to the nations as a possession and the ends of the earth as the inheritance of believers. Already in early Christian exegesis this language was connected with the Abrahamic land promise (Gen. 17.8) and reinterpreted in Acts 7.2-8, 45; 13.32-33 (Western text) to refer to the establishment of the church and the mission to the Gentiles. See Allan J. McNicol, 'Rebuilding the House of David: The Function of the Benedictus in Luke-Acts', *ResQ* 40/1 (1998), pp.25–38. In Rev. 7.9 John connects the vindicated followers of the Lamb to the Abrahamic promises as 'a number which no one can count'. But, in Rev. 21.7 this promise is extended to anyone who will share or κληρονομήσει 'inherit' the new creation. Since the entire creation is a universal temple filled with God's presence both the Abrahamic promises and the entirety of Ps. 2.8b finds its ultimate fulfilment in this reality. Cf. G. K. Beale, *The Temple and the Church's Mission: A Biblical Theology of the Dwelling Place of God*, NSBT 17 (Downer's Grove, Ill: Apollos/Intervarsity Press, 2004), pp.365–73.

79   J. P. M. Sweet, *Revelation*, p.96; Beale, *The Book of Revelation*, p.268.

'subdue' them with an iron rod. In this text we encounter two linguistic issues of considerable significance: (1) the appropriate translation of ποιμαίνειν, and (2) the nature and function of the iron rod.

As noted below, we have chosen to translate ποιμαίνειν as 'subdue'. But a reader will note that the English translators show no uniformity in their translations of this verb in this context. Generally speaking, there are two major options for the rendering of ποιμαίνειν in English.[80] One may take a cue from the immediately preceding phraseology in Revelation 2.26b and understand ποιμαίνειν as an analogue to the guidance of a beneficent king, in the sense of being given power (RSV 'rule'). This meaning stresses the power of beneficent shepherding authority. Interestingly enough, probably echoing the popular reading of Psalm 23, this is how much contemporary culture responds to this metaphor. Indeed, ποιμαίνειν is used in the sense of 'to provide nourishment, rule, or shepherd' in Revelation 7.17 and in some other places in the New Testament (Matt. 2.6; Jn. 21.16; 1 Cor. 9.7). This is also probably the sense that the faithful are promised to reign (βασιλεύσουσιν) in Revelation 22.5. But it is open to question whether this usage applies here.[81] This is because when John utilizes Psalm 2.9 elsewhere, in 12.5 and 19.15, he understands it is a decree in the sense of 'subdue' or even 'demolish' the nations in a definitive judgment. The critical verse that underscores the point is 19.15. There, in the description of the rider on the white horse, his coming in judgment against the forces of the beast and his allies is stated in a parallel construction based on Psalm 2.9. The wording in Greek is: καὶ αὐτὸς ποιμανεῖ αὐτοὺς ἐν ῥάβδῳ σιδηρᾷ 'He will subdue them with an iron rod'. The parallel phraseology καὶ αὐτὸς πατεῖ τὴν ληνὸν τοῦ οἴνου τοῦ θυμοῦ τῆς ὀργῆς τοῦ θεοῦ 'he will trample the winepress of the fury of the wrath of God', confirms this interpretation. Revelation 2.27a is totally in keeping with this reading; and the parallel drawn directly from Ps. 2.9 in Revelation 2.27b 'as (rejected) clay pots are demolished (by the potter); also confirms this. Thus this text functions as a promise to the believers in Thyatira that the faithful will defeat their enemies and will participate in a rule over them.[82]

---

80   Colin J. Hemer, *The Letters to the Seven Churches of Asia in their Local Setting*, JSNTSup 11 (Sheffield: JSOT Press, 1989), p.124.

81   The Semitic *Vorlage* of ποιμαίνειν in Ps. 2.9 is a matter of considerable conflict. Aune, *Revelation 1–5*, pp.210–11, gives a fair discussion of the issues. The point needs to be underscored that where John uses ποιμαίνειν in the other two direct echoes of Ps. 2.9 in the Apocalypse (12.5, 19.15) he is consistent in understanding it to mean 'subdue' or 'smash'. Evidently this is how the author of the Apocalypse read his (probable) Semitic text no matter what particular vocalization he attached to it.

82   Also ποιμαίνειν is used in the sense of destroy in several texts of the LXX (Mic. 5.5[6]; Jer. 6.3; 22.22) as well as Pss. Sol. 17.24, as Beale, *Revelation*, p.267, points out. George Wesley Buchanan, *The Book of Revelation: Its Introduction and Prophecy* (Eugene, Oregon: Wipf & Stock,

This powerful promise to the believers at Thyatira that those who persist in the faith will see their enemies subdued forcibly understandably bothers commentators. One commentator (among many) refers to this text as 'the great paradox, the supreme irony, already present in the ambivalent ποιμαίνειν: to smash and to shepherd'.[83] He is not alone. But, to find a dialectic between smashing and kind shepherding, in the ambiguity of the meaning of ποιμαί νειν, as judgment vis-à-vis grace, which some do, would seem to attribute to John an oversupply of subtlety.[84] In light of Revelation 2.27b it would appear that John, anticipating the fulfilment of Psalm 2.9, envisions a time when the forces of Christ (the Lord's anointed) will witness a destructive blow of the nations, presumably in an eschatological conflict of critical future significance. Specifically, how John envisions the nature of this conflict will be traced in the next chapter.

This brings us to the issue of the precise nature and function of the 'iron rod'. The iron rod often refers to the 'iron tipped' rod or staff of a shepherd which may be used as a club or a staff to bring wandering animals into line. On the other hand this reference could be understood to be a scepter (as it appears in some royal Near Eastern iconography) of the Lord's anointed (in analogy with Psalm 2 as a royal Psalm).[85] Perhaps it is a combination of both ideas. The Davidic king comes with authority expressed in his scepter to destroy his enemies. As the shepherd uses the rod to subdue any opposition he encounters, so the Lord's anointed and his army of followers will exercise the same power over the nations.[86]

This reading that the followers of the Lamb will subdue the nations is totally in keeping with the third aspect of the initial promise to the believers at Thyatira dependent upon Psalm 2.8-9. Echoing Jeremiah 18.1-11, as well as Psalm 2.9, John is saying that as a defective clay pot is shattered by the master potter, the nations, standing in rebellion to the Lord, defective in their relationship to the Creator, will suffer crushing defeat.

Revelation 2.26b-27 represents a careful appropriation of Psalm 2.8-9 by the prophet John. It comes in the context of the struggle of early Christian communities in Asia against the impact of the Roman imperial power and its inter-

---

2005), pp. 116–17, notes that the metaphor of the king as shepherd implied not only that shepherds cared for their flock, but that they defended them strongly with rods against intruders. This latter understanding of the use of the rod seems to be what is meant here.

83   W. J. Harrington, *Revelation* SP 16 (Collegeville, Minn: The Liturgical Press, 1993), p.66.

84   George Caird, *A Commentary on The Revelation of St. John the Divine* HNTC (New York: Harper & Row Publishers, 1966), p.46; J. P. M. Sweet, *Revelation*, p.96.

85   Grant A. Osborne, *Revelation*, p.685. John Collins' translation of the *Sibylline Oracles* in *The Old Testament Pseudepigrapha* 1, *Apocalyptic Literature and Testaments*, ed. James H. Charlesworth (Garden City, NY: Doubleday & Company, 1983), p.424, renders a similar reference (Sib. Or. 8.248) as 'an iron shepherd's rod'.

86   Aune, *Revelation 1–5*, p.210.

twined sub-strata of the sponsorship of various cults, imperial and otherwise. On the basis of the promise of Psalm 2.8-9 that the Lord's anointed will have authority over the nations, the believers in a small church in the province of Asia are told that they will have a share in the decisive and absolute rout of their enemies. This theme will emerge again as a central strand of the story in the major heavenly vision of 4.1–22.5.

The use of Psalm 2.8-9 in Revelation 12.5

Another major usage of Psalm 2.8-9 occurs in Revelation 12.5, a passage which affirms that God's 'anointed one', his son, is destined to subdue the nations.

In Revelation 12.1-6 two important figures in the drama of the last half of the Apocalypse (the pregnant woman and the dragon) are introduced. Without nuancing the discussion it is clear that the woman represents the people of God (in some respect) and the dragon is Satan. We enter the flow of the narrative at a critical point. The pregnant woman is about to give birth and the dragon stands poised ready to devour the child (12.4).

Subsequently, in 12.5a, the woman gives birth to a son. The description of her son as a υἱὸν ἄρσεν, a 'male child', is an unusual construction and again probably reflects the use of scripture. First, there is the clear allusion to Psalm 2.8-9 that follows directly the reference to the 'male child' who will 'subdue the nations with a rod of iron'. The general subject matter involves a major theme of Psalm 2 (the authority of God's anointed over the nations). On this basis it is defensible to claim that the appearance of υἱόν 'son' in Revelation 12.5 is an echo of υἱός μου 'my son' of Psalm 2.7. This point is substantiated by the use of ἄρσεν 'male child' in apposition with son. Commentators duly note the incongruity of the Greek grammar since ἄρσεν 'male child' is a neuter adjective while υἱόν 'son' is a masculine noun.[87] Even though John is famous for his solecisms, he later uses τὸν ἄρσεν 'the male child' properly as a masculine accusative.[88] The unusual use of ἄρσεν in 12.5 emerges because John is echoing another scriptural reference ἔτεκεν ἄρσεν 'she brought forth a son' (LXX Isa. 66.7).[89] Contextually, in Isaiah, this verse is in a unit housing a rousing promise of the restoration of God's people, and the defeat of their enemies. The basic image is the birth of a child. It seems impossible for a woman to give birth without labour; yet God is able to bring new life seemingly without effort: both to restore Jerusalem and defeat its enemies. John seems to echo this text as his authoritative basis to underscore the idea that the Lord's anointed (Ps. 2.7), God's son, is fully capable of bringing the restoration of the people of God of his day to full realization. Thus the allusion is appropriate.

---

87   David E. Aune, *Revelation 6–16*, p.687.
88   Beale, *Revelation*, p.641.
89   Beale, *Revelation*, pp.640–41, correctly notes that already in Rev. 12.2 there is an echo of Isa. 66.7 with the use of ὠδίνουσαν τεκεῖν 'through labour pains to bring forth'.

We now address directly the use of Psalm 2.8-9 in Revelation 12.5. A significant feature of the anticipated restoration, in keeping with the allusion to Psalm 2.8-9, is the defeat of the powers causing the subjection of the nations. We learn in Revelation 12.5 that the son is μέλλει 'destined' to ποιμαίνειν 'subdue' the nations with a rod of iron. Here there is obviously a close connection with the subject matter of Revelation 2.26-28.[90] In 2.28 God's anointed (Christ) is presumed to have authority over the *nations*. And in 2.26-27 his followers are promised that they will share in his victory by ruling over them. Returning to 12.5, the focus now shifts to the exaltation of Christ. According to the seer this event inaugurated the fulfilment of the promise to subject *all nations* to his dominion.[91] It is obviously anticipatory. But in Revelation 19.5 we are thrust forward, following the narrative flow of John's vision, to the climactic future eschatological victory for the Lamb and his people. By this time in the flow of the narrative the promise is brought to completion. There, both the son and the army of the saints engage in the final eschatological battle. It is to this crucial text we now turn in some detail.

The use of Psalm 2.8-9 in Revelation 19.15
Revelation 19.15, with its direct echo of Psalm 2.8-9, occurs within the wider unit of the eschatological triumph of the heavenly Lord Jesus over the nations (19.11-21). Critical commentators find connections between this unit and the earlier passages of Revelation 16.14-16 and 17.14 where we have anticipations of an eschatological conflict of great magnitude between Christ and those who are arraigned against him. But, although these eschatological events were already anticipated, it is difficult to escape the impression that this passage inaugurates John's actual description of how he perceives events of the end of the age. This is because it is housed in a narrative that has many of the appearances of climaxing chronological progression (i.e. 19.11–21.8: from parousia to the new Jerusalem). Revelation 19.11-21 is a vivid account of the visible appearance of Christ seated on a white horse coming with the armies of heaven to defeat his enemies. It begins the final action sequences of the book. It links the momentous struggles against evil that have already taken place during the great tribulation with an elaboration, in stages, of the defeat of evil and the coming of the new creation which is about to unfold.[92]

90   Fekkes, *Isaiah and Prophetic Traditions*, p.115, gives several examples to illustrate that 'John's use of scripture exhibits a clear pattern of conscious repetition which often involves a base text and the recapitulation of its various units or key words.' In subsequent passages, the use of Ps. 2.8-9 first in Rev. 2.26-27 and then in 12.15 and 19.15 is a good example of this procedure.

91   The explicit reference to 'all the nations' occurs several times in Revelation (12.5; 14.8; 15.4; 18.3, 23). It seems to be nothing more than a linguistic preference to express the comprehensiveness of the victory of God's anointed and his people.

92   Most commentators understand that the rider on the white horse is a reference to the parousia of Christ. No one disputes that the rider is Christ (see 19.13, 16). But R. J. McKelvey, *The*

Connection between Psalm 2.8-9 and the defeat of the nations already set forth in Revelation 2.26-27 and 12.5 are underscored again in 19.15. The action opens in 19.11 with the general description of the rider on the white horse coming from heaven with his armies. The rider on the white horse is called Faithful and True. The identity of this rider as Christ is beyond doubt (19.11-14; cf. 1.5; 3.7, 14). The reference to the white horse echoes 6.2 where this image represents the first of a series of God's judgments on *pax Romana*. Perhaps the reappearance of the white horse suggests that the parousia is the penultimate judgment.[93] In any case the coming of Christ clearly affirms his sovereign power over his enemies. The text states explicitly that, as the Divine Warrior, he judges righteously and will wage war against them (19.11).

Astonishingly, John describes the rider (Christ) as dressed in a robe sprinkled with blood[94] *before the battle.* Is John alluding to the earlier battle at the cross through which Christ has won the ultimate victory over Satan (5.12; 12.5, 11)? Or is his coming in his parousia viewed primarily as a holy war against his enemies.[95] As the Word of God came from heaven precipitating the destruction

---

Millennium and the Book of Revelation (Cambridge: Lutterworth Press, 1999), pp.77–81, gives a spirited defence of the position that this is *not* a parousia unit but a general use of holy war imagery to describe the eschatological defeat of evil. It is true that some familiar parousia imagery such as the coming of Christ on the clouds and the gathering of the elect from all nations is missing. But one essential ingredient of parousia scenes is the destruction of the Lord's enemies (cf. 2 Thess. 1.8) and this seems to be the focus here. Rather than view 19.11-21 as either a specific description of the parousia or a general use of holy war imagery to describe spiritual warfare, it is likely that John is simply making the more general point that the enemies of the people of God will be routed in a final eschatological victory. Usually, in early Christian thinking, this takes place at the parousia.

93   Pierre Prigent, *Commentary on the Apocalypse of St. John* (trans. Wendy Pradels: Tübingen: Mohr Siebeck, 2004), p.539.

94   The textual tradition is mixed. Nestle-Aland with its reading of the perfect passive participle drawn from βαπτίζειν 'to dip' or 'to immerse' is favoured by many. However, various forms of the perfect passive participle of ῥαντίζειν are also well attested in ancient texts – especially in the versions. Cf. Carroll D. Osborne, 'Alexander Campbell and the Text of Revelation 19:13', ResQ 25 (1982), pp.129–38, who gives an exhaustive listing of the textual evidence. The reading of a form of ῥαντίζειν appears in the Greek versions of Aquila and Symmachus of Isa. 63.3. Isa. 63 is a key text echoed strongly in this passage. The latter usage probably was the original reading. The various readings of 'dipped' or 'drenched' may come into the text through the influence of Targumic interpolations with early Christian commentators drawn from Gen. 49.11.

95   The text of Isa. 63.1-3 clearly pictures Yahweh as a survivor returning from a battle in blood-spattered garments or as someone who has trodden a winepress, returning to exercise retribution on his enemies (cf. Lam. 1.15). John uses similar terminology in 14.19-20. The martyrs have suffered in battles in the past. Now the enemies will suffer. The idea of the blood-stained warrior is a common OT theme (cf. Aune, *Revelation 17–22*, p.1057). What is astonishing, as compared with the Targums, is how restrained John is in his use of the language of vengeance! Nevertheless, this is clearly no anticipation of a victory celebration of the way of suffering-servant type Christian martyrdom winning out in the end. The time for definitive defeat of the enemies by the warrior-messiah is at hand. Most likely because of the anticipatory language of 14.19-20 and the common dependence of this text and 19.11-21 on Isaiah 63.1-6 the bloody robe refers to the blood of the enemies and not to the cross of Christ. The fact this is a description before the actual battle is not

of the Egyptians at the Exodus (Wis. 18.15-19), so Christ the Word of God, comes to vanquish his enemies (19.13). Heavenly armies clothed in white pure linen follow him (19.14).

A key exegetical issue is whether the heavenly armies are angels, or the faithful ones who earlier, by the heavenly altar, had called for vindication (6.9-11). References in apocalyptic writings to the presence of angels at the glory of the last day are ubiquitous. This also tumbles over into scripture (2 Thess. 1.7; Matt. 25.31; Jude 14). However, it is difficult to escape the conclusion that the focus, for John in this text, is on the martyred saints. It is often overlooked that the *maśkîlîm* of Daniel 11.33-35, after being cleansed and refined through martyrdom, are made white (i.e. clean). Throughout Revelation, John views the followers of the Lamb as their antitype. In the immediate context at 19:8 the 'bride of the Lamb' is clothed in clean pure linen; and similar terminology is used in other places to describe the clothing of the faithful who are vindicated (3.4-5; 6.11; 7.9, 13-14). Thus, it is evident that John wished to stress that the presence of the martyrs of 6.9-11 is central to the constituency of the heavenly army.[96] But it is noteworthy that they are unlike their leader in one key aspect. They are not sprinkled in blood. They *follow* their leader. Christ will wield the sword, not his followers. This will remain so until the very end.

In this unit Revelation 19.15 is a crucial text that echoes directly Psalm 2.8-9 and contains the strong reference to the defeat of the nations. It opens by describing the rider on the white horse having a sharp sword protruding from his mouth.[97] This reference reflects directly Isaiah 11.4, a strong messianic text. Through metonymy John is referring to what comes from the rider's mouth (his sovereign authority) as a sword (cf. Isa. 11.4 LXX and Wis. 18.15-19). The text is saying that Christ is coming in judgment to destroy the rebellious nations (19.15, 21). Earlier in our discussion of Psalms of Solomon 17 we had noted that this psalm envisioned a restoration of a Davidite in Jerusalem along the lines set forth in Psalm 2.8-9 (cf. Pss. Sol. 17.23-24). According to the Psalms of Solomon, in his victory the king shows magnanimity to all those people who acknowledge his kingship and respect the glory of the Lord (Pss. Sol. 17.34). For a warning to his enemies we are told that the king will πατάζει 'strike' the earth by the word of his mouth (Pss. Sol. 17.35). Thus, already in Psalms of Solomon there is a clear exegetical connection between the power of the Word

---

a matter of ultimate importance in John's visionary world (note the regular use of anticipations in chapters 6–16). See Fekkes, *Isaiah and Prophetic Traditions*, p.198.

96   Heavenly figures are also clothed with pure linen in Revelation (15.6). In the Apocalypse, what is unusual, and thus a point of emphasis, is the repeated allusions to the clothing of the vindicated martyrs.

97   A number of minuscules and versions add δίστομος 'double-edged' from Rev. 1.16 and 2.12. This reading would solidify further the identification with Christ but does not materially change the thrust of the passage.

of the Lord and the defeat of the nations. A similar interpretive tradition also occurs in Revelation 19.15, although we do not claim it is directly dependent upon the Psalms of Solomon.

The wider literary context here is critical for interpreting this verse. Revelation 16.12-16 (the sixth seal) and 17.11-13, 15-18 are in the immediate background! In the latter a powerful figure emerges. He comes from across the Euphrates and gathers together a coalition of client kings and provincial leaders from the tribes and nations to launch an assault against Babylon, i.e. Rome (cf. 16.12; 17:12). They destroy Rome (17.16-17). But now, shortly after, 'in one hour', drunk with their power, they set their sights on the real enemies of idolatry, the people of God. By the use of metonymy, the people of God are embodied in their leader, the Lamb, 'Lord of lords and King of kings' (17.14; 19.16). Given the propensity of the author of the Apocalypse to anchor his vision in the text of Psalm 2, where the 'kings of the earth' and 'the nations' are synonymous (Ps. 2.2, 8), it is probable that he sees the kings who set themselves against the Lamb as the antitype of Psalm 2. At the parousia of Christ they encounter defeat.

Revelation 19.15 concludes with two paratactic clauses giving additional descriptions of the judging activity of the rider on the white horse (Christ). Both clauses commence with the emphatic linguistic construction καὶ αὐτός 'he himself', which gives added weight to what Christ does.[98] As already noted, the first description, 'And he himself will crush them (the nations) with a rod of iron', echoes again directly Psalm 2.9.[99] The second description, 'And he tramples the winepress of the anger of God the Almighty One' (Rev. 19:15b), also connects with Psalm 2, although some of the basic imagery seems to be drawn more directly from Isa 63:2-6.[100] In Psalm 2.12 the kings of the earth (see Ps. 2.2, 10) are urged to serve the Lord with fear lest he (i.e. the Lord) come upon them with fear and wrath. In Revelation 16.15 the wrath and anger of God promised to be visited upon these kings (cf. 14.20). Now, in 19.15-21, their defeat by the King of kings (19.16) takes place. This seems to cement the connection of Revelation 19:15 with Psalm 2. Although this is not technically a prophecy and fulfilment schema, the prophet John appears to indicate that in

---

98   Fekkes, *Isaiah and Prophetic Traditions*, p.197, traces this use of the emphatic 'I' back to the key text of Isa. 63.1, 3.

99   The Greek phraseology καὶ αὐτὸς ποιμανεῖ αὐτοὺς ἐν ῥάβδῳ σιδηρᾷ, 'and he will crush them with a rod of iron' paraphrases Ps. 2.8-9 (cf. Pss. Sol. 17.24 for another reference to 'the rod of iron' in inverted order to Revelation but clearly in a messianic context). Beale, *Revelation*, p.962, notes that similar linguistic connections are made in Isa. 11.4 and 49.2. However, literary connections with Psalm 2 or Rev. 19.15 in these texts are unclear.

100   John has used Isa. 63.3 in Rev. 19.13, and he could also have moved to Isa. 63.5-6 through the use of gezērâ sāwâ. There is a common usage of θυμός 'wrath' and ὀργή 'anger' in the LXX both in Ps. 2.12 and Isa. 63.5-6. Notice also a compound form of πατεῖν 'trample' in Isa. 63.3 (cf. Rev. 14.19 for the winepress metaphor). Both Ps. 2 and Isa. 63.1-6 have the common theme of the defeat of the nations.

these events the word of Psalm 2 has, as *sensus plenior*, come to culmination in the defeat of the nations at the parousia of Christ.

To conclude the unit on the parousia in Revelation 19.16, John announces that the rider on the white horse has both on his garment and thigh the inscription, 'King of kings and Lord of lords'. This is the description of the Lamb found in reverse order in Revelation 17.14. Besides recapitulating 17.14, John may also be echoing Isaiah 60.12 as well as Psalm 2 as an anticipation of what will take place in the ensuing verses. Isaiah 60 is a word about the new Jerusalem that John understands to be fulfilled in the new creation of Revelation 21.1– 22.5. But with the coming of the new Jerusalem, it must be made absolutely clear that there will be no place there for the rebellious nations. This is the burden of Isaiah 60.12:

> For the nations and kings who will not serve you will be destroyed.
> Those nations will be utterly devastated.

Sure enough, the provincial leaders and kings that are loyal to the forces of emperor worship gather against the Lamb (Rev. 19.19). And just as surely they are routed.

Addendum on Revelation 11.18 and Psalm 2
An additional echo of the use of Psalm 2 by the author of the Apocalypse occurs as part of the praise of the 24 elders in 11.18 during the sequence of the seventh trumpet. The context is similar to the song of praise of those who come out of the great tribulation in 7.11-17. There is an announcement that the kingdom of the world has become the kingdom of the Lord and his Christ (11.15). The 24 elders pour out praise to God 'who is' and 'was' (11.17). Noticeably, the usual additional description of God as the One who 'is to come' of 1.8 and 4.8 is absent. The cycle of events covered in the vision of the seven trumpets and the first two woes has run its course (cf. 9.12; 11.14). The penultimate judgment of the third woe is at hand. The future, as it were, is already here.[101]

In announcing judgment in 11.18, John returns to Psalm 2 to structure his argument. In Psalm 2.2 the kings and rulers of the earth set themselves against the Lord's anointed. But, in heaven, the Lord decides and promises to come in anger and wrath to destroy these enemies and place his anointed king in Zion (Ps. 2.3-6). Similarly, in Revelation 11.18 the time has come for the full demonstration of divine ὀργή 'wrath' against the nations or the destroyers

---

101   One of the mysteries of research on the book of Revelation is what is entailed in the third woe since the author does not state it directly in the text. We understand this to commence at 12.1 incorporating the penultimate events of the judgment against the dragon and his allies (12.1–19.21). The final judgment, of course, comes in 20.11-15.

of the earth.[102] The latter reference provides the clue to the understanding of the identity of the nations. This reference echoes Jeremiah 51.25 (28.25 LXX) where Babylon is indicated as the one in which corruption is set τὸ διαφθεῖρον πᾶσαν τὴν γῆν 'to destroy the whole earth'. In Revelation 19.2 John will apply this indictment directly to Babylon (Rome). In the latter text Babylon is pictured as a harlot upon whom God avenges the blood of his servants. Thus it is clear that when we read in 11.18 that God is visiting his anger on the nations and destroyers of the earth, the reference is primarily to those provincial leaders and client kings operating under the auspices of Babylon who are responsible for the death of the martyrs in the crisis of the great tribulation. An assurance is given that they will receive their just deserts.

The prophet John has structured carefully his discussion of the crushing of the nations on Psalm 2. In no uncertain terms John views the nations as being thrown into the great winepress of the wrath of God. But our analysis allows us to make an important nuanced distinction. Both in this unit, and in the previous discussion about the nations holding sway under the power of the beast, John is not making a blanket indictment of every person and tribe upon the face of the earth. Sometimes, as in the Old Testament, the language can appear sweeping, but the focus falls on the real enemies of the Lamb, who promote the power structure of the Roman Empire. These may be described as 'the earth dwellers'. They promote a system of debilitating idolatry that holds in subjection 'the nations'. But, for John, this reality is temporary. The nations will not always stand corrupted by the dragon and his allies. Help is on the way! In the parousia of the Lamb followed by his saints (19.11-16) those who actively uphold the Roman power structure will be destroyed by Christ, the Divine Warrior. Many ordinary people, held captive by the evil powers, will be freed from the control of Babylon.

Summary

As we opened this chapter we noted that a central theological focus of the Apocalypse revolved around a vision of the transition of power; specifically,

---

102   There is a clear play on the words ὀργή 'anger' and διοφθείρειν 'to destroy' in 11.18. The anger of God comes on angry nations and, in apposition, it comes to destroy those who are destroying the earth. This word play on anger and destruction (of the wicked) serves as a linguistic boundary for a chiastic construction wherein it is announced that it is the καιρός 'proper time' for the dead ones (in the Lord) to be judged and to receive their appropriate reward. It is noticeable that the faithful are called δούλοις 'servants' and prophets. The latter echoes the two prophetic witnesses earlier in the chapter, the former the martyrs in 6.11 and 7.3 (cf. 10.7). Thus, this terminology, along with the reference to the 'saints' and those 'fearing your name', is not a subtle reference to categories of ministry within the Asian church but reflects the general flow of the narrative.

the movement of the allegiance of the nations from Caesar's control to the lordship of Christ. John's visions form a narrative that emerges in a context of a set of eschatological expectations being in the process of realization for the people of God. The people of God are a minority. But they are drawn 'out of' all nations and peoples to form a contrast-society (5.9; 7.9). They are held in contempt by the majority of the peoples and nations who increasingly allow the Caesars to be venerated in the emperor cult (13.7; 14.6). But the rise and consolidation of Roman imperialism and claims to power over the nations is only temporary. Rome, this toxic prostitute, the seducer of kings and nations, will collapse (14.8; 16.19; 18.3, 23; 17.16). All of this is thought to be in keeping with the expectation of the prophets – especially the writer of Psalm 2 – who supposedly previews the outcome of the transition of power with respect to the kingdom. The malevolent leaders of the nations reject the sovereignty of the God of Israel. In their vanity they plot to eradicate his people. But in a holy war (i.e. the coming of Jesus in his parousia) they are defeated (2.26-27; 12.5; 19.15; 11.18). Housed in an account that is charged with drama, this must have been impressive to the earliest hearers and readers. The leaders to whom the nations and even some in the church gave their allegiance are routed and destroyed. A transition of power is under way. Inevitably the nations will be called to shift their allegiances.

To whom is this addressed? Certainly, we are not the first to observe that there is a kind of dualism, perhaps bordering on fatalism operating in the Apocalypse.[103] The forces of Rome are resolved irrevocably to shake their fist at the God of heaven (cf. 16:9, 11, 20).[104] They are not prepared to change. On the other hand John goes out of his way to say that the people of God are sealed and their names are found in the book of life (Rev. 7:3; 9:4; 20:12). They long for assurance, and their allegiance is unconditional. But in the churches there is another group. They are the waverers. Can they accept John's strict constructionist view of the Christian faith? A summary is not the place to go into detail about them. Because of those who hold to the doctrines of Jezebel/Balaam (the mid-church of the seven) or those who have cooled in their allegiance because of the attraction to the dominant culture (first and seventh church), the description of this transition of power should be a point of vital interest. In this chapter we have pointed out instances where this is the case. As we trace the ultimate outcome of John's vision of the allegiance of the nations, we will draw additional attention to this audience as critical for the shaping of this eschatological tractate.

---

103 Lambrecht, 'The People of God', p.381.
104 The only possible exception is Rev. 11.13 which will be discussed later.

CHAPTER 3

THE ULTIMATE DESTINY OF THE NATIONS IN REVELATION

The Eschatological Battle

Our survey of the function of the nations in the Apocalypse in the last chapter has arrived at some well-founded conclusions. First, we saw that the Lamb created a universal community drawn from all peoples and nations. Its constituency is a people redeemed by the cross and committed to follow Christ's way in sacrificial love (5.9; 7.9).

Secondly, despite the emergence of this community, the imperial power wielded by the leaders of the empire continues to win the allegiance of the general populace of the nations. Like a siren, the power of Rome leads the nations to venerate the system. In the Eastern provinces emperor worship is one of the most potent forms of this veneration. Given this reality, few among the nations, even though various groups may be disenchanted with Rome's tyrannical exercise of power, are prepared to change course and follow the Lamb (11.9). In terms of early Christian faith, the nations refuse to repent (9.20-21). Thus, the burden of John the prophet is to convince his hearers and readers within the churches of Asia that those who follow this pathway will come to a door that opens into defeat and destruction. This was designed to be of special interest to those in the churches who were tempted to make alliances and compromises with the operative contemporary powers. John chronicles his vision of the fate of the empire and the nations seduced by its power in 11.19–19.10. It is a road that leads to destruction. The form and structure of the case against the empire and the nations is built piecemeal from the prophetic oracles against Babylon in the Old Testament prophets. Babylon ends in a conflagration.

Yet Babylon's destruction is carried out by forces and powers antithetical to God and the Lamb. Before the new Jerusalem appears as the replacement of Babylon the forces and powers that destroyed Babylon, still idolatrous, prepare to do battle against the Lamb. This comes in Revelation 19.11-21.

How John perceives the battle as taking place is still a matter of considerable discussion.[1] There is a tendency among some critical commentators to

---

1   The issue is addressed by Kevin E. Miller, 'The Nuptial Eschatology of Revelation 19–22', *CBQ* 60 (1998), pp.312–16. Miller argues that Rev. 19.11-21 represents a concluding phase of the spiritual struggle between the Lamb and the dragon that entered the initial stage at the cross. But

spiritualize Revelation 19.11-21.[2] Yet the evidence that the narrative world of the text presumes that an actual battle will take place is much stronger than usually thought. We are prepared to highlight some of the exegetical evidence to bolster this claim.

As early as Revelation 1.7 there is an intimation of the importance of this battle. This verse, coming at the outset of the book, highlights the parousia of Christ as a Divine Warrior.[3] Thus, in the opening salutation of the book there is an intimation of a coming critical conflict. It is generally recognized that this is a text which to some degree draws its terminology from language and ideas in Zechariah 12.10, 12 (MT), conflated with Daniel 7.13-14 and, perhaps, echoing Matthew 24.30.[4] In Zechariah 12.10-12 the text refers to the mourning of the inhabitants of Jerusalem over the loss of their king. The wider context narrates that the nations are gathered against Jerusalem to engage in a battle against the Lord (Zech. 14.1-3). The Lord purges his people in Jerusalem and defeats the nations (Zech. 12.1–14.11). On that day his kingship will be manifested over all the earth (14.9). Revelation 1.7 echoes deeply key features of the structure of thought of the latter chapters of Zechariah. It stands between several strong Christological statements (1.5 and 1.12-18) that presume that Christ is acting on behalf of Yahweh. The fact that these statements occur at the beginning of the Apocalypse is significant. They signal to the reader that a major body of thought that stands behind the doctrine of the parousia of Christ in Revelation 19.11-21 is Zechariah 12–14. And central to this text is the idea that those who were responsible for the death of the Davidic king will capitulate to the Lord (Zech. 12.11). Whether they are repentant or not they are subject to his rule.[5] The emphasis of Revelation is that this theophanic appearance of Christ will have implications not only in Judea but universally.[6] Thus, as early as Revelation 1.7, it is hard to escape the conclusion that the oppressors of the heavenly king will be a significant factor in the narrative account of the Apocalypse. The fact that Revelation 1.7 and 19.11-21 serve as bookends to the narration of considerable conflict in the book is not without significance. This is especially

---

the struggle is primarily for the hearts and minds of humankind. The sharp sword of the rider of the white horse (19.15) is the power of the proclaimed word of God. Aune, *Revelation*, pp.1060–69, posits that an earlier stage of 19.11-21 in Jewish exegesis could reflect an actual battle between the Messiah and his enemies. But a final editor has glossed the text. In its present form it promotes a metaphorical reading of the references to armies and war somewhat congruent with the approach of Miller.

2   Prigent, *Commentary on the Apocalypse of St. John*, 546–9; Boring, *Revelation*, pp.195–200; Bauckham, *The Climax of Prophecy*, pp.232–7; Fekkes, *Isaiah and Prophetic Traditions*, pp.121–2.

3   This intimates to the reader that at some time in the narrative that rulership will become evident.

4   Bauckham, *Climax of Prophecy*, pp.318–26; Jauhiainen, *Use of Zechariah in Revelation*, pp.102–7.

5   The important question in Rev. 1.7 as to whether κόπτειν 'to mourn' functions as an expression of fear or a sign of repentance will be addressed in the discussion in Chapter 4.

6   We refer to the wording 'Every eye will see him', and 'all of the tribes of the earth will mourn on his account'. Dan. 7.13-14 may have been a contributing factor to this emphasis.

true with respect to the original readers in the seven churches. It functions as a not-too-subtle warning to those who are seeking accommodation with the dominant culture (2.16; 2.26-27; 3.9, 21). This is a lost cause. Do not go there! The edge of this strong critique of military power is lost when one engages in a purely metaphorical reading.

This theme of the rout of the opponents by the Divine Warrior in a final battle also makes sense of the development of John's narrative. The three central visions of seals, trumpets, and bowls of wrath presume a conclusion such as this. The opening section of the seven seals (four horsemen of the Apocalypse) portray a negative assessment of the effects of Rome's expansionist policies from the perspective of a strong dissident (6.1-8).[7] The martyred dissidents cry out for vindication (6.9-11). By the sixth seal a theophany provides the first intimation of a divine response (6.12-17). All classes of society that give allegiance to the imperial system shudder in fear. Revelation 6.12-17 brings us to the edge of the beginning of the Day of the Lord that will crystallize the defeat of the Lord's enemies. All of the action that follows until the actual parousia of Christ in 19.11-21 is a development and expansion in great detail of the impact of the woes and times of testing inaugurating the coming of the Day of the Lord.[8] What is noteworthy for our purposes is that we meet practically the same people of Revelation 6.12-17 again at the end of the conflict in Revelation 19.17-18. It is as though we have two sides of the same coin. On one side the conflict is initiated. On the other it is resolved. In the feast of the grisly banquet (19.17-18), itself a parody of the messianic banquet (19.6-9a), we have the ultimate outcome of the conflict. In between we are given one of the most gripping minority reports on the corrosive effects of the Roman Empire emerging from its earliest centuries.

Interspersed with this withering critique are vignettes on the sealing and preservation of the people of the Lamb (7.1-17; 9.4; 11.15-18; 12.10-12; 14.1-5; 15.1-4). No doubt these texts were meant to function rhetorically for the benefit of the churches. Both true believers and accommodationists, in their own ways, were exhorted to take heed. Nevertheless, the major emphasis of Revelation 6.1-19.21 is the collapse of the ubiquitous forces and powers of the empire that underwrote the idolatries of that age. Thus it is no surprise that John saw it all coalescing in the destruction of Rome and the parousia of Christ at the Day of the Lord against his foes.

Interpreters could wish for additional descriptions in the narrative about the nature of this final battle. But the failure to furnish details of the actual warfare 'is a well known literary and dramatic device' of this kind of esoteric literature.[9]

---

7   M. Jauhiainen, 'Recapitulation and Chronological Progression in John's Apocalypse: Towards a New Perspective', NTS 49 (2003), p.548.

8   As argued by J. Lambrecht, 'A Structuration of Revelation 4:1–22:5', *L'Apocalyptique Johannique et L'Apocalyptique dans le Nouveau Testament*, BETL 53, ed. J. Lambrecht (Leuven: Leuven University Press, 1980), pp.77–104.

9   Adela Collins, 'Eschatology in the Book of Revelation', *Ex Auditu* 6 (1990), p.70.

And the fact that the author of the Apocalypse regularly echoes earlier precedents in scripture, such as the Exodus, destruction of Babylon, and the sacking of Jerusalem, creates a strong presumption that the reference to the eschatological conflict are far more literal than mere metaphors for spiritual conflict.

Finally, it is useful to recall our earlier analysis of the use of Psalm 2.9 in the narrative. In Revelation 2.26-27, 12.5, and 19.15 the reader is left in no doubt that the Lord and his redeemed people will defeat decisively the army of the nations. The key metaphor is that the divine shepherd will use his rod to smash them. What is noticeable is that in Psalm 2.6, several verses earlier, we read that the Lord has set his king on Mount Zion. Already, in Revelation 14.1 there is a reference to Mount Zion as the place of safety for the one hundred and forty-four thousand; but in this text it is unclear whether we are to understand that this is a geographical location. The emphasis in Revelation 14.1-5 is security, not place. But if we understand that, in addition to Psalm 2, the author of Revelation is drawing upon Zechariah 12.1–14.11 as a prophetic oracle anticipating the eschatological conflict, then we can construe the outline of a scenario of what John sees as taking place. As in the earlier parousia text of Revelation 1.7, when the Lord comes, he comes to purge his people and to defeat the nations. The coming to Zion is now recast in universal terms. It is a creative mutation of an old biblical theme of the restoration of Zion (Ps. 87). The old Jerusalem is unclean and polluted and must be purged (cf. 11.1-2, 8, 13).[10] A new Jerusalem, ruled by the Lamb and the victorious people of God, is about to appear (21.1–22.5). A new day is dawning upon the resounding defeat of the beast and false prophet.

With the resounding defeat of the idolatrous powers the nations are adrift. What is their role to play with the expectation of the emergence of the new Jerusalem? This is answered in Revelation 20-22.

Freeing the Nations from Satan's Deception

The structure of Revelation 20.1-15

With the defeat of Babylon, the beast and false prophet, the struggle against the enemies of the Lamb now moves to closure. The dragon is still left. Revelation 20 centres on his final eclipse and defeat. The chapter has four clearly delineated pericopes: (1) Satan is bound (20.1-3); (2) the millennial reign of the faithful (20.4-6); (3) Satan's release and final rebellion (20.7-10); and (4) the last judgment (20.11-15). What is clear immediately is that three out of four of the pericopes focus on the dragon (Satan) and his defeat. That is the central focus. Only after full recognition of the reality of his demise are we able to receive a glimpse of the vindication of the righteous in 20.4-6.

---

10   P. W. L. Walker, *Jesus and the Holy City: New Testament Perspectives on Jerusalem* (Grand Rapids, Michigan: Eerdmans, 1996), pp.248–65.

Three of these four pericopes are introduced by a stock formula καὶ εἶδον 'and I saw' (20.1, 4, 10 [11]). Similar phraseology occurs in the final action narrating section of the book which occurs from 19.11–21.8 (19.11, 17, 19; 20.1, 4, 11, 12; 21.1, 2)[11] This kind of formula occurs as a regular feature in John's very simple paratactic style. Here it functions to connect a series of different visions. It is clear that the series has some chronological progression (viz., the eschatological battle followed by the grisly banquet [19.11-18] and the binding and release of Satan [20.1-3, 8] culminating in the final judgment). But this should not be overdone. Just like the other story-telling units there is frequent retrospection and overlap in the time sequences of the action narrated. Here, John is utilizing freely early Christian motifs as to what happens subsequent to the parousia of Christ. It functions as a climax to the last phase of his extended treatment of the Day of the Lord.

In my view what is paramount is not so much the sequence of the 'action passages' but the way the author features the fortunes and destinies of the two women cities, Babylon and the new Jerusalem, in the closing chapters of the book. The defeat of Babylon precedes, in an anticipatory way, the final action sequence of the book (17.1–19.10). The wording of the initial unit on the evil woman city (17.1) bears a remarkable similarity to the wording of the introduction to the new Jerusalem in 21.9.[12] Moreover, the two uses of the perfect of γίνομαι 'it is finished', coming from the throne of God, which precede the introduction of the description to the two women cities, add a striking coda to this parallelism (16.17; 21.6). Finally, the ending of the elaboration of the contrasting roles of the women cities has many linguistic and thematic similarities (19.8-10; 22.6-9).

Our point is simply this: as the elaboration of the destiny of the evil woman city (17.1–19.10) is closely linked up with the action sequence of the seven bowls of wrath against Babylon in 15.6–16.21, so the appearance and destiny of the new Jerusalem (21.9–22.5) is closely linked with the action sequence of the parousia and subsequent events in 19.11–21.8. Thus, in my judgment, 19.11–21.8 should be read in much the same way as an interconnected unit. To be sure, there are elements of chronological development here. The devil must be consigned to perdition before the full glory of the holy city is revealed. Some things necessarily take place before others, but chronology is secondary. What is primary is John's total description of the last phase of the Day of the Lord.

11   See especially A. J. P. Garrow, *Revelation: New Testament Readings* (London: Routledge, 1997), pp.34, 61–5. Garrow views the unfolding of the message of Revelation as coming primarily in three 'story-telling' units (12.1–14.5; 15.6–16.21; 19.11b–21.8). The remaining sections of the last half of the book either anticipate or give additional clarification of what occurs in the 'action passages'. I like the term 'action passages' and will use it several times later in this monograph.

12   On this point there is considerable agreement among the commentators. The Greek text of 17.1 opens with 12 words almost identical with 21.9, the text which introduces the description of the second woman city. Also, the syntactical and verbal elements of the angelic interpreters are very similar. If ever there were structural markers in a text, this is it!

The appearance of the new Jerusalem cannot be detached from this. Revelation 19.11–21.8 is inextricably linked and united with 21.9–22.9.

The function of the Millennium (Revelation 20.1-10)

Our goal here is mainly to focus on what is said about the nations in this crucial text. But in order to do this one cannot escape taking an interpretive stance on the reference to the one thousand years, or as it is widely known: the millennium. The secondary literature on Revelation 20 is enormous.[13] Two areas of concern are of central importance. First, the origin and function of the concept itself. Second, for our purposes, the even more important question: John's pre-understanding of the role and the destiny of the nations themselves during this last phase of the Day of the Lord.

Commentators routinely point to a number of references both in Jewish apocalypses and early Christian writings with respect to a temporary messianic reign on earth upon the advent of the messiah.[14] Clearly these concepts were widespread but it is almost impossible to tell whether John's composition reflects their influence directly. Already in Paul's eschatology there are hints of three different τάγματα 'orders' or 'stages' of the establishment of the full messianic reign that may have circulated in some circles of early Christianity (1 Cor. 15.22-24). The first stage is the resurrection of Jesus. The second is the parousia. The third stage is the τέλος 'end' when the kingdom is given up to God.[15] This schema has certain similarities with John such as a stepped progression of the emergence of the kingdom of God from its inauguration at the resurrection of Christ (Rev. 1.5, 5.10) to its consummation in God's new world after the parousia. But it remains unclear whether, for John, there is a

---

13   For a fairly recent monograph on Revelation 20 see J. Webb Mealy, *After the Thousand Years: Resurrection and Judgment in Revelation 20*, JSNTSup 70 (Sheffield: Sheffield Academic Press, 1992). It contains bibliographical listings of major works. A substantive review and expansion of the discussion filling in some gaps in the discussion is the work of Greg K. Beale, 'Review Article: J. W. Mealy, *After the Thousand Years*', EQ 66 (1994), pp.229–49.

14   2 Bar. 29.1–30.5; 4 Ezra 6–7; Sib. Or. 5.414-30; Ascen. Isa. 4.1-18; Justin Dial. 81.3-4 are the main texts roughly contemporary with John. As such many consider the thousand years' reign of the faithful as a handy expedient for mediating between the OT prophetic view of the rule of God coming fully in Jerusalem in ordinary time and the full-blown apocalyptic images of the earth being destroyed and God bringing a totally new creation. See Aune, *Revelation*, pp.1104–8.

15   Peter Stuhlmacher, 'Eschatology and Hope in Paul', EvQ 72/4 (2000), pp.319–20, also posits as evidence of Paul's belief in a third stage after the parousia Rom. 5.17 and 1 Cor. 6.2-3. He thinks these texts confirm the existence of this third stage in interpretation. Nevertheless, 1 Cor. 15.22-24 is the key text. Stuhlmacher considers that for Paul the major function of the stage after the parousia is the redemption of 'all Israel' (Rom. 11.26) through the establishment of the centre of the messianic kingdom in Zion. Whether this reading of Paul is correct or not, it would appear that the Pauline emphasis on the future obedience of Israel has shifted in the Apocalypse to more of an emphasis on the messianic kingdom based on Zion being drawn from 'all peoples' (cf. Rev. 21.3) rather than the redemption of ethnic Israel itself. This may also suggest that John was not particularly interested in a line of exegesis that posited historical developments between the parousia and the end.

penultimate interregnum between the parousia of Christ and the full consummation of the kingdom in the new Jerusalem. The fact that the opening section of the action unit in 19.11–21.8 begins with the parousia and ends with the judgment of the wicked and coming of God's new world seems in many ways to be not much more than an echoing of early mainstream Christian eschatology that ties the end-time events closely to the parousia. Thus, the burden of proof would seem to fall on those who would take 20.1-10 with its six references to a thousand-year period, occurring in one pericope in a highly symbolic book, to conclude that this denotes a literal period of time between the parousia and the consummation. 1 Chronicles 16.15, speaking of the covenant with Abraham, affirms that it lasts for 'one thousand generations', obviously a metaphor for God's unfailing covenantal commitment to his people. One should not overlook the obvious point that since, for John, twelve is the number for the people of God (Rev. 21.12, 14) and when it is squared and multiplied by one thousand it produces the number of the vindicated from the great tribulation (Rev. 7.4-8; 14.1; 20.4).[16] What we are suggesting is that the thousand years' reign in Revelation 20 is a useful symbol for expressing the full vindication of those who wore the mark of the Lamb during the tribulation. It is the return to paradise. It is protological as much as eschatological.[17] It represents the culmination of the expectation that the righteous will finally be vindicated (6.9-11; 7.9-17; 11.11-13; 12.11-12; 14.1-5; 15.2-4). What is in heaven (notice no place is given in 20.4-6) is now complete. God's reign has extended in its fullness to the earth. In contrast with the relatively brief period of the great tribulation (symbolized by three and a half years), one thousand years points to the overwhelming qualitative superiority of the Lamb's victory and reign; and so, even here, in this quintessential esoteric passage, a pastoral concern emerges. The text functions to remind readers that Satan's power after the parousia will be eclipsed permanently. John is underscoring to his readers that, in retrospect, adherence to their commitment to the contrast-society of the Lamb is the only worthwhile value that will stand in the long run. Ultimately, emperor worship, and what it symbolizes, is only a blip on the radarscope of eternity. The true victors will be the armies of the Lamb. Readers from the seven churches of Asia are urged to take note.

---

16   Bauckham, *Climax of Prophecy*, pp.36, 397–400, through a complicated process also argues that 144, the 12th square number, is the representative number in Revelation for the new Jerusalem (cf. 21.17). Thus, from the selection of the faithful in 7.4-8 through the millennial reign of a thousand years into the new Jerusalem, the numbers 12 and 144 multiplied by a thousand seems to function as a symbol for the reign of the faithful people of God.

17   Others have seen the thousand years as an ancient version of world history being divided into seven thousand years (a day = 1,000 years) ending in a seventh (or eighth) day of timeless rest (Ep. of Barn. 15.3-9; 2 En. 33.2). Or perhaps, even behind that, is the idea in Jewish exegesis, based on Ps. 90.4, 15, that the span of Adam's life, because of his sin (Gen. 2.17), was just short of an allotted one thousand years (Gen. 5.5; Jub. 4.29-30). Now, true Adamic existence, interrupted as a result of sin, upon the binding of Satan, returns (Rev. 20.4-6). As long as this is understood as contributing to the literary use of the symbol we are open to such interpretations.

The Place of the Nations During the Millennium (Revelation 20.3, 8)

In Revelation 20.3 the angel from heaven casts Satan into the pit. The angel closes and seals it ἵνα μὴ πλανήσῃ ἔτι τὰ ἔθνη 'in order that he (Satan) cannot continue to deceive the nations anymore' until the end of one thousand years. Revelation 12.7-9 is especially helpful for understanding the context of 20.3. In this text Satan is deposed from a place in the heavenly court. For a short while he wreaks havoc on the whole earthly habitation through his deception of the nations (12.13–13.18; cf. 13.14; 18.23; 19.20). But with his allies (the beast and the false prophet) now in the lake of fire, the time has come to recognize his power is eclipsed.[18]

The language of an evil figure being consigned to a pit and sealed there has a number of parallels in the Greco-Roman world of this era.[19] It is not a unique motif. However, our major question is John's perception of the status of the nations themselves. There is a widespread view that when the Divine Warrior (Christ) defeats the kings of the earth (19.19) in the eschatological conflict at the parousia, that the reader is to assume that the nations were obliterated.[20] Therefore, the reappearance of the nations in Revelation 20-22 is often treated as a *non sequitur*, or is explained as a recapitulation of some sequence of events before the parousia.[21] However, such a reading coming immediately after the eschatological war of 19.17-21 is very difficult. The conflict in Revelation

---

18   It is important to notice the use of the verb πλανᾶν 'to deceive' in most of these verses. The verb first appears in 2.20 where the charge is made against the prophetess Jezebel that she teaches God's servants to engage in fornication and eat foods dedicated to idols. Ian Boxall, '"For Paul" or "For Cephas"? The Book of Revelation and Early Asian Christianity', in *Understanding, Studying and Reading: New Testament Essays in Honour of John Ashton* (ed. Christopher Rowland and Crispin H.T. Fletcher-Louis), JSNTSup 153 (Sheffield: Sheffield Academic Press 1998), pp.214–17, addresses this issue in detail. Boxall argues that clearly John, a Christian Jew, was opposed both to the accommodation with eating foods sold in pagan marketplaces and social/commercial interaction with pagan idolaters generally accepted by many Gentile Christian believers in Asia. These beliefs could well be found among many of the converts of the Pauline mission. Paul and his followers seem to be more open to this line of thinking. John brands this *Tendenz* as 'the deep things of Satan' (2.24). It is just another expression of the same deceit that Satan and allies use to keep the nations captive. Upon the defeat of the beast and the false prophet (cf. 19.20) in the eschatological war a step is made to free the earth from the influence of this scourge.

19   Aune, *Revelation*, pp.1082–3.

20   J. W. Mealy, *After the Thousand Years*, p.25, states that 'there is no question of any non-Christian surviving the judgment of the parousia as described in Rev. 19.11-21'. *Idem* p.90, 'Who participates in the battle against the returning Christ and his armies? The answer to this question is both clear and consistent with everything that has gone before: every single person remaining on earth participates.' Although this view is extreme, a version of this remains a fundamental presupposition of many major interpretations. The present author strongly resists this reading. In my view 19.11-21 is a description of the aftermath of a battle not the obliteration of most of humankind.

21   Is Rev. 20.1-10 to be read as a description of what takes place after the parousia or does it function as recapitulation, a heavenly perspective of the triumph of the righteous in the life of the

19.17-21 echoes Revelation 17.14 (viz., the similar terminology for the Lamb in 19.16). It refers to the battle between the Lamb and the kings of the earth and their armies. The key term here is the phrase 'kings of the earth'. As we have seen, Psalm 2.2 is the basic paradigm informing John's theology at this point. In Psalm 2.2 these rulers set themselves against the Lord's anointed. In this text, under the influence of Psalm 2 (cf. 19.15), this phraseology functions as a practical equivalent for the leaders of the earth dwellers,[22] who as we have noted earlier, constitute the core of the opposition to the Lamb. As a great army they make their last stand. From Revelation 6.10 onwards the earth dwellers are the ones who have concentrated on persecuting the people of God to the point of martyrdom. On the other hand, noticeably, there is no reference to the nations in Revelation 19.17-21, although they are a transparency for the rebellion of Gog and Magog in 20.7-9.[23] To be sure, the nations have been deceived by the beast and false prophet into submitting to emperor worship (13.7; 14.6). But with the demise of the false prophet and his allies who hold their position of power in Babylon, their situation is much more ambiguous. They can no longer submit their allegiance to Rome. They have no alternative but to recognize who is the ultimate Lord. With the defeat of the idolatrous powers the tables are turned. This is the major burden of the appropriation of Dan. 7.9 in 20.4-6.

Revelation 20.4-6 is a victory celebration. A straightforward reading would indicate that integral to the victory celebration of those who refused to bear the mark of the beast is their assumption of power over the nations. Psalm 2, a paradigmatic text for the Apocalypse, is now fulfilled (1.5-6; 2.26-27; 3.21; 5.10; 12.5 and 19.18). The Lamb (God's son) is now the evident ruler over the kings of the earth. The martyrs (6.9-11) now have the answer to their prayers.

Revelation 20.4 is an appropriation of Daniel 7.9. But instead of the Ancient of Days taking a seat on the throne both the martyrs and those who did not worship the beast (the faithful through the recent crisis) take their well-de-

---

church since the incarnation of Christ? With respect to the latter view Ulfgard, *Feast and Future*, p.155, states '20.4-6 does not refer to a *future* period of time, but that it is another way of speaking about the present era (continuing into the future) brought about by Christ...'. Texts such as Lk. 10.18 can be read to conclude that since the ministry of Jesus and the later proclamation of the gospel, Satan cannot prevent humans hearing and obeying the word. Satan is still active in this world in countless ways, but he is unable to stop the faithful reigning with Christ. But this seems to be a very unlikely reading of the text. There is nothing at Rev. 20.1 that would indicate a major shift takes place moving us back in the narrative sequence to the time after the reign of Christ. A normal reader would understand 20.1-3 is precipitated by the parousia of Christ and the defeat of the early powers. C. H. Giblin, 'The Millennium (Rev. 20.4-6) as Heaven', *NTS* 45 (1999), pp.554–5, cogently comments on the Augustinian identification of the millennium with the present existence of the church on earth. Giblin notes, '...one may urge the problem of identifying a group of Christians already martyred and then regarded as "blessed and holy" with the church on earth'.

22   The qualification that they belong to 'the earth' is also an indication for the reader of Revelation that they are opposed to the way of God.

23   The λοιποί 'rest' (19.21) refers not to all of the peoples on earth but to the entire complement of the various classes of people who align themselves in opposition to the Lamb (6.15; 19.18).

served places (cf. Dan 7.27). Probably this is not strictly a tribunal. But it is more than a mere reception of the honour and dignity so previously withheld during the previous regime.[24] The faithful now possess the kingdom (cf. Dan. 7.22; Rev. 20.5). As kings and priests they revel in the blessings of the kingdom. Psalm 2.8-11 is fully realized. The nations are their inheritance.[25] Final judgment will be administered by God himself to the rest of the created order (20.11-15). The people of God have entered their victory lap.

Turning directly to Revelation 20.7-10 it is worth noting that, despite the change in topic, these verses are not introduced with the characteristic καὶ εἶδον 'and I saw' phraseology. This indicates that 20.4-10 is in some way interconnected. Although it is somewhat clumsy in its editorial setting, 'when the thousand years are ended', Revelation 20.7-10 complements 20.4-6. These verses highlight the importance of Satan. That is the *Tendenz* of the text. Freed temporarily from the abyss, Satan pieces together a coalition of forces for a final last-ditch stand. But it is of no use. Against the people of God he is powerless. The pericope is another way of highlighting the strength of the victory of the faithful. That is the point of connection between 20.4-6 and 7-10.

In order to build his imagery, the prophet John evokes the Gog prophecy of Ezekiel 38–39 as a basis for the description of what happens.[26] Echoing Ezekiel 38.22 and 39.6, hailstones, fire and brimstone pour down from heaven against the forces of Gog and Magog (Rev. 20.9). The Gog prophecies in Ezekiel function as an attestation of the truth of Yahweh's protection for Israel against the profanation of the nations.[27] In her restoration to full covenant relationship Israel is now fully secure. Gog and his forces march against her only to be annihilated.[28] In a similar way, the people of God, safe and secure in 'the camp of the saints', are invulnerable to the forces of the same deception which once caused terrible havoc across the creation.[29] Restored to their land Ezekiel

---

24   Contra J. Roloff, *The Revelation of John: A Continental Commentary* (trans. John E. Alsup; Minneapolis. Fortress Press, 1993), p.227.

25   Osborne, *Revelation*, p.705 draws attention to two powerful texts, Wis. 3.7-8 and 1 Qp. Hab. 5.4. Both of these texts speak directly about the rule of the saints over the nations. There is no doubt this was a strong sentiment in the Jewish world that nourished the prophet John.

26   D. Smith, 'The Millennial Reign of Jesus Christ: Some Observations on Rev 20:1-10', ResQ 16 (1973), pp.222–4.

27   Also Ezek 36.6-7, 15, 20-24, 30.

28   S. Boe, *Gog and Magog: Ezekiel 38–39 as Pre-Text for Revelation 19:17-21 and 20:7-10*, WUNT 2/135 (Tübingen: Mohr Siebeck, 2001), pp.274–300. What is important here is not that Boe points out more important connections between Rev. 20.7-10 and Ezek. 38–39; but, with the exception of the birds feeding on the carcasses in the grisly banquet precious little of the Gog prophecies are echoed in Rev. 19.17-21. This militates against the idea that Rev. 19.17-21 and 20.7-10 are either doublets or visions alluding to the same event. Indeed, as is often noted by commentators, the grisly banquet itself is probably a literary counterpoint to the messianic banquet of Rev. 19.7-9.

29   The two references in Rev. 20.9 to the place of safety for the people of God (ἡ παρεμβολὴ τῶν ἁγίων 'the camp of the holy ones' and 'the beloved city') are worthy of notice. The former is

represents Yahweh as showing his face so that his holy name will no longer be profaned among the nations (Ezek. 38.23; 39.7, 21, 23, 27-29). This seems to be the outcome of the episode in 20.7-9. True to his nature, to the end, the devil is a deceiver. But his deceptions have run their course. He is ready to be consigned to the lake of fire (Rev. 20.10). The time of the trampling of the Gentiles (nations) has come to an end (Rev. 11.2).

Thus the primary function of Revelation 20.1-10 is to argue that Satan no longer has any power. The role of the nations is a key element in that explanation. In Revelation 20.3 Satan is stripped of his power to deceive the nations. The purpose of his cameo appearance in 20.8-9 is simply to manifest his impotence. He marshals the nations, but it is to no avail. They cannot make inroads against the people of God. Thankfully, Satan's *coup de grâce* comes in 20.10 when he is thrown into the lake of fire. The nations for evermore will be under the control of the Lamb and his followers.[30] This will be underscored in the description of the new Jerusalem (20.9–21.5).

The Anticipation of Victory (Revelation 15.2-4)

The reality of the triumph of the Lamb and the faithful, coming to fruition with their dominion over the nations in Revelation 20.4-6, is already anticipated in 15.2-4. Indeed, since 15.2-4 is a song of praise in heaven, it is tapping into the major motif of the call for the victory of the faithful already emerging in heaven in 7.9-11, 11.15-19 and 14.1-5. Now, in 15.2-4 we are thrust forward, as the scene proleptically anticipates the actual time of triumph of the Lamb's coming after the great tribulation. Appropriately, the celebration consists of a song: the Song of Moses and the Lamb. Of course the song echoes directly the Song of Moses after Pharaoh's defeat in the Exodus (Exod. 15.1-18). In

---

used commonly as a term for army barracks where troops would be quartered in tents (Acts 21.34). Given the frequent allusions in Revelation to Exodus, the wilderness journey, and especially the motifs drawn from the Feast of the Tabernacles, contra Steven S. Smalley, *The Revelation to John: A Commentary on the Greek Text of the Apocalypse* (Downers Grove, Illinois: InterVarsity Press, 2005), p.514, this probably is a reference to the triumph of God in preserving his people in absolute safety at the end of the age. In short, it refers to the eschatological people of God at rest under God's protective care. The 'beloved city' is simply an explanatory gloss of the former reference. It is the only occurrence of this phrase in Revelation although it is unmistakable that this is a clear echo of the important place Jerusalem holds among the people of God (Rev. 3.12; 11.2, 21.2, 10; 22.14). For the Jewish writer of the Apocalypse Jerusalem is the locale *par excellence* for the people of God. John is capable of evoking the prophetic critique of its shadowy side (11.8; cf. Isa. 1.10). But here he is not making a critique. 'The beloved city' stands impregnable against the now impotent evil one.

30   As Richard Bauckham and Trevor Hart, *Hope against Hope: Christian Eschatology at the Turn of the Millennium* (Grand Rapids: William B. Eerdmans, 1999), p.135, note, 'This time the citadel of the saints proves impregnable.' The people of the Lamb stand fully vindicated; and without a shadow of a doubt, the nations are subjected to them.

John's *narrative* time the parousia has not yet taken place; so the scene is set not on earth but within heaven's dome, which has the appearance of a sea of glass. Unlike Revelation 4.6, where the sea is clear as crystal, this time the sea is mixed with fire. No doubt, given passages such as 8.3-5, the occurrence of δικαιώματα 'judgments' in 15.4, and the frequent connection between judgment and fire throughout the book (cf. 20.10), this refers to God's punishing wrath. But it is difficult not to see another idea present as well. God's throne room rings with a song of victory after the faithful have passed through a fiery conflagration that involves martyrdom. As a reminder of this time the sea is mingled with fire.

Through a process of *gezērâ sāwâ*, to create his song, John moves from Exodus 15.11-14 to Jeremiah 10.6-7a (MT), where God is invoked as the king of the nations.[31] Bauckham has described the exegetical process in considerable detail.[32] The reference to βασιλεύς 'king' also echoes Revelation 11.15. In this text, the sounding of the seventh trumpet announces that the kingdom of this world has become the kingdom of our Lord (God) and his anointed one (Christ). His rule will be forever. Now in Revelation 15.3, epexegetically, the same point is made. We are informed that God's rule (through his agent the Lamb) is over the nations. In keeping with the context of dependence upon Jeremiah 10 God is recognized as the true king of the nations even though through the folly of idolatry they did not recognize him.

Having asserted the sovereignty of God over the nations, Revelation 15.4 opens with a rhetorical question:

'Who can conceive that anyone will not fear and magnify your name, O Lord?'

Since much of the wording is from the Song of Moses, the immediate referent must be to Exodus 15.14-16. There the nations are represented as being in terror and awe at Yahweh's victory at the Reed Sea. Proleptically, a similar reaction in Revelation 15.4a is attributed to the nations after the Lamb comes and makes them subject to his sovereignty. John artfully draws on two key biblical passages concerning the recognition of God's glory by the nations (Jer. 10.6-7 and Ps. 86.8-10) to supply key terminology to fill out the rhetorical question. This verse is at the edge of the beginning of several chapters where the earthly enemies of the Lamb are about to be routed. But, even before the conflict, the note of triumph in the Lamb's victory is confidently asserted.

---

31   There is a major textual issue as to whether we should read king of the ἐθνῶν 'nations' or king of the αἰώνων 'ages' in Rev. 15.3. As part of the *gezērâ sāwâ* process, John possibly moved from 'nations' in Exod. 15.14, not only to Jer. 10.6-7, 10 but also to Ps. 86.9-10 and 98.1-2 (all texts on nations). We have echoes of all these texts in Rev. 15.4. On this basis we conclude that 'nations' seems to be the appropriate reading. The manuscript evidence is divided. The suspicion is that later scribes conformed the reading 'king of the ages' to 1 Tim. 1.17.

32   Bauckham, *Climax of Prophecy*, pp.296–307.

The basis for this word of confidence is substantiated by three causal clauses of result all beginning with the same Greek word ὅτι that may follow an A B A¹ B¹ construction.[33]

> Because you alone are holy.
> The result is that all nations will come and worship before you,
> Because your righteous judgments are apparent.
> The result is that all nations will come and worship before you. [text understood]

The meaning of the first clause is evident. Suffice to say it also should be read in connection with all of 15.3. The interpretation of the last two clauses is disputed. On a simple reading, the text is saying that on the grounds of the victory of the Divine Warrior, the nations will give homage to the Lord. His judgments are just. This reading is supported by both a linguistic and thematic connection with Revelation 20.4. In the latter text, directly complementing Daniel 7.9 ('thrones are set in place') and Daniel 7.22 ('judgment was given to the saints of the most high'), John narrates what is implied when Revelation 15.4 is fulfilled. In Revelation 20.4-6 the faithful on behalf of the Lamb will exercise dominion over the created order.[34]

On the other hand, Richard Bauckham has argued strongly that this text celebrates God's victory primarily on the grounds of the effect of the martyrdom of the Lamb's followers upon the nations.[35] The nations at last come to see the winsome appeal of the sacrifice of the Lamb through the power of the committed faith of the martyrs. Upon this recognition, they freely submit to God's sovereignty. But, as interesting as this reading may be, it does not seem to be warranted by the text. This is true with respect to the Old Testament motifs of Exodus 15 and the pilgrimage of the nations themes which furnish the basic conceptual framework of Revelation 15.2-4.[36] Broadly speaking in the Old Testament, the Gentiles come to Zion to praise the Lord, because such actions are part and parcel of an appropriate recognition of Yahweh's universal sovereignty. They do it out of a sense of recognition of awesome power, much the same way as the leaders of small vulnerable powers line up today for an opportunity to visit the President of the United States. There is nothing in these verses that indicates that the nations will turn to the Lamb on account of the power of the martyr's witness (cf. 16.9, 11, 21).

---

33   Mounce, *Revelation*, p.286.

34   The Greek words κρίμα ἐδόθη 'and to them judgment was given (by God)' in Rev. 20.4 connect with δικαιώματα '(your) righteous judgments' in Rev. 15.4 (cf. Ps. 98.2). In 15.4, proleptically, God is praised for bringing his righteous justice to the created order by exercising his sovereign power over the nations. Rev. 20.4 views this victory retrospectively. Probably because of 20.8 there is no specific reference to the exercise of rule over the nations in 20.4.

35   Bauckham, *Theology of Revelation*, pp.98–104; *idem, Climax of Prophecy*, pp.296–307.

36   In addition to Jer. 10.6-7; Ps. 86.8-10 and 98.1-2, see Isa. 2.2-4; 60.1-3; 66.19-21; Zech 8.20-23; 14.9.

The Nations Fall Under the Sway of the Lamb (Revelation 21.3, 24-26; 22.2)

Since Revelation 17.1 John has focused on the fate of the evil woman-city Babylon and her allies. In a plodding methodical march (in the opposite order in which they were introduced) Babylon, the beasts and the dragon are destroyed (17.1–20.10). A punitive judgment of the unrighteous follows (20.11-15). One must keep in mind the limits of the vision of the prophet John. His focus is shaped within the parameters of both his scriptural and first-century world. Babylon (Rome) was the embodiment of all things evil. It has seduced and beguiled the nations. It must be replaced by another city in which the nations are to find peaceful repose. This city emerges in Revelation 21.9–22.5. Revelation 21.1-8, the last unit in the 'action section' commencing in 19.11, is a brief interpretation of that intervening time which anticipates the full appearance of the new Jerusalem.

There is no direct reference to the nations in Revelation 21.1-8. However, there is an interesting reference in Revelation 21.3 to people (peoples) that has important implications with respect to our project.

The structure of Revelation 21.1-8 can be carefully delineated. In 21.1-2 John has a twofold vision introduced by his characteristic word εἶδον 'I saw'. Corresponding to what John sees in 21.1-2 are two auditory responses.[37] The interplay of 'seeing' to expound upon what the prophet 'hears' or vice versa is characteristic of the composition of Revelation. The first auditory response (21.3-4) is that of a voice from the throne (an angel?). The second auditory response comes from God himself (21.5-8). What is important to note is the emphasis on the word καινός 'new'. The word occurs three times in 21.1-7. As Creator, God is continually interacting with the world. In the Bible 'new' can be understood in two ways: (1) total replacement; (2) renovation of the old. Usually, for the idea of replacement, the word νεός 'brand new' is used. The word καινός connotes a sense of massive change in essence or quality. It comes closer to the idea of renovation.[38] The distinction is not absolute; and clearly John indicates that at the parousia the renovation of the creation will be at a radical level.[39] Yet, by using καινός, John probably is saying while there is continuity with the old, the new essence is eternal as opposed to the old order that was subject to decay and transition.[40] This reading is also in keeping with Isaiah

---

37   Roloff, *Revelation*, pp.234–5. The distinction between the new creation and the new Jerusalem is primarily a semantic discussion for purposes of illustration. Nevertheless, it is clear that John's interest is not so much in new creation as in new Jerusalem. The new order of things provides the basis for the emergence of the new Jerusalem which is the central focus of what is to come.

38   Beale, *Revelation*, p.1040.

39   The old 'sea' of chaos will be no more. The first heaven and earth will pass away (21.1).

40   This would be in keeping with Rom. 8.18-23 and even a critical reading of 2 Pet. 3.10-11. Cf. Bauckham, *Jude, 2 Peter*, pp.315–22; also, Allan J. McNicol, 'All Things New', *Christian Studies* 21 (2006), pp.46–8. Roy A. Harrisville, *The Concept of Newness in the New Testament* (Minneapolis: Augsburg, 1960), pp.100–108.

65.17, which John clearly echoes in 21.1. The concept of renovation or a radical shaking up of the old order seems to be the paramount concern of the text.[41]

Revelation 21.3

Coterminous with the new creation is the new Jerusalem. Babylon was the embodiment of the centre of influence of the 'earth dwellers' who sought power throughout the created order. Upon the demise of Babylon a terrible lament pours forth from this quarter (18.2-24). On the other hand, the new Jerusalem is the embodiment of the people of the new creation.[42] Its difference from Babylon is shown in that it is not of this order. It comes from above (21.2).

Although the full explication of the structure and function of the new Jerusalem as the bride of the Lamb comes in Revelation 21.9-22.5, several clues about its actual constituency emerge in 21.3. The verse opens with the announcement of a voice from the throne. This is probably the voice of an angel because it is distinguished from the voice of God 'the one sitting upon the throne' in 21.5.[43] There follows immediately the statement that 'the home of God is among humankind'.[44] Having just observed the important *inclusio* of the two announcements of God in Revelation 1.8 and 21.5-8, another

---

41   See Brevard S. Childs, *Isaiah* OTL (Louisville, Kentucky: Westminster John Knox Press, 2001), pp.538-9. Note also that Isa. 65.18, which seems to be in apposition with the new creation of Isa. 65.17, refers to Jerusalem.

42   Robert H. Gundry, 'The New Jerusalem: People as Place, Not Place for People', NovT 29 (1987), pp.254-64; Beale, *The Temple and The Church's Mission*, pp.385-93. However, it is important to observe that for John the city or the people may not be read as an either/or proposition. John considers the climactic events of the new age, inaugurated by Christ, as bringing to fulfilment the ideal hopes of Israel. Israel constitutes the people of God. The early Christian community is Israel restored to play its fulfilled role taking the central place in the total biblical story. As John envisions the last phases of the eschatological events, in the context of reading prophets such as Isaiah, Ezekiel, Daniel, and Zechariah, he inevitably conflates the future glory of life in the new creation with people and place. The new Jerusalem is a revived Jerusalem as a place populated by faithful renewed people. Its origin is in heaven but it exists on a renewed earth although the descriptions and dimensions given are highly symbolic.

43   This is the first direct reference to God speaking since Rev. 1.8. The threefold repetition in 21.5 (twice) and 21.6 that it is God speaking highlights its importance. This is also underscored by the reference to God as the Alpha and the Omega (1.8 and 21.6). Not only does this mark off a massive *inclusio* incorporating the message of both the sealed and open scrolls but Rev. 21.5-8 functions as the great climax of the major heavenly vision within the book (4.1-22.9). Its message is that from beginning to end God is all in all. Also, worthwhile to notice again is that at the end of the action sequence of the seven bowls of wrath, announcing the end of Babylon, there is the important phraseology 'It is done' (16.17). Now, upon the announcement of the coming of the new Jerusalem, God announces to John, 'It is done' (21.6).

44   The English translation of 'home' appears in the NRSV. It is the translation of σκηνή which primarily, in the context of biblical writings, means 'tent' or 'dwelling'. There is a word play on this terminology in Rev. 21.3 that underscores this usage. Literally 21.3b reads, 'Behold the *tent* of God is with humankind and he God will *tent* with (i.e. dwell) with them.' The sentence alludes to the anticipated coming of the new Jerusalem among humankind. As a point of reference it is anchored

inclusio is worthy of notice. This is between Revelation 3.12 (the promise to the church in Philadelphia) and 21.3. In 3.12 the promise to the faithful believer is to become a pillar in the ναός 'inner sanctuary' of God. This is a metaphor for direct access to the presence of God. Earlier in Revelation the great multitude of 7.9-17 worship in this inner sanctuary as the one sitting upon the throne σκηνοῦν 'shelters' them (7.15; cf. 15.5). In 3.12 we read that the name of 'the city of my God, the new Jerusalem which comes down from my God out of heaven', is written on the believer.[45] Revelation 21.3 is an exposition of the coming of the new Jerusalem to earth where now, as the climactic eschatological event, God will give shelter to his people. It is critical that we observe that this promise in 3.12 is given to the faithful believer (cf. 2.7, 11, 17, 26; 3.5, 21). Then in Revelation 21.7 it is stated, upon the coming of the new Jerusalem, 'that he who conquers will inherit these things and I will be his God and he will be to me as a son'. John understands Revelation 21.1-7 as the fulfilment of God's promise for the faithful believers. Those in Revelation 21.8 (the unfaithful in the churches?) are subject to the second death.[46]

This brings us to Revelation 21.3b. 'They (humankind) will be his peoples. And God himself, their God, will be with them.'[47] The unit echoes strongly the

in the experience of Israel in the wilderness when the Lord was present in the tabernacle in a direct way (Exod. 39.32–40.38; cf. Exod. 29.45; Lev. 26.11-12). Based on this motif Israel came to celebrate this time of God's special presence with them in the Feast of Booths or Tabernacles (Deut. 16.13-16; cf. Exod. 23.16; Lev. 23.40). It provides a basis in John's Apocalypse for the expression of an unmediated relationship between God and his people. First, this takes place in the liturgy of the heavenly tabernacle (7.15-17; 12.12; 15.5). Now in 21.3 it finds a place in the new Jerusalem which comes down from heaven to earth.

45   It is true that in the later exposition on the new Jerusalem (21.22) it is stated that there is no sanctuary in the city, but it is worthy of notice that the city, in the shape of a cube, is one big sanctuary and, filled with the divine presence, is the absolute expression of unmediated access to God.

46   Much of the terminology listed with respect to the 'unfaithful' of Rev. 21.8 is applicable to John's critique of the problem areas in the seven churches in 2.1–3.22 and not necessarily the wider culture. Note Ian Boxall, '"For Paul" or "For Cephas"', pp.205–17.

47   There are two textual issues here. One of these is especially significant for our purposes. The last two words of 21.3 in Nestle-Aland (fourth revised edition), αὐτῶν θεός 'their God', are in brackets. Aune, *Revelation*, pp.1110–11, has a thorough survey of the massive variations in the ancient textual tradition. The issue cannot be solved definitively. Since final resolution is not germane for the purposes of our analysis we accept the reading of the current standard Greek text. The second issue, however, is of critical importance. It can be stated clearly. Do we accept the manuscript evidence in favour of λαός 'people' as singular or the manuscript tradition that has the plural λαοί 'peoples'? The manuscript evidence leans in favour of the plural reading, but not decisively. A number of the ancient versions have the singular, which is a sign of very early usage. Also, despite Aune's claim, *passim*, established biblical usage is in favour of the singular. In the context John would have to change the well-established scriptural concept of the 'people of God' deliberately to make a theological point if he chose the plural. In 18.4, the nearest usage of λαός, John clearly shows he is capable of using the singular in the established way. Here, in the taunt narrative, he is speaking retrospectively of the people of God called not to submit to the deception of the beast during the great

Old Testament prophetic vision of Yahweh ruling peacefully over his people (Israel) restored to Jerusalem. The Hebrew prophets speak of a time that when the sovereignty of Yahweh comes to Jerusalem nations will acknowledge the glory of the king and his God (Ezekiel 37.27; 43.7; Zech. 2.10-11 [LXX 2.14-15]).[48] Built on this web of exegesis the writer of the Apocalypse envisions Israel, under the messiahship of Christ, as an entity that now incorporates all peoples. The hopes of the prophets have been expanded and deepened. In this final phase of the eschatological expectations of the early church the traditional hopes of the prophets have been stretched to the limits. The people of God, those bearing the name of Christ, are now both the new temple and the new holy city (cf. 3.12).

To summarise, Revelation 21.3 is a key verse that brings into focus John's vision of the coming of God's new world. The play on σκηνή 'tent' in both noun and verbal forms is prominent in this text. In the Johannine world God has come in Christ and 'tented' among us (Jn. 1.14). In the Gospel of John Jesus promises to send the Paraclete in order that Christ will continue to dwell with his disciples (Jn. 14.1–17.26; 20.21-23). But in Revelation the prophet John goes farther. In 7.14-17 we are brought to the heavenly sanctuary where the Lamb stands at God's throne sheltering those who were faithful during the great tribulation. In the midst of this praise a future day of full vindication is anticipated. We read ὁ καθήμενος ἐπὶ τοῦ θρόνου σκηνώσει ἐπ' αὐτούς 'the one sitting upon the throne will dwell with them'. This promise is fulfilled in Revelation 21.3. The victors are clearly delineated not only as those who have come out of the great tribulation but who have 'washed their robes and made them white in

---

tribulation. This reference to God's people corresponds to the 144,000 who are sealed off to escape the wrath of God in 7.11-17 and 14.1-5. Thus, in my judgment, the singular would be appropriate in this text. However, along with most interpreters, it is probable that the plural 'peoples' should be the accepted reading. The breadth of the manuscript evidence is superior and, in light of established usage, the singular 'people [of God]', it conforms to the maxim of accepting the *lectio difficilior* as the more difficult reading. Yet, by accepting the plural reading it is important to determine how it functions in this text. Bauckham, *Climax of the Covenant*, pp.311–13 understands this text as a fulfilled promise that all nations, as a result of the witness of the church, have become 'the people(s) of God'. He argues that because λαοί stands in apposition with τῶν ἀνθρώπων 'of the humans' it subsequently anticipates the references to the ingathering of the nations in 21.24, 26 and 22.2. Yet, it is doubtful whether this is the direction in which the narrative is moving. E. J. Schnabel, 'John and the Future of the Nations', *BBR* 12/2, pp.266–7, notes that the two previous chapters (19–20) are filled with accounts of strong judgment on the ungodly. This culminates in 20.11-15 when all who are not in the book of life are consigned to the second death in the lake of fire. Then, in 21.1-2 the new creation and new Jerusalem arrive from heaven. It is hard for an attentive reader of the narrative to see that any 'action passage' before the end of chapter 20 provides an occasion for God embracing 'all nations' in a new covenant as some claim. A more appropriate reading is that the new Jerusalem, having its origin in heaven, now appears among humans. In keeping with the earlier announcement in 5.9 and 7.9, it announces the near fulfilment that the new Jerusalem is a universal community incorporating all people(s) of every tribe and nation.

48   In Zech. 2.14-15 LXX the text speaks of ἔθνη πολλά 'many nations' joining themselves to the Lord and becoming his λαός 'people' on that day.

the blood of the Lamb' (7.13; cf. 7.9; 12.11; 22.14). On earth, with the shepherd, they share rule over the nations after the Lamb defeats the forces of the dragon (Rev. 20.4-5). The promise to wipe away all tears (7.17) has come to fruition (20.4).

Revelation 21.24-26
In the action sequence of Revelation 19.11–21.8, all those who refuse to wear the mark of the beast during the great tribulation, in the presence of the Lamb exercise dominion over the new order (20.4-6). The locale is the new Jerusalem which comes from above to be the centre of the renewed creation on earth. The last pericope of the action unit (21.1-8) serves as an introduction to a detailed exposition in 21.9–22.10. Since 21.1-8 provides a brief contextual summary of the concluding phase of John's eschatological depiction, we agree with Fekkes that 21.9–22.5 should be described as an expansion or appendix to the summary in 21.1-8).[49] Within the appendix on the new Jerusalem the division into two distinct units on *Architectural Traditions* (21.9-21) and the *Temple-City* (21.22–22.5) is satisfactory.[50] The references to the nations appear in the latter unit on the glories of the temple-city.

In Revelation 21.22 John makes the critical announcement that there is no temple in the city.[51] But one should not be misled. There is no need for a temple because the city itself functions as a temple where the direct presence of the divine (God and the Lamb) is pervasive. Then, in Revelation 21.23 by use of epexegetical καί John expands his description of the implications of the divine presence abiding in the city. The verse is important for our purposes because it reflects compositional dependence upon the text of Isaiah 60, a key source for John's exposition. Isaiah 60 is a celebration of the restoration of Zion, the return of the exiles from the Diaspora, and, above all, the recognition of its glory by the nations. I propose to give evidence of this dependence of the use

---

49   Fekkes, *Isaiah and the Prophetic Traditions*, pp.93–4.
50   Fekkes, *Isaiah and the Prophetic Traditions*, pp.95–101; cf. Herms, *An Apocalypse For The Church*, p.241, prefers the terminology 'outward features' for 21.9-21 and 'inward "living conditions" of that city' (21.22–22.5) with respect to John's summary of the new Jerusalem. On the other hand Philip L. Mayo, 'Those Who Call Themselves Jews', *The Church and Judaism in the Apocalypse of John*, PTMS 60 (Eugene, Oregon: Wipf & Stock, 2006), p.172, makes the division at 22.1 where the shift in themes to a new paradise emerges. Since there are various themes emerging in the unit it is not a compelling argument to select randomly this particular image as a basis for making a structural decision.
51   The fact that there is no temple in the new Jerusalem is a major differentiation from OT texts, especially Ezek 40.1–48.35, and from the Qumran materials, including the Temple Scroll (11Q18) and the texts on the new Jerusalem. Cf. 1 Enoch 90.28-29; Sib. Or. 3.657-701; 5.420-433. With respect to the latter, see Michael Wise, Martin Abegg, Jr., and Edward Cook, *The Dead Sea Scrolls: A New Translation* (San Francisco: HarperCollins, 1996), pp.180–84. Some of these differences may be obviated by the fact that John considers the entire new Jerusalem, the people of God in the new creation, as a temple-city. Cf. Beale, *The Temple and the Church's Mission*, pp.365–73; also Hirschberg, *Das eschatologische Israel*, pp.262–72.

of Isaiah 60 in my analysis of Revelation 21.24-26. But, already in 21.23 John creatively uses the beginning and end of Isaiah 60 to provide the setting for his discussion of the role of the nations in the new Jerusalem (Isa. 60.1-2; 16-20). In Isaiah 60.1-2 the image of divine light dispelling darkness is used to describe the descent of God's glory into Jerusalem as the basis for its future greatness. Then in 60.19-20 the prophet describes the Lord's glory as so powerful that the sun and the moon will no longer be needed for light. This is also echoed in Zechariah 14.7, a pericope that has similar themes to Isaiah 60 and may even be dependent upon it. Revelation 21.23 makes a similar point. It is now God and the Lamb who manifest their divine radiance in the new Jerusalem. Consequently there is no need of the sun or moon.[52] This immediately leads one to Isaiah 60.3 – a critical verse that provides the foundation for the argument in Revelation 21.24-26. Indeed, it is no exaggeration to say that Revelation 21.22-22.5, a text that narrates the spiritual purpose of the city for John, is meant to be the true fulfilment of this critical chapter of Isaiah.

It is through the use of Isaiah 60.3 that John introduces further details about the role of the nations in the new order. The Hebrew text of Isaiah 60.3 may be translated as follows:

> And Gentiles will walk to your light
> And kings to the brightness of your sunrise.

Oddly enough, the translation of the Greek Bible (LXX) reverses the subjects so that the kings come to the light and the Gentiles or the nations to your (Jerusalem's) brightness.[53] As is typical of John, he seems to prefer a text closer to the *Vorlage* of our present Hebrew text. This is an expression of the motif of the pilgrimage of the nations to Jerusalem in the end-times that is important for the Isaianic corpus, which John utilizes as a vehicle for spiritualization.[54] This also functions as the framework for his view that the universal sovereignty of Yahweh will not be complete without the full recognition of the nations. Isaiah argues that because of both the future universal recognition of Yahweh and the future glory of his house in Zion, a day is coming when the nations will acknowledge appropriately Jerusalem's significance. In Isaiah 60.5-6, 11, 14, and 16, the nations will bring their wealth as gifts – including gold and frankincense

---

52   The last unit on the temple-city (21.22–22.5) ends with a repetition of the same thought. Thus this use of terminology echoing Isaiah 60.1-2, 19 that functions as an *inclusio* returns as an *inclusio* in Revelation on the importance of the city. This seems to be a delicate editorial feature of the author. Cf. Aune, *Revelation*, p.1169; Johnson Puthussery, *Days of Man and God's Day: An Exegitico-Theological Study of* ἡμέρα *in the Book of Revelation*, Tesi Gregoriana 82 (Rome: Gregorian University Press, 2001), p.243, observes that with regard to the other city (Babylon) that it discards the light: 'the light of a lamp shines no more' (Rev. 18.23).

53   Aune, *Revelation*, p.1171.

54   Isa 2.2-4; 18.7; 49.23; 55.5; 60.1-16; 61.5-6; 66.18-23. Cf. R. J. McKelvey, *The New Temple: the Church in the New Testament* (London: Oxford University Press, 1969), p.173.

to Zion. Indeed, the city's gates will be open day and night. This wealth will stream into Zion and contribute to its greatness (Isa 60.11-14).[55]

Returning to Revelation 21.24-26, characteristically, we are claiming that in his description of the emergence of the new Jerusalem the prophet John views this text as the eschatological fulfilment of Isaiah 60. He makes changes to his Isaianic *Vorlage* to communicate the theological vision that this is the ultimate expression of the divine presence resting within the human community. First, picking up the theme of light in Revelation 21.25, John asserts that the nations will walk 'in' or 'through' its light instead of coming to the light of the city in Isaiah 60.3. The use of the genitive διά 'through' is probably meant to describe a manner of life in keeping with God and the Lamb's way. Bauckham argues that this translation comes closer to the Hebrew preposition for 'in' of Isaiah 2.5, 'come let us walk in the light of the Lord'.[56] The latter is a classical text of the pilgrimage of the nations (Isa. 2.2-5). The total effect of John's glossing of these Isaianic texts is to say that the nations come to the new Jerusalem not simply on the basis of the sheer recognition of its power but because they accept and live by the precepts which come from it.[57] At last we have come to the conversion of the nations. For Paul, the ultimate fulfilment of the covenants with Abraham was the ingathering in the present of the Gentiles through faith and baptism (Gal. 3.26-29). But John expands this insight into an almost breathtaking eschatological vision. The renewed Israel, incorporating the nations, without the encumbrance of the beast and his allies, now embodies the precepts of the Lamb. Of course, this is impressionistic language evoking an ideal reality. After all it is a new heaven and a new earth. The central insight is that, in keeping with God's original intentions, finally the created order will work. We do John a disservice if we speculate about the nature of this new world. He is not addressing anthropological issues such as whether people have been transformed into a new dimension, continue to procreate or are subject to death. Rather, the vision is theological. Once the nations were subject to Babylon; now the nations live by the precepts of the Lamb. The changes in lordship which eventuates in a vast difference in moral outcomes of the nations is his main focus.

In Revelation 21.24b and 26 John continues to use Isaiah 60.3b to continue to affirm the full allegiance of the nations to the Lamb. The kings of the earth bring their glory into Jerusalem (21.24b). There is a repetition of a similar idea in 21.26 where the text adds 'honour of the nations' to the glory that the kings (unquestionably the subject) bring into the holy city.

---

55   The reference to the perpetually open gates in Rev. 21.25 is another direct echo of Isa. 60.11. Noticeably, in the heart of this text, Isa. 60.12, John states that the nations that do not serve Yahweh will be utterly laid waste. As we have argued earlier, John drew heavily on this text to furnish a basis for the outcome of the Lamb's war against the beast and his allies (Rev. 19.11-21).

56   Bauckham, *Climax of Prophecy*, pp.314–15, contends that John gets there by gezērâ sāwâ. We do not contest this point, although it is not decisive for our argument.

57   Bauckham, *Climax of Prophecy*, p.315, makes a similar point. The use of περιπατεῖν in a familiar expression for 'living faithfully' found in early Christian paraenetic texts (Rom. 13.13; Gal. 5.16; 1 Thess. 2.12; Eph. 4.1; cf. Rev. 3.4).

The role of the kings of the earth in Revelation has recently been the subject
of a lengthy analysis by Ronald Herms.[58] The phraseology οἱ βασιλεῖς τῆς
γῆς 'the kings of the earth' appears in various case forms in Revelation 1.5,
6.15; 17.2, 18; 18.3, 9-10; 19.19; 21.24. In addition, the phraseology of 'the kings
of the whole inhabited order' appears to be a simile (16.14); and several general
mentions of kings (10.11; 17.12-14, 16; 19.16, 19) generally can be taken to
have the same reference.[59] Our specific interest is in the rhetorical role of this
terminology in the book of Revelation.

By far the most frequent usage of the phrase 'kings of the earth' in Revelation
refers to the leaders of the nations who offer full allegiance to the empire. By
and large the term 'the earth' is burdened with negative overtones in Revelation.[60] Thus, in a key pericope in 6.15, we are introduced to these 'kings of the
earth' who stand at the apex of power among all social classes in the empire.
Ultimately, deceived by Satan, having given themselves over to Babylon, they
suffer a similar fate as their sponsor (19.19-21). Yet there are two pericopes (1.5
and 21.24-26) where the 'kings of the earth' do not appear to have a negative
usage. Since both usages impact our project directly we will give attention to
them.

Revelation 1.5a, as we noted in the previous chapter, the opening salutation
of the letter functions as part of two triads on Christ and his people.

Christ 1.5a	Salvific Accomplishments 5b-6a
1. Faithful witness	1. Loves us
2. First born from the Dead	2. Freed us from our sins by his blood
3. Ruler of the Kings of the Earth	3. Made us a Kingdom and Priests

Again manifesting his strong dependence upon scripture, the threefold triad on
Christ can be traced directly to John's use of Psalm 89.37-38 (88.37-38 LXX).
This psalm speaks of the sun and moon standing as a faithful *witness* to the
eternal kingship of the family of David. This is supplemented by Psalm 89.27-28
[88.26-28 LXX] where the Davidite is promised to become the *firstborn*, the
highest of the *kings of the earth* (cf. Ps. 2.2). Since the author of the Apocalypse
regularly works with Psalm 2 it is worthy of notice that immediately preceding
Psalm 89.28, where the Davidite is the King *par excellence*, it is said that he will
address God as 'my Father' (cf. Ps. 2.7). Clearly the author of Revelation views
Jesus Christ as the Davidite who fulfils the words of this psalm in his life, death,
and resurrection. He thus is King of Kings (19.16). He is infinitely superior to
those who claim kingship in the context of the empire.

---

58   Herms, *An Apocalypse for the Church and the World*, pp.197–256. This includes an
Excursus on the use of Isaiah 60 in the Isaiah Targum and 1 QM 12.13-14.
59   Herms, *An Apocalypse for the Church and the World*, pp.197-8. Note also the usage in 4
Ezra 15.20-21.
60   Cf. the phraseology 'the inhabitants of the earth' (Rev. 3.10; 6.10; 8.13; 11.10[2]; 13.8, 12, 14[2];
17.2, 8).

In Revelation, language about kingship and kingdom can have more than one referent. In several instances followers of Jesus are considered to be participants in the kingdom (1.6; 5.10; 11.15; 12.10). The beast also has a rival kingdom (16.10; 17.12, 17, 18). But, although the faithful are given thrones in the millennium (20.4-5) nowhere are they referred to specifically as kings in Revelation.[61] Therefore, it is highly unlikely that the reference to Jesus as ruler of the kings of the earth refers to Christ's present lordship over Christian believers who are the antecedents of 'kings'.[62] At the outset the reader is informed that Jesus Christ, enthroned in heaven, is far superior to any king, including the emperor. This is a fundamental presupposition that is echoed in many shapes and forms throughout Revelation.

In Revelation 21.24b and 26, John, utilizing Isaiah 60.3b, glosses the text to continue to affirm the full allegiance of all nations to the Lamb. In Isaiah 60.3, 5, 9, and 11 the amount of goods and wealth of the nations are indicators of Jerusalem's power and significance.[63] John had seen this kind of wealth in Babylon (Rome) and was not impressed (18.11-13). He prefers to spiritualize Isaiah's terminology. For John glory and honour (Isa 60.19) are appropriate terms for the majesty of God and the Lamb (4.9, 11; 5.12, 13; 7.12). Perhaps the portion of Isaiah 60.6, 'And will proclaim the praise of the Lord', is also being echoed.[64] In any case, the thought is clear. The nations are bringing the appropriate praise, thanksgiving, and honour to God and the Lamb. Humankind moves to the praise of God. The main vision of the book begins in chapter 4 and opens with these bursts of praises to God in the heavenly sanctuary. As we approach the end of the Apocalypse this praise is heard on the renewed earth coming from the most distant expanses of the nations and their kings.[65]

---

61   Clearly as Rev. 20.4 indicates the thrones function as seats of judgment. This is a clear echo of Daniel 7.

62   As argued by Elizabeth Shüssler Fiorenza, *Priester für Gott: Studien zum Herrschafts- und Priestermotiv in der Apocalypse*, NTAbh 7 (Münster: Aschendorff, 1972); *idem, Justice and Judgment*, p.78. This reading seems to be plausible only if a very obscure reading of 1.6 βασιλεῖς 'kings' rather than the massively attested βασιλείαν 'kingdom' is accepted. The reading of 'kings' seems to have entered the textual tradition through conformity with some translations of Exod. 19.6 in later versions of the Greek Bible.

63   A similar belief emerges at Qumran in 4Q 504 col.4, 'Having seen your glory…all the nations shall bring their offerings: silver, gold, and gems, even every precious thing of their lands, whereby to glorify your people and Zion, your holy city, as well as your glorious temple', *The Dead Sea Scrolls: A New Translation*, p.412.

64   Beale, *Revelation*, pp.1094–5, also draws attention to Isa. 49.6-8, 23 as another potential echo. In addition Ps. 2.10-11 should definitely not be overlooked. Fekkes, *Isaiah and Prophetic Tradition*, p.270, makes a case that John has translated 'wealth' in Isa. 60.11 into 'glory'. If so, it represents a spiritualization that is compatible with John's exegetical procedure.

65   As if to reinforce the sovereignty and all-encompassing holiness of God's presence in the new Jerusalem, John highlights its purity in Rev. 21.27. As with his paranetic asides in 21.8-9 and 22.14-15 it is inconceivable that anyone impure can be present.

Nevertheless, as we have already highlighted, the fact that John spiritualizes the material gifts (Isaiah 60) brought by the kings of the nations to Jerusalem has led many to claim that the new Jerusalem functions only as a metaphor for the ideal existence of the people of God.[66] Here, the people of God live in unmediated union with God and the Lamb. It is the logical extended description of the marriage feast of the Lamb that surfaces in 19.6-9 (cf. 21.2, 9).[67]

Although there is no doubt that John highlights the people of God in an idealized situation in his description of the new Jerusalem, it is open to question that this is all that the metaphor entails. Rather than retrace the lengthy discussion about whether Jerusalem is people or place, we would assert two points in favour of the view that the new Jerusalem should be understood in a multivalent sense. First, there is the matter of the parallel descriptions of the two cities in 17.1 and 19.9. In 17.1 an angel shows John 'the judgment of the great prostitute'. Here John refers to the fate of Babylon (Rome). The destruction of an actual city is narrated in no uncertain terms in the following chapters. In 21.9 an angel shows John the bride. This is followed by a lengthy description of the new Jerusalem, indeed idealized beyond ordinary reality, but still a city. For the analogy to be appropriate an ordinary reader would probably conclude that places are being compared. Second, we should remember that our reading of Revelation 11 indicates that there are clear echoes of the destruction of the holy city no matter what conclusions the author drew from this tragic event (11.1-2, 8, 13).[68] The prophet was a Jew. He considered the church was Israel renewed and he freely used traditional texts in Isaiah, Ezekiel, and Zechariah on the restoration of Jerusalem as the framework for his discussion of the last phase of eschatological fulfilment of God's people. Steeped in these traditional expectations he calls this the new Jerusalem. It is both people and place. Thus, as the nations once looked to Babylon as their mentor, now they are drawn by the light of God's glory to a new city. Their offerings are now the earthly counterparts to the heavenly doxologies resonant in Revelation 4–5.[69]

Once again there is the consistent theme of a correlation of first and last things. The perfect rule of God that existed in the creation will return in a perfect way at the end. The way is now open for the nations and kings of the earth to submit to their shepherd's rule (Ps. 2.10-11). This they do in 20.24-26.

---

66   This, of course, is a play on Gundry's 'New Jerusalem: People as Place, Not Place for People', pp.254–64. For Gundry, Jerusalem as an actual entity is not visualized in any sense of being restored. Cf. McKelvey, *The New Temple*, pp.171–6.

67   Mayo, 'Those Who Call Themselves Jews', pp.173–80. Mayo is in favour of the view that the city is meant to be a spiritual entity but summarizes and intersects fairly with other positions. Especially helpful is his observation that in Ezek. 44.9 the nations are excluded from the temple. The fact that John makes such a point of stating that they will enter the new Jerusalem indicates how strongly he believes in divine acceptance of people from every tribe and nation.

68   Marko Jauhiainen, 'The Measuring of the Sanctuary', pp.524–6.

69   Fekkes, *Isaiah and the Prophetic Traditions*, pp.272–3.

Revelation 22.2-3

As he moves to close his description of the new Jerusalem, John, in the light of Genesis 2, utilizes the theme of the new Eden (22.1-3). The pericope falls into two parts. First, in 21.1-2 the focus is on the reappearance of the river and the tree of life (Gen. 2.9-14; 3.22; cf. Ezek. 47.1-12; Zech. 14.8; Joel 3.18). Second, in 22.3a the nations are freed from their earlier curses because of their infidelity. With respect to the new Edenic theme the terminology has parallels in other apocalyptic works of the time.[70] John's description relies heavily on images drawn from Ezekiel 47.1-12. In Revelation it is anticipated that the life-giving stream of paradise, now centred at the throne of God and the Lamb on Mount Zion, will flow east. On both banks, under the collective image of the restoration of the tree of life, stand a series of fruit trees.[71] Subtly echoing Ezekiel's fruit of each month (Ezek. 47.12) this orchard produces 12 different varieties. And, in an additional echo of Ezekiel 47.12, these fruits are for healing. However, John makes a significant gloss on Ezekiel. In John, the fruit is not for healing alone, but the healing of the nations. This brings us to a significant observation. Shortly before the critical text of Psalms of Solomon 17, which represents an important interpretation of Psalm 2 in post-biblical Judaism, there occurs in 14.3-4 these words:

The holy ones of the Lord will live by the law forever.
As his holy ones they are the paradise of the Lord, the trees of life.
Their planting is well rooted forever.
They will not be uprooted as long as there is heaven.

This text echoes Proverbs 3.18, where one who lives under the control of wisdom is likened to a tree of life. Using the theme of a planting, by *gezērâ sāwâ* it is possible to move from Psalms of Solomon 14.4 LXX (φυτεία 'planting') to Isaiah 60.21 LXX (φύτευμα 'what is planted', cf. Isa 61.3, 11), the basic text for much of John's description of the new Jerusalem.[72] In short we suggest that John understands the tree of life, just like the new Jerusalem, as metonymy for the faithful community living in restored Zion, God's new world (cf. Rev. 2.7; 3.12; 22.14, 19). The dominion of the Lamb manifested in his covenantal community now serves as the light or the means to bring healing to the nations. In Isaiah 60.22 we come to the climax of the vision of the restoration of the new Jerusalem. Isaiah states that the most insignificant ones of God's people LXX (λαός = Isa. 60.21) will multiply into the thousands; the least will become a great ἔθνος 'nation'. In the context of cosmological changes (Isa. 60.19-20) God will transform Zion and its people to become a mighty nation. They are truly the Lord's planting. In turn, the

---

70   2 Bar. 4.1-7; 4 Ezra 8.52.

71   This reading of the text is preferable to the alternative idea that the river and street are side by side with the trees on a bank between the two.

72   Childs, *Isaiah*, pp. 493, 499, notes that the Hebrew text has several different readings, 'shoot of his planting' and 'my plantings' are variants. The NRSV, referring to the righteous who possess the land, are called 'the shoot of the plantings of the Lord'. He also notes the 1Q Is^a reads 'the planting of Yahweh'.

seer adds that this transformation will be indelibly recognized and acknowledged by the nations (Isa. 54.3; 60.9, 11-12; 61.6; 62.2). It will result in their healing. John seems to have interpreted Isaiah's vision of the new Jerusalem to include the coming of the various nations (i.e. humankind) to hear and live by the word of the Lamb and his people. Finally, his interpretation of Isaiah 60 has moved to completion. The nations and their kings now live in the light of the brightness of the Lord (22.5; cf. Isa. 60.3, 19-20).

Consequently, Revelation 22.3a appropriately brings this exegesis to closure. The Lamb and his servants are around the throne of God and exercise dominion over the creation forever (Rev. 22.3b-5; cf. Isa. 60.19). Perhaps echoing Zechariah 14.11 the ban of destruction is lifted (22.3a), the prophet envisions a time when the earlier pronouncements of destruction against the holy city are lifted. The curse of war is ended. In the new Eden John claims this promise as fulfilled. The nations receive nourishment from the Word of the Lamb and his people. Eden is restored. God's creation now works as he intended it.

Summary

The isle of Patmos was only an outpost in the total expanse of the great Mediterranean basin. As confining a place as it may be, it did not hinder the prophet John from constructing a massive vision about what was to come in the last days. As a member of a small counter-cultural community of believers in Jesus as Lord, John saw clearly the underside of the fist of Roman imperialism. Tapping into a reservoir of hostility toward the ideology of *Pax Romana*, John charts his perception of the course of affairs in the immediate future. To the surprise of no one conversant with his theology, what happens to Rome is vastly different from the prevailing popular ideologies.

Distributed across the vast expanse of the empire are numerous peoples, tribes, and nations. The nations, along with their provincial rulers and leaders, are enmeshed in a system that is idolatrous to the core. Despite Rome's claim to be blessed by the dæmons and gods, it is very much of this world. Throughout these visions the partisans of emperor worship are referred to as 'earth dwellers'. Nothing about them belongs to the one God of heaven.

John, a prophet schooled in the traditions and thought categories of the sectarian Jewish world of the second temple period was well equipped to make a grim assessment of Rome's ultimate destiny. He places the conflict between Rome and the church in the context of the conflict between Israel (the people of God) and Babylon historically anchored in the exilic period.[73] Of course, this choice for his biblical framework has an overlay of a set of beliefs whereby he trans-

73   Peder Borgen, 'Polemic in the Book of Revelation' in *To See Ourselves as Others See Us: Christians, Jews Others in Late Antiquity* (eds. Jacob Neusner and Ernst S. Frericks; Chico, California: Scholars Press, 1985), pp.200-201.

forms Israel into a people who see their history linked to the coming of Jesus, the Christ. Given his strong theological grounding in early Christian faith, it is remarkable how few direct echoes of the earliest Christian literature have found their way into John's Apocalypse. Rather he chooses to anchor his frame of reference in the world of the scriptures of Judaism especially the prophets of the exilic and early post-exilic period. As we have noted, there are multiple allusions to motifs drawn from Ezekiel, Isaiah, Zechariah and Daniel intermingled with the use of key Psalms. This is in contrast to very few traceable allusions to the Gospel tradition. The prophetic vision of the defeat of Babylon and the restoration of Jerusalem in the context of the new creation is the dominant motif underlying the whole project. Even his free use of the Day of the Lord motif as a basis on a macro-level for ordering the various phases of the end is dependent on the prophets.

Housed within this framework one can begin to 'tease out' the outline of how John conceived that this new order would emerge. First, there would be a restoration of repentant Israel to the land. Second, Yahweh would purge unrepentant Israel and launch a holy war against its enemies. Third, a king of the Davidic order (Christ) would take his place in a restored Jerusalem. Fourth, not only would Jewish exiles return from the Diaspora but other nations would make a pilgrimage to the holy city to worship the one God.

Procedurally, based within this framework, John is transported through an open heaven into another world. On this plane the Lamb rules triumphant in the heavenly throne room. The Lamb hears the cries of those few from the tribes and nations who are loyal to him through the brief but intense time (three and a half years) of forced submission to perceived Roman idolatry. And then, in fulfilment of the prophetic expectations of key passages such as Psalm 2, Daniel 7, and Isaiah 60-63 as a Divine Warrior, the Lamb launches a holy war against those kings and nations who persecuted and martyred his people. The defeat of Rome, its successors, and its spiritual sponsors will be absolute. The nations, once captivated and deceived by Rome's power, are either destroyed or in disarray over this turn of events. Free from their subservience to idolatry the book ends with the tribes and nations sublimated to the lordship of the Lamb. They embrace the principles and practices of the people of God who now exercise dominion in the new creation.

Our survey of the texts on the role of the nations is now complete. But there are several major questions emerging from this analysis that remain to be addressed. First, there is the question of the abrupt change in the status of the nations. They move from total defeat in 19.11-21 to unlimited access to the new Jerusalem in 21.24-26! How do we understand how the prophet frames the conversion of the nations? Is he working out a wider biblical picture? Second, there is an important question about the specific addressees of the text. To whom is this text being addressed? Almost certainly it is not the nations. They would hardly be expected to read it! John writes to the seven churches. But why should the destiny of the nations be such an important factor in his discussion? In the next two chapters we will give attention successively to these two issues.

No doubt some, even in the seven churches, were wary of this comprehensive eschatological vision anchored in a sectarian view of reality! Why did it survive? Certainly not because it was a piece of anti-Roman propaganda! And to add fuel to the fire, as the early centuries wore on, even the churches which had placed it in their canon would find it difficult to determine clearly that John's prophecy was fulfilled. Where was the evidence that Rome's power was diminishing? When things finally began to come apart, the great Augustine, in his momentous *City of God*, mourned over the loss of Rome nearly as much as the merchants and kings of Revelation 18!

Perhaps there was something else about this vision of the 'conversion' of the nations that gave it power. That is, in the minds of many, it brings to completion the biblical story about God's promise to bless the nations (Gen. 12.3). Steeped deeply in his reading of the Psalms and the prophets, in some way, John was able to take standard early Christian eschatology and project it onto an almost poetic plain. Many of the seer's hearers probably would take special pleasure in the knowledge that the nations would be destroyed. They had no love for the future of the empire! They would be suspicious of one who spoke about the salvation of the people of Rome and her clients. John left the churches with a delicate balance they could accept. Through the return of Christ, the Divine Warrior, the nations would be subjugated to his control. In the course of their subjugation the age-long purposes of God to bless the nations would be fulfilled. The secret purposes for the destiny of the people of God vis-à-vis the nations, that God announced to the prophets, and which even they only grasped partially, now becomes housed plausibly within the parameters of a universal vision for the destiny of humankind. In my view that is what made this work evocative and intrinsically appealing to Christian communities centuries later.

CHAPTER 4

THE SCRIPTURAL FRAMEWORK OF THE CONVERSION OF THE NATIONS IN REVELATION

An Overview

Our analysis of the new Jerusalem unit in Revelation 21.1–22.5 indicates it is the product of a writer deeply steeped in the Jewish world of the first-century era. It is possible that the various traditions about the form and structure of the new Jerusalem, if not even some of the text itself, came to John from sources circulating among groups within sectarian Judaism of the time.[1] Certainly it is reasonable to conclude that he was familiar with these traditions and was in conversation with them.

It is generally accepted that the prophet John was a Jew who lived in Roman Greater Syria and that he moved later to the province of Asia. The Apocalypse reflects general familiarity with the esoteric writings circulating within Jewish sectarian circles in the first century. There is no question that John still shared many of the convictions and presuppositions of his heritage within Israel. Indeed, his theological perspective was that Christianity was the true version of Judaism.

Peder Borgen puts it bluntly when he goes so far as to say:

Thus the thinking in the book of Revelation indeed resembles the self-understanding of the Qumran community that they were the true Israel within Judaism.[2]

From John's perspective it was appropriate to utilize the heritage of the prophetic scriptures and models of interpretation utilized within sectarian Judaism as the basis of his exposition.

---

1   Peter Hirschberg, *Das eschatologische Israel*, pp.291–2, states, 'John knows only Israel as the people of God.' In addition, we have argued that the prophet was steeped in the writings of the sectarian Judaism of the era. However, since this is a comprehensive visionary work, the matter of discovering and delineating oral or written sources behind the Apocalypse is daunting. Our own research indicates the probability that in the new Jerusalem unit John was aware of other source traditions on this subject. Hirschberg, *passim*, pp.240–78 discusses the relevant texts that have emerged from Qumran. But what is of ultimate significance is the final product which John carefully composed.

With historic Jerusalem in ruins there were still the passions and intense convictions within the Jewish community, nourished in scripture, for its restoration. It surely is no accident that the capstone of John's great literary work is a description of the new Jerusalem. Within this context he speaks about the nations bringing their glory to the holy city and walking by its light. Here he echoes the earlier scriptures and centuries of exegesis in Second-Temple Judaism. Yet, it is also here that we encounter our central problem. The texts, although somewhat opaque, presume the presence and conversion of the nations (21.3, 24-26; 22.2-3). How can this be? The description of the nations' entrance into the holy city is unrestricted; yet it comes after the earlier action sequences of the narrative speak of their smashing defeat. There are major questions about this massive shift in the narrative. What lies behind this massive shift in the destiny of the nations?

Given the fragmentary content and lack of context for these verses, we suggest that analysis may be helped by placing these texts in a broader framework. We should recognize that these verses are but pieces of a much wider picture which was operative in the circles in which John travelled. The full picture emerges only when one takes into consideration his lifelong immersion in the prophetic scriptures and their exposition in sectarian Judaism.[3] As already noted, a key factor in the treatment of the nations in Revelation are the parallels drawn between their allegiance to Rome with their earlier submission to Babylon. In fact, Babylon functions as a transparency for Rome in Revelation. The Israel of the biblical period had to face squarely the overwhelming influence of an idolatrous world power that had nothing but contempt for the people of Yahweh. As one who viewed himself at the core of faithful Israel in the first century, John faces a similar situation with Rome. It makes sense to conclude that in the Apocalypse John is utilizing a similar construct drawn from scripture to frame his discussion of the conversion of the nations.

Procedurally, in this chapter, we wish to trace the contours of an outline of the big picture from which John was working and in which he presumed the conversion of the nations would function.[4] This will entail an analysis of some key texts in the prophets which deal with the change of the nations from oppressors of the holy city to compliant recognition of the holy presence and universal sovereignty of Yahweh in the new Jerusalem. This will be fortified by evidence that these texts continued to be nourished in later Second-Temple Judaism. We contend that their widespread availability means that there is no barrier to the conclusion that John would be aware of the kind of eschatological reflection taking place in

---

2   Peder Borgen, 'Polemic in the Book of Revelation', p.209.

3   Besides the use of scripture, in his assessment of the nations' alliances with Rome, John utilized other traditions operative in both the wider Greco-Roman culture and the sectarian Judaism of the period. Notable are the legends about the return of Nero (*Nero Redivivus*) which are embedded in the Sibylline Oracles. For a lively overview of this issue which breaks new ground, Bauckham, *Climax of the Covenant*, pp.384–452; cf. Klauck, 'Do They Never Come Back?' pp.683–98.

4   To do this comprehensively would, of course, require another monograph. We will be selective in our treatment dealing with what we consider to be the crucial texts.

esoteric Second-Temple Judaism. Specifically, we will attempt to show that John's account of the pilgrimage of the nations to Jerusalem reflects themes drawn from such key texts as Isaiah 60, 66, and Zechariah 14. There we find featured the pilgrimage of compliant nations coming to the new Jerusalem in recognition of the sovereign power of Yahweh. When this is placed within the frame of Christian-Jewish exegesis of the late Second-Temple period the matrix of interpretation is similar to what we find in Revelation. In short, we will argue that John has simply reformulated these earlier texts to reflect his Christian-Jewish view of reality. In so doing, he is drawing on this earlier broader picture to make his argument that followers of the Lamb, the true Israel, will be joined by proselytes from the nations, formally in alliance with people like Babylon, in giving glory to God.

The Destiny of the Nations in Exilic/Post-Exilic Judaism

The incorporation of the nations into a recognition of the sovereignty of Yahweh and his representative (the Davidic king) in an eschatological setting cuts a strong swath through the Psalms and Prophets. The terminology of these texts varies but the German phraseology *Völkerwallfahrt*, usually translated 'conversion of the nations', is sufficiently inclusive to describe the central focus of these texts. In its broadest sense *Völkerwallfahrt* is the recognition of a movement in Judaism toward a deeper understanding of the implications that belief in one God has universal dimensions for all people. It involves the conviction that the recognition of Jerusalem, her king, and above all the sovereignty of Yahweh, are worthy of ultimate recognition – not only by Israel but the whole creation. With the exile and the subsequent emergence of Judaism as a faith system, this recognition by others was problematic as the people of Judah remained small and, for most of the Second-Temple period, in political captivity to larger Near Eastern powers. Subsequently, speculation about the *Völkerwallfahrt* often becomes intermingled with the substance of Jewish eschatological reflection about the future shape of God's new world.

The Psalms
Already in the Psalms the praise of God is embedded in many of these compositions. In Psalm 2.10-11 the kings and rulers are exhorted to honour the Lord because he has installed his representative in Zion. Psalm 2 is a text that is critical for the interpretation of Revelation, but the expectation becomes widespread in the Psalms that there is a time coming when the families among the nations will celebrate the reign of the Lord in Zion (Ps. 22.25-31; 86.8-10; 96; 102.12-22).[5]

---

5   Fekkes, *Isaiah and Prophetic Traditions*, p.99, lists also Ps. 47.7-9; 68.29; 72.9-11; 122.3-4; 138.4-5; cf. Christopher J.H. Wright, *The Mission of God* (Downers Grove, Illinois: InterVarsity Press, 2006), pp. 474–84.

Although the dating of many of the Psalms is problematic, at the very least this represents a widespread rhetorical recognition of the universal sovereignty of Yahweh over both Israel and the Nations.

The Prophets

It is among the prophets that the full theological weight of the conversion of the nations is found. Nowhere is this so strong as Isaiah.[6] It begins with the classical expression (almost at the opening of the book) in 2.2-4[7] of the nations coming to Zion to be taught by the Lord as the source of his law. It ends in 66.18-23 where the nations become Yahweh's emissaries to the ends of the earth. Isaiah is a veritable cornucopia of expressions of concern for the nations. These include oracles as diverse as the incorporation of Egypt into the worship of Yahweh (Isa. 19.16-25); the provision of a banquet in Zion for all peoples where death is defeated (25.6-8)[8]; all nations coming to know that there is one God: Yahweh (45.4-6)[9]; Yahweh's salvific plans through his chosen servant include bringing light to the nations (42.1-6; 45.22); and universal praise expressed through gifts brought to the Lord in Zion by the nations (60.1-22). This is only a sampling in the book of Isaiah of the richness of the announcements about the eschatological salvation that await the nations. Christopher Wright is even so bold to say, after examining Isaiah, that this theme is strong enough to structure the whole Bible.[10] Similar expressions, although not so pervasive, emerge in Ezekiel 37.28; 39.21-9; Zechariah 2.11 (LXX 2.15), 6.15; 8.20-23 and 14.12-19. It is even found in the prophet Joel 3.2-5 [LXX].

As we have noted our goal is not to be exhaustive in our survey of texts on the *Völkerwallfahrt*. For our purposes it is enough to make the point that concern for the incorporation of the nations into ultimate recognition of Yahweh in a restored Zion was pervasive in the prophetic scriptures. Any faithful Jew of the late Second-Temple period interested in forming an eschatological vision of the last days could hardly miss this emphasis.

Among the prophetic texts on the destiny of the nations that would be closely scrutinized by the prophet John would be Zechariah 14.1-21 and Isaiah 66.17-24. Coming at the end of their respective books, a late Second-Temple-era Jew would, of course, read these texts in a general literary sense, as a prophetic anticipation

---

6   Christopher T. Begg, 'The Peoples and the Worship of Yahweh in the Book of Isaiah' in *Worship and the Hebrew Bible*, JSOTSup 284 (ed. M. Patrick Graham, et al.; Sheffield: Sheffield Academic Press, 1999), pp.35–55.

7   Note the parallel in Micah 4.1-4.

8   Cf. 'And the Lord God will wipe away all tears...' (Rev. 21.4).

9   Christopher Begg, 'The Peoples and the Worship of Yahweh', p.47.

10   Wright, *Mission of God*, p.455, 'It is God's mission in relation to the nations, arguably more than any other single theme, that provides the key that unlocks the biblical grand narrative.' Without going that far we can surely say that such an intense reader of prophetic texts as John could hardly miss the significance of these themes as he sought to shape his eschatological vision (cf. Isa. 49.6; 52.7-12, 15; 55.5; 56.6-8).

of the end-times.[11] Such texts would be fruitful for him, not because they reflect the historical circumstances of the post-exilic period, but because they dealt with themes such as the restoration of Zion, return of the exiles, a new creation, and the *Völkerwallfahrt*. For a late Second-Temple Jew struggling to erect his eschatological framework, clarity on all these concepts would be crucial to determine. This is precisely the situation in which the prophet John found himself.

Both texts, at the end of Zechariah and Isaiah, came after earlier hopes for the restoration of Judah were dwindling or at the point of collapse. The excitement for renewal that came at the end of the post-exilic period had receded. Although the temple was rebuilt and its liturgical life was operative in some sense, Judea was only a shadow of the perceived glorious days of the Davidic kingdom. Given the vicious struggles between various factions in post-exilic Judaism, hope for immediate renewal subsided. But the dream for restoration was far from dead. Ironically, in the context of this setting, this delay of the end allowed eschatological hopes to become more developed and extensive. One thing was certain: for these people, true restoration would take place as a way of vindicating a small remnant who considered themselves to be faithful.[12]

Zechariah 14.1-21

At the heart of the announcement in Zechariah 14 is the core conviction that Yahweh will restore Jerusalem not only to its former glory but better than ever (14.4-8, 10-12, 16-19; cf. 12.4-9; 13.1). For the present the people of Jerusalem are plagued by inner turmoil, apostasy and betrayal (14.1-2; cf. 11.4-17). But the time is coming when the corrupt in Judah will be purged by an invasion (14.1-2). While the nations gather at Jerusalem conducting their purge, Yahweh will launch an attack against them and vindicate the faithful remnant (14.2b-3a, 12-15; cf. 13.8-9). The net result will be the emergence of the new Jerusalem.[13] It will even have cosmic implications (Zech. 14.6-8). The order of the first creation will be substituted with the order of a new creation. But, paradoxically, some features represent a return to Eden (14.6-8). Here we find a rich source for the terminology used in Revelation.[14] Yahweh manifests himself as king. The kingdom of God is established (14.9). Through convulsions in the land around

---

11   Paul Hanson, *The Dawn of Apocalyptic* (Philadelphia: Fortress Press, 1975), p.388.

12   Marko Jauhiainen, *The Use of Zechariah*, pp.56–61. The repetition and use of the phraseology 'on that day' in Zechariah must have helped later readers in Second-Temple Judaism to view these texts as a prediction of the end-times! It would add to speculation about not only the time of their coming but the precise shape and form.

13   Paul Hanson, *The Dawn of Apocalyptic*, p.382 gives an elegant description of Zechariah 14. 'Thus exalted and located at the source of the life-giving stream which turns the surrounding area into a paradisiacal garden, the earthly Jerusalem has begun to be transformed into the heavenly Jerusalem located at the *axis mundi* where heaven and earth are conjoined. The transformation represents a powerful thrust in the direction of a mythopoeic view of salvation.'

14   This would include the absence of night (14.6; cf. Rev. 21.25; 22.5); the presence of living waters (14.8; cf. Rev. 22.1); the lifting of the ban (14.11; cf. Rev. 22.3); and depending on the translation of Rev. 21.6b changes in the cosmic order tantamount to a new creation (cf. Rev. 21.1-2).

Zion (the direct result of Yahweh's action) a way is opened up for the compliant nations to stream forth in a procession to keep the Feast of Tabernacles (Zech. 14.16, 20-21). The Feast of Tabernacles now seems to be much more than a celebration of God's covenanting protection for his people in the wilderness. It becomes a renewal of God's covenant with the nations, which commenced originally with Noah.[15]

What is striking is the extent to which Yahweh works change among the nations. First they are gathered in Jerusalem against God's people to purge them. Then, the Divine Warrior appears in a theophany. The nations are humbled and defeated. Finally, living in the context of a new order, they engage in a yearly pilgrimage to Jerusalem. They become full participants in the festival of the Feast of Tabernacles without observing the usual preconditions for observing the purification rites demanded by Torah (14.20-21). Regular cooking pots become just as acceptable for use in worship as the sacred bowls of the temple.[16] The reality of one God for Jew and Gentile is apparent.

Isaiah 66.18-24
Isaiah 66.18-24, as with Zechariah 14, brings closure to a book with a vast number of prophetic oracles given at many different times and under widely varied circumstances. Before we take up the eschatological vision in these closing verses in Isaiah an additional point of clarification about some of these earlier oracles ought to be made. The continuity between Zechariah 14 and Isaiah 60-62 has come to the attention of Paul Hanson. He concludes that a similar body of traditions which informed the authors of Isaiah 60-62 at an earlier time also was utilized by Third Isaiah and the author(s) of Zechariah 14.[17] An integral part of this synthesis presumes that a democratization of the servant traditions in much of Second Isaiah had taken place at the end of the exilic period.[18] The earlier announcement from Yahweh that the Servant is a light to the nations to bring salvation to the ends of the earth (Isa. 42.6; 49.6-8) is sublimated in Isaiah 60–62 and later texts. It now takes the form wherein the faithful in Jerusalem become a people-covenant who are feared and honoured by the surrounding nations. Nations will come to their light and kings will acknowledge their 'rising brightness' (Isa. 60.3). Wealth from the nations will pour in continually (Isa. 60.6, 9, 11, 16-17, 21-22; 61.5-7; 62.2, 6-7, 11-12). And, as in Zechariah 14, some from the nations will even be given access to Yahweh's house.[19]

---

15   W. Harrelson, 'The Celebration of the Feast of Booths According to Zech XIV 16-21', in *Religions in Antiquity: Essays in Memory of E. R. Goodenough* (ed. Jacob Neusner: Leiden: E.J. Brill, 1968), pp.93–4.

16   Harrelson, 'Feast of Booths', pp.93–4.

17   Paul Hanson, *The Dawn of Apocalyptic*, pp.385–96.

18   Adrian M. Leske, 'The Influence of Isaiah on Christology in Matthew and Luke', in *Crisis in Christology: Essays in Quest of Resolution* (ed. William R. Farmer: Livonia, Michigan: Dove Booksellers, 1995), p.243.

19   Childs, *Isaiah*, pp.457–8 stresses that this access does demand a basic conformity to certain ritual demands of Torah. But even this is a debated point among specialists on these texts.

It has been argued that these oracles in Third Isaiah were nurtured among visionaries in Jerusalem in the post-exilic period.[20] Our concern does not extend to identifying specifically the setting of these oracles in post-exilic Judaism. Our desire is to determine how someone like the prophet John would hear these texts. We intend to show that there is strong evidence that as with Zechariah 14, such a text as Isaiah 66 was extremely influential in providing the basis for the eschatological framework out of which John envisioned the nations coming to the new Jerusalem.

Isaiah 66.18-23 is not a coherent body of material. It shifts subjects a number of times and an ordinary reader is not always sure when transitions are taking place or what precipitates them. Given the fact that this text concludes Isaiah, it is more than likely that extensive editing has taken place in this pericope.[21] But if a later Second-Temple reader is looking at these verses in conjunction with the endings of Zechariah and Ezekiel 37-48, the redactional history of the text is a peripheral point of concern. What is significant for our purposes is that this text expands considerably the role of the nations in Isaiah's eschatological description of the end-times over Ezekiel and even Zechariah.[22]

The major point of entrance into the text in Isaiah 66.18 is that Yahweh is coming to gather all nations and tongues.[23] It is announced that they will see the Lord's glory. Presumably this refers to the divine presence radiating in restored Zion (Isa. 4.5; 6.3; 24.23; 40.5; Ezek. 44.4; cf. Ps. 102.15, 16). The nations will be present before the Lord gathered in Jerusalem. How this will occur is the central thrust of the whole pericope.

This unit is part of a wider chapter that celebrates Jerusalem's rebirth (cf. 66.10-24). This is facilitated by Yahweh's prior coming in wrath to purge evildoers (66.15-16).[24] Such a situation parallels generally Ezekiel 37-39 and especially Zechariah 14. In the case of the latter a faithful remnant is preserved as the foundation for Jerusalem's rebirth (14.2a, 6-11) when the Lord defeats his enemies (14.5b, 12-13). But Isaiah 66.19 expands this scenario with considerable attention to the response of the nations to the return of the Lord's glory. First, a sign (1Q Isaᵃ. and LXX 'signs') appears. This sign(s) or signal

---

20   Paul Hanson, *The Dawn of Apocalyptic*, p.393.

21   Typical of this concern for tracing the editing process in the formation of the text is Claus Westermann, *Isaiah 40–66: A Commentary*, OTL (Philadelphia: The Westminster Press, 1969), pp.422–9. Westermann sees the text as a compilation of three separate units (66.17 going with 65.3b-5, 7b; 66.18, 19, 21 go together; 66.20, 22-24). For purposes of our interpretation the important point he makes is to separate verse 20 from 66.18-19, 21.

22   Zechariah has the nations coming up to the holy city once a year at the Feast of Tabernacles (Zech. 14.16-18). Ezekiel does not even allow them on the temple premises (Ezek. 44.9).

23   James M. Scott, 'Paul's *Imago Mundi* and Scripture' in *Evangelium-Schriftauslegung-Kirche* (ed. Jostein Adna, et al.: Göttingen: Vandenhoeck & Ruprecht, 1997), p.370, traces the reference to 'tongues' back to Gen. 10.5, 20, 31 and the Table-of-Nations tradition. Thus it is clearly a reference to all humanity.

24   Roger Aus, 'Paul's Travel Plans to Spain and the "Full Number of the Gentiles" of Roman XI:25', *NovT* 21/1 (1979), p.238, note 24.

has been interpreted in many ways.[25] We will be content to say that it refers
to some announcement or indication that the mission to the nations inviting
them to come to Zion and acknowledge that Yahweh is Sovereign has begun.
The text is somewhat loose grammatically but it is clear that those who are sent
are the survivors ('the saved' LXX) from the theophanic coming of the Lord
in Judgment (Isa. 66.6, 15-16). These would be proselytes emerging from the
assault on Zion by the nations and, as a result of the theophany, changing and
becoming compliant to Yahweh.[26] The listing of the particular nations seems
to be dependent upon Ezekiel 27.10, 12-13 and 38.2-5. In turn, this could be
traced back to the Table-of-Nations tradition incorporating representatives of
the three sons of Noah. It appears here as an indication of the mission's universality.[27] Thus the earlier promises of nations (through their representatives)
coming from the ends of the earth to see the glory of the Lord will be fulfilled (Isa.
40.5; 60.1-3). The hearers in the nations will bring with them an offering. Once
again Isaiah 60.4-10 is clearly echoed. But now the offering will not be of material
gifts or animal sacrifices but of 'your brothers' (66.20), fellow countrypersons
of the citizens of Zion (viz., Diaspora Jews).[28] Thus the circle is complete. All
peoples, Diaspora Jews and Gentiles come to the remnant of Zion to acknowledge Yahweh's sovereignty. From among this circle will even be chosen priests
and Levites (66.21).[29] The nations at last have access to the full faith benefits and
privileges extended from the beginning to the chosen people of God.

This astonishing body of claims is reinforced in the concluding verses of the
book of Isaiah. In Isaiah 65.22 the author, in similar fashion to Zechariah 14.6-8,
refers to a new order to the creation (cf. Isa. 65.17). What remains in unbroken
continuity for perpetuity is not seedtime and harvest (Gen. 8.22) but Yahweh's
people and his name.[30] They are the abiding realities of the new creation. In the
context of the cultic liturgy 'all flesh' will recognize Yahweh's glory.

---

25   Joseph Blenkinsopp, *Isaiah 56–66: A New Translation with Introduction and Commentary*,
AB 19b (New York: Doubleday, 2003), p.314, thinks it evokes earlier texts in Isaiah and speaks of
a signal for the outreach to the Gentile world to begin (cf. Isa. 11.12; 49.22). Begg, 'The peoples
and the Worship of Yahweh', p.52, alludes to Isaiah 19.21 where the pillar at the border of Egypt
functions as Yahweh's commitments to the nations. Westermann, *Isaiah 40–66*, p.425, equivocates.

26   Blenkinsopp, *Isaiah 56–66*, p.314.

27   James M. Scott, 'Paul's *Imago Mundi* and Scripture', p.370.

28   Begg, 'The Peoples and the Worship of Yahweh', p.53, notes that this mission to the
Diaspora is the nations' equivalent to the cereal offering that the Israelites present in a clean vessel
at the house of the Lord (cf. Isa. 66.20). It is interesting to observe the parallel to the ending of
Zechariah in 14.20-21.

29   Whether these include Diaspora Jews or Gentile proselytes is unclear from the text.
Childs, *Isaiah*, p.542, on the basis of Isa. 56.6ff. thinks it is the latter. In any case it represents the
recognition of acceptance of the people of Judah of the implications of the belief in universality of
one God.

30   Begg, 'The Peoples and the Worship of Yahweh', p.54, interprets the 'your descendants' of
Isa. 66.22 as a reference to Israel. R. N. Whybray, *Isaiah 40–66* NCB (Greenwood, South Carolina:
Attic Press, 1975), p.292, says this is the view of the majority of commentators. However, both the
Greek and Hebrew read literally 'your seed'. This clearly echoes the Abrahamic promises and Isa.

The Destiny of the Nations in Later Second-Temple Judaism

The second-century BCE writer Ben Sira, speaking of the prophet Isaiah, reflected:

> By the Spirit of might he saw the last things and comforted those who mourned in Zion. He revealed what was to occur to the end of time and the hidden things before they came to pass (Sirach 48.24-25).[31]

The prophet John, a Christian Jew of the first century of the present era, would be comfortable with this statement about the significance of the prophets. With respect to their reflections about the role of the nations (Gentiles) in key texts in Ezekiel, Isaiah and Zechariah, we have noted that they fall within a complex of thought that emerges in the exilic and early post-exilic prophets. This complex consists of a set of belief structures that would be used by later seers and interpreters, including John, to form their views about the end-times.

Let us summarise the chief features of this complex.

1. The nations assemble against the holy city and the Lord's anointed; the nations are defeated.
2. The Lord brings a new creation with analogues to elements of the first creation.
3. The covenant with the house of David and his servants is renewed in the form of a people-covenant.
4. Jerusalem and its temple are renewed beyond its former glory.
5. The covenant with the nations is renewed. They come to Zion to acknowledge the sovereignty of Yahweh.

Because of his Christian confession John will utilize these features for different purposes. For example, his vision of the new Jerusalem has no specific temple. In John's world there is no need for sacrifices. The temple has now become a Temple-City. It comes from heaven filled with the presence of God and the Lamb. John retains the form of this structure but the content is different because of his theological concerns.[32] Nevertheless, overall, in his vision of the climactic

---

48.19 which involves all peoples. Since this promise concerning the eschatological future follows the incorporation of the nations into the community of Yahweh in 66.19-21 it seems more likely that 'your seed' refers to all people: both Jew and Gentile.

31   This echoes Isa. 42.9. For Ben Sira this not only referred to the return from the exile, but also suggested deep insight into what would take place in the last days. This was a typical assessment of what some within the Judaism of the Second-Temple era thought of the prophets (cf. Dan. 12.4-11; Sirach 3.21-24). Christopher Rowland, *The Open Heaven: A Study of Apocalyptic in Judaism and Early Christianity* (New York: Crossroad, 1982) expanded this as going beyond insight into matters about the end-times. Rowland claimed that the Second-Temple seers reflected about the nature of the universe and other areas of knowledge. Nevertheless, Rowland would not deny that there remained a keen interest in searching for divine insight into the process of the last things in esoteric circles of the Judaism of this era. This remains at the heart of their esoteric exegesis.

32   Celia Deutsch, 'Transformation of Symbols: The New Jerusalem in Rv 21.1–22.5', *ZNW* 48 (1987), p.125. Also, there is no need for the nations to bring ethnic Jews home to Zion from the Diaspora. The church universally is Israel.

events of the end-times, John's account of what emerges stands in remarkable continuity with the prophetic promises.[33] We will chart the details in Revelation shortly with special attention to the conversion of the nations. But before we do this we will note cursorily that this process of exegesis was operative in the Judaism of late Second-Temple period that nourished John.

Psalms of Solomon 17[34]

We believe that Psalms of Solomon 17 is a good example of exegesis of the late Second-Temple era that incorporates key eschatological themes. Our analysis will follow a slightly different order of the themes than those listed above. Psalms of Solomon 17 falls into two major areas. In 17.5-20 the author laments over the terrible situation into which Jerusalem has fallen. Nevertheless, he accepts this as just punishment for their sins. Then in 17.21-46 the author anticipates the return of a Davidite to the throne of Jerusalem. He will purge Jerusalem, vindicating the faithful remnant and exercising strong judgment against the nations. In the course of narrating these expectations, the discourse dovetails with earlier prophetic accounts in the texts we have discussed.

First, the return of a Davidite to the throne is an expression of a central hope of Second-Temple Judaism. The author refers to a son of David ruling 'servant Israel' in 17.21. The latter echoes the Isaianic servant passages and evokes the image of the people-covenant. But the key emphasis is on Psalm 2. The author uses two central metaphors from Psalm 2.9 to describe the action of the (Davidic) king against sinners. He will destroy them with 'an iron rod' and smash them as a potter demolishes a defective pot (Pss. Sol. 17.23-24). Equally striking in 17.32 is a reference to the king as the χριστὸς κυρίου 'anointed of the Lord'. This directly echoes Ps. 2.2.[35] Without question the expectation of the return of a righteous leader to restore the house of David stands at the centre of Psalms of Solomon 17.

Second, as with Isaiah 66.7-8 and Zechariah 13.8-9, 14.2b-3a and 12-15, there will be a purging of Jerusalem to restore the faithful remnant. In Psalms of Solomon 17.22 there is a prayerful entreaty to give the king strength to defeat the unrighteous rulers and to purge Jerusalem from the Gentiles 'who trample her to destruction'.[36] It may be recalled that in Zechariah 14.1-2 Yahweh uses the nations as his agent to purify Jerusalem. This theme of purging Jerusalem is followed in Psalms of Solomon 17.26-28a with the announcement that God will gather a holy people and judge them justly (cf. 17.30b; 35b-36, 40).[37]

---

33   Deutsch, 'Transformation of Symbols', p.126.

34   We discussed the context and importance of this text earlier in Chapter 2.

35   There are other linguistic and thematic echoes to Psalm 2 as well as in Pss. Sol. 17. Janse, 'You are my Son', p.56, draws special attention to 17.29-30.

36   The Greek phraseology is similar to Lk. 21.24 and, more distantly, to Rev. 11.2.

37   The author of Psalms of Solomon was not enthralled by the Jewish leadership in Jerusalem before Pompey took control. He considered it to be corrupt (Pss. Sol. 17.5-10, 20, cf. 2.3). Consequently the leadership in Jerusalem needed to be purged. The Romans may be considered to be a vehicle for this purging.

Third, there is a strong emphasis in this text on the future role of the nations (Gentiles). Despite the fortuitous role the nations played in destroying a corrupt leadership in Jerusalem, the author of the psalm envisions strongly the subjection of the nations to the rule of the Davidic king. Indeed, this seems to be the central point of 17.21-46. Once again Psalm 2 plays a major role. Jerusalem is the place where the Davidic family rules. The Davidic king, as Yahweh's agent (son), is the visible expression of his sovereignty. This sovereignty is operative not only in the city but functions as an inheritance stretching to the ends of the earth (Ps. 2.8; cf. Pss. Sol. 9.1, 17.20). The nations rage (Ps. 2.1-2). But, in the expression of Pompey and his Roman forces, they must be defeated (Ps. 2.9; Pss. Sol. 2.23b-25). God will not let them coalesce with his pure people (Pss. Sol. 2.27-8). They will be under his yoke (Pss. Sol. 17.30). God is vindicated in his condemnation of the nations (Pss. Sol. 8.23).

Yet, finally, despite the obvious emphasis on Yahweh as Judge who subjugates the nations, there is a word of hope for them. As in Isaiah 66.19 where Gentile proselytes are sent to invite the nations to come to Jerusalem in recognition of Yahweh's sovereignty, the Davidic king charges the subdued peoples to come from the ends of the earth to acknowledge his glory (cf. Isa. 55.5). Again, just as Isaiah 66.20 intimates, the nations will gather the Jews from the Diaspora to see what God has done in the restoration of Jerusalem (Pss. Sol. 17.31).[38] Then the Lord will show mercy upon all the nations who come to him in fear (Pss. Sol. 17.34).

Given the historical situation of Pompey's boot held firmly on Jerusalem's neck one can readily understand the neutral feelings of the author of the Psalms of Solomon toward the nations. However, despite this historical reality, the author can still visualize not only Jerusalem, but also the whole world, as Yahweh's inheritance. The door remains open for Gentiles who fear the Lord. There are differences between this eschatology and Revelation. What is striking is the absence of any dramatic theophanic coming of the Lord to change the allegiance of the nations which we see in the later prophets and Revelation. However, this does emerge in several of the apocalyptic writings which we will note briefly.

Late Second-Temple Esoteric Writings

The esoteric writings of the late Second-Temple era are vast. We intend to highlight only several texts that echo the *Völkerwallfahrt* envisioned by the earlier prophets. This pilgrimage of the nations to Jerusalem is reckoned to be one of the key elements of the complex events which would take place in the end times. Thus in Tobit 13.11, in a hymn of praise which echoes Isaiah 60, this belief is spelled out:

> Many nations will come from afar to the name of the Lord God bearing gifts in their hands, gifts for the King of heaven.

---

38   It is significant that the material gifts of Isaiah 60 now become people.

The various strata of traditions that are incorporated into 1 Enoch are rich with accounts about the role of the nations in the last days. Thus, in 1 Enoch 10.21–11.2, as part of the renovation of the creation, it is stated that all nations will learn, bless, and worship the Divine One. As a result 'the storerooms of heaven' will be open to humankind. Picking up from such texts as Isaiah 49.6, and other servant traditions, the Son of Man is described in 1 Enoch 48.4-5 as 'a light to the Gentiles'. On this basis, upon his theophanic appearance all on earth will fall down and worship him (1 En. 57.3).[39] In another strata of 1 Enoch (1 En. 90.30, 37-38), in a strong allegorical passage, the 'wild animals' and 'birds of heaven', euphemisms for the Gentiles, are reconciled to the primordial glory of the original order of the creation.[40] Nickelsburg views this as a contemporizing analogy to Daniel 7 by the author of this text, especially 7.27.[41] Finally, in the Testaments of the Twelve Patriarchs there are several striking references to the *Völkerwallfahrt*. Starting with the paean to the eschatological priest in *Testament of Levi* 18.9, as a result of his priesthood in the new era, we are told that the nations 'will be multiplied in knowledge' throughout the earth. Speaking of the significance of Judah, *Testament of Napthali* 8.3 says that in the last days his descendant (the New David) will rule universally and he will gather the righteous from among the nations. There is even an unconditional promise that the Most High would save Israel and the nations (*Testament of Asher* 7.3).

Of course, intermingled with these accounts of expectations of the conversion of the nations in the last days are statements of judgments against them (4 Ezra 7.36-44). The Book of Jubilees sees no hope for salvation without circumcision (Jub. 15.26-27). As we have stressed throughout, this distinction between the righteous ones and the evil-doers continues a traditional motif and remains a central focus of Second-Temple Jewish exegesis. Our point is more minimal. There is enough evidence to indicate that the effects of texts like Isaiah 60, 66 and Zechariah 14 persisted in the centuries that followed. The idea that the nations would be compelled to honour Yahweh in the last days was irrevocably imbedded in Second-Temple Judaism.

We have given special attention to several key exegetical passages in exilic and post-exilic Judaism on the role of the nations in the end-times. In order to view the complete picture we have had to highlight various related features of the eschatology of that period. At the core of this picture is the conviction that the nations would ultimately abandon their idolatry, and within limits stipulated by Torah, recognize Yahweh, Zion and its leadership, as the basic ground of their ultimate commitments. One may call this action 'conversion'.[42]

---

39   Deutsch, 'Transformation of Symbols', p.121, points out that 1 Enoch is not consistent in its treatment of the nations. Some texts speak about the total destruction of kings and princes at the theophanic appearance of the Son of Man and the new creation.

40   cf. 1 En. 91.14.

41   George W. E. Nickelsburg, *1 Enoch 1: A Commentary on the Book of 1 Enoch Chapters 1–36, 81–108*, Hermeneia Series (Minneapolis: Augsburg Fortress, 2001), p.407.

42   Borgen, 'Polemic in the Book of Revelation', p.209. This is true in the general sense that one abandons a particular faith system to embrace another as ultimate. The Greek ἐπιστρέφειν

We are arguing that the prophet John sees himself in continuity with this body of exegetical tradition; only for him the 'conversion' is to true Israel: those who accept that Jesus is the messiah and who conform their lives with a lifestyle in keeping with that belief. As noted, from time to time, this will entail transformation and re-ordering of some features of this eschatology. Yet the overall body of thought strongly persists and brings into clearer light John's fragmentary references to the conversion of the nations.

Since we have identified the key features of this complex of motifs nourished within Second-Temple eschatology it is now time to discuss how the prophet John connects with and appropriates this tradition. To create the basic picture we will examine the key motifs following the order of the five areas of our basic table (see p.93).

The Defeat of the Nations

Before the nations come into the new Jerusalem and give praise to the Lord they must first suffer defeat. In Revelation this takes place with the parousia of Christ in 19.11-21. Earlier the nations gave allegiance to Babylon (Rome). Terminology drawn from Jeremiah 50.1–51.64 and similar polemics in the prophetic scriptures are used to describe the defeat of Babylon (Rev. 17.1–19.10). The destruction of Babylon is followed by the assault of the nations and their defeat by the Lord's anointed (19.11-21). This is considered to be prefigured in Psalm 2 (cf. Rev. 19.15). As we have noted in Chapter 2, Psalm 2, with its overtones of the nations raging against the Lord and his anointed followed by their ultimate defeat, is a key text contributing to the basic sensibility of the Apocalypse (cf. Rev. 2.26b-27; 11.15, 12.5 as well as 19.15). This theme is echoed strongly in texts that we have noted from the prophets (Isa. 63.1-6; 66.15-16 and Zech. 14.2b-3a; 12.15). No doubt traditions of the holy war against the nations, which are widespread in the Hebrew Scriptures, are also at work in the background.

As we have argued earlier, one should not infer that the defeat of the nations in Revelation 19.11-21 implies that they all perished. For an ordinary reader of the Apocalypse, in its present literary form, Revelation 20.1-15 immediately follows. Here the emphasis is on the reversal of the present situation for both the followers of the Lamb and the nations. On the one hand, the followers of Jesus who persisted faithfully through the recent crisis are vindicated. They reign with Christ in triumph through the millennium (Rev. 20.4-6). On the other hand the nations who currently manifest great power are impotent. They

'to turn around' or 'to change a course of action' is the word most often used by the ancients (Acts 3.19). This position is underscored by A. D. Nock, *Conversion* (London: Oxford University Press, 1963 [paper]), pp.13–14. This understanding of conversion should not be confused with various forms of revivalism operative in the West, especially North America, in the last several centuries.

no longer have the capacity to deceive (20.1-3). They are unable to trouble the saints safely residing in their secure shelter in God's new world (20.7-10). Satan is banished (20.10). Those among the nations, whose names are not found in the book of life, after the resurrection are consigned to the lake of fire (20.11-15). Yet, even after the new creation, as an analogue with the first creation, the nations persist. Only in the new creation they will have a different role.

The New Creation

Within the text of Isaiah the concept of God as Creator and Sovereign of the universe is well known (cf. Isa. 42.5; 45.12, 18). What emerges in Isaiah is not only a concern to uphold God as Creator but to articulate that his ongoing work in history will involve dramatic new actions. Revolving around the restoration of Israel these eschatological events are so significant that the only analogies are with the first creation. This whole idea is encapsulated in the contrast between 'the former things' (Isa. 41.22; 42.9; 43.9, 18; 46.9; 48.3) and 'the new things' (Isa. 42.9; 43.19; 48.6). In addition, the 'new things' will be qualitatively superior to what Yahweh has done before.[43] This anticipation of a marvellous new order is so powerful that it can only be viewed as being embedded in a renovation of the cosmos. This vision bursts forth in Isaiah 65.17-18 and 66.22. In short it will be 'a new heavens and a new earth'. But it is not totally new. As Childs notes, for Isaiah, the new heavens and new earth are always seen in relation to God's faithful people who yearn for a transformed Jerusalem (cf. Isa. 66.19-22; Zech. 14.4-8, 10-12, 16-19).[44]

The prophet John grounds his eschatological vision for the end-times firmly in this context. The defeat of the powers that held the nations under its control is so far reaching that it is reckoned to have cosmological implications. In Revelation 20.11, the banishment of the evil is the prelude to the disappearance of the (old) earth and sky (cf. Rev. 21.1). In Revelation 21.1-2 John sees a new heaven, a new earth, and a new Jerusalem coming down from heaven. This transcendent language evokes the idea of radical renovation of the created order rather than total destruction and re-creation.[45] This can be clearly seen from what follows. There we find the emphasis on a new Jerusalem, the return of Eden, and a pilgrimage of the nations to join the vindicated people of God. All of these themes have earlier precedents in the biblical story.[46] The new creation is a classic case of envisioning a new world order with precedents continuing from

---

43   Paul D. Hanson, *The Dawn of Apocalyptic*, p.156.

44   Brevard S. Childs, *Isaiah*, p.539.

45   See Allan J. McNicol, 'All Things New', pp.45–50, for a fuller explanation of these texts.

46   Roy A. Harrisville, *The Concept of Newness in the New Testament* (Minneapolis: Augsburg, 1960), p.100. In this kind of esoteric literature a return to ideal beginnings (protology) is almost as important as the obvious emphasis on eschatology.

the past. It will not be the same as the past. It will be better. The nations will be a totally different order. They no longer will give their allegiance to a subversive power. Their new allegiance to God and the Lamb will result in wholeness.

The Renewal of the House of David as a People-Covenant

The concept that Yahweh has chosen David and his descendants as his ambassador(s) on earth has deep resonance in scripture. Often this is referred to as 'an everlasting covenant' (2 Sam. 23.5; Ps. 89.3-4, 29-37; 132.11-12).[47] It taps into the potent language of the father-son relationship (2 Sam. 7.14; Ps. 2.7). Yahweh is the father and the king deputises as his representative on earth. Following the custom of the ancient world the son re-presents the full authority of the father. In the New Testament the father-son language (often with Davidic overtones) is picked up. God is Father and Jesus Christ is spoken of as his Son (cf. Matt. 3.17 par.; 11.27, 17.5 par.; Acts 13.33; Rom. 1.3-4; Heb. 1.5; 5.5). The Apocalypse of John also presumes that Jesus stands firmly within the Davidic tradition (Rev. 3.7; 5.5 [Isa. 11.1, 10; Gen. 49.9]; 22.16). There are even echoes of the father-son terminology although it strictly refers to language appropriate to the godhead (Rev. 1.6; 2.18, 27; 3.5, 21).

Our focus here is not so much on Christology; rather, we desire to draw attention to a development emerging out of the servant traditions in Second Isaiah. As Isaiah unfolds in the latter chapters the servant traditions crystallize in the formation of a people-covenant incorporated among the faithful to the Davidic traditions. The eternal covenant with the house of David is now broadened and becomes inclusive of the faithful in Israel. The people of God emerge as both partners and beneficiaries of the eternal covenant. A key text is Isaiah 55.3. The LXX reads, 'I will make with you an διαθήκην αἰώνον "eternal covenant" in keeping with the faithful mercies extended to David.' The addressees are 'the servants of the Lord' (Isa. 54.17).[48] Several verses later (Isa. 55.5) we read these critical words addressed to the covenant people which echo earlier servant passages such as Isaiah 49.6b:

Behold, you shall call nations that you know not and nations that knew you not shall run to you because of the Lord your God, and of the Holy One of Israel, for he has glorified you.

---

47   Brevard S. Childs, *Isaiah*, p.434, notes that the Hebrew bᵉrît 'ôlām 'eternal covenant' occurs in the Pentateuch Exod. 31.16 and Lev. 24.8. Interestingly, it occurs also in Gen. 9.16 in connection with the covenant with Noah. It is also dispersed in some strands of the prophets (Jer. 32.40; 50.5; Ezek. 16.60; 37.20, and Isa. 61.8).

48   Childs, *Isaiah*, pp.430–31, argues convincingly that the 'servants of the Lord' in Isa. 54.17 are the ones addressed in Isa. 55.3. Isa. 54.17 speaks of a 'heritage' for the servants of the Lord. Childs notes that the servant of Isaiah 53 was promised a posterity and fruit for his labour. Building on this promise of a heritage, the author of Isaiah 54 sees the future servants as the continued legacy and extension of the work of the servant of Isaiah 53. Thus it is entirely appropriate to call these 'the people-covenant'.

Second Isaiah is filled with similar motifs. In Third Isaiah this terminology is deepened and fortified with language about the new creation. In Isaiah 61.8, Yahweh promises to enter into an everlasting covenant with the purged people who will inhabit Zion. Zion's fame among the nations is so exalted that the nations not only are drawn to it in awe but they come with righteous lives bringing gifts (Isa. 60.3-6, 21-22; 61.9-11; 66.18-23, cf. Zech. 14.16-19).

For the prophet John, who reads these texts much later, the faithful in the churches constitute the people-covenant. If they conquer, they are the inheritors of the promises in the prophets given to the people of God. All of this comes to a climax in Revelation 21.1–22.5. Upon the coming of the new creation (21.1-2) the promises given to each one of the seven churches of Asia are fulfilled (21.7).[49] Furthermore, in 21.7 the terminology of the LXX for receiving an inheritance, κληρονομεῖν, used to describe the benefits available for the people-covenant, appears (Isa. 54.17; 60.21). Those benefits are spelled out tentatively in Revelation 21.3-7. But if we look further they also involve a comprehensive spectrum of promises articulated in the prophets that now come to fulfilment in the new Jerusalem for both the people of God in covenant and the converted nations (21.9–22.5).

Thus, in Revelation 21.7b we have come full circle. The anticipation of the reception of benefits for the revised house of David is realized for those in the people-covenant. With Psalm 2.7 and 2 Samuel 7.14 echoing in the background, the people of God enjoy full divine unmediated presence analogous to the relationship between father and son.[50] But for the new Jerusalem to be the new Jerusalem the prophets envisioned, the nations, in righteousness, must be there. They are (21.24-26).

Zion and its Temple is Restored

In Jewish eschatology of the Second-Temple era, the theme of the revived Zion and a restored temple is a regular feature (Testament of Dan. 5.12-13; 4 Ezra 7.26; 2 Bar. 32.2-6). Indeed, a revived Zion with its awesome temple is a basic presupposition for the pilgrimage of the nations who come in awe to acknowledge the presence of Yahweh in an exalted setting. To survey these texts comprehensively would be a massive task. Indeed, the literature alone on Revelation is daunting. There is a recent monograph dedicated to the subject placing major emphasis on Jewish texts overlapping the time of the first century.[51] Our

---

49   The phraseology ὁ νικῶν 'the one conquering' in Rev. 2.7, 11, 17, 26; 3.5, 12, 21 returns in 21.7.

50   Grant R. Osborne, *Revelation*, p.740 notes that usually in Revelation the 'father-son' terminology is reserved for God and Jesus (Rev. 1.6; 2.27; 3.5, 21; 14.1). Thus the subtle change from father to God in Rev. 21.7. This change is similar to Ps. 2.7 but not 2 Sam. 7.14.

51   Pilchan Lee, *The New Jerusalem in the Book of Revelation: A Study of Revelation 21-22 in Light of its Background in Jewish Tradition*, WUNT 129 (Tübingen: Mohr Siebeck, 2001). Somewhat more dated but still valuable is R. J. McKelvey, *The New Temple*, pp.9–41.

concern is not to feature these temple traditions (important as they may be) but to focus upon the conversion of the nations. We will simply trace the broad contours of the theme of the new Jerusalem/Temple so that we will have a better perspective of how it fits into John's landscape vis-à-vis the place of the nations.

After the devastation of Jerusalem and the temple in 588–587 BCE there emerges in the prophets a fervid anticipation of its restoration as the *sine qua non* of God's presence with his people. Among the hierocratic leaders, Ezekiel's architectural plan (Ezekiel 40-48) was highly prized. It did feature some restrictions on the place of the Gentiles (cf. Ezek. 44.9) even though other parts of the plan speak of the return of paradise (Ezek. 47.1-12). Haggai narrates the restored temple's glory as greater than the one before (Haggai 1.15b–2.9). The early chapters of Zechariah visualize a restored city and temple which by its sheer grandeur will attract the nations (Zech. 1.16; 2.11-12; 4.6-10; 6.12-13; 8.21-23). Especially poignant is Zechariah 2.11-12 MT:

> And many nations shall join themselves to the Lord in that day and I will dwell in the midst of you…and the Lord will inherit Judah as his portion in the holy land and will again choose Jerusalem.

On the other hand the more visionary and esoteric writers of Isaiah 40–66 and Zechariah 9–14 also maintain the hope for a restored Jerusalem and temple. In Isaiah 54 the Jerusalem of the exilic period is described as a barren woman; but in its restored splendour it will be bedecked with precious stones and jewels (Isa. 54.11-12; cf. Rev. 21.11, 18-21). And in a well-travelled text (Isa. 60) foreigners accompanied by their kings will bring their wealth to Zion as gifts as his glory will be seen upon it (Isa. 60.2; cf. Zech. 14.9, 16-19). Speaking of chapter 60, Childs notes that Isaiah's vision of the new Jerusalem 'is not a rebuilt earthly city, but the entrance of the divine kingdom of God'.[52] This same theme, so dominant in exilic and early post-exilic Judaism, continues to dominate throughout Second-Temple exegesis.[53] Without question a restored temple and city is the essential presupposition in Jewish exegesis for the conversion of the nations. It is difficult to visualize one without the other.

As the full counterpoint to Babylon, the new Jerusalem plays a significant role in the closing chapters of Revelation (Rev. 21.1–22.5). Since its origin is in heaven it is a vital part of the new creation (21.1-5). John draws upon a wealth of images, both in scripture and the esoteric Jewish literature of the era, for his descriptions of its architecture, materials (built from paradise), structure, and function (21.9–22.5).[54] Its most notable feature is that it has no temple separate from the city (21.22). A temple in which a god dwelt was an essential precondition for any ancient city. It constituted the city as holy.[55] However, as John explains, unlike

52   Brevard S. Childs, *Isaiah*, p.500.

53   Celia Deutsch, 'Transformation of Symbols', pp.111–15.

54   Peter Hirschberg, *Das Eschatologische Israel*, pp.244–90 has an exhaustive analysis of these details.

55   Celia Deutsch, 'Transformation of Symbols', p.125.

when Ezekiel watched the divine glory leave the first temple (Ezek. 10.1-22; 11.22-25), God and the Lamb have returned and are present (21.22). In fact, the new Jerusalem is a Temple-City having the geometric dimensions of the holy of holies (Rev. 21.15-18).

If one works within the boundaries of Jewish exegesis of the Second-Temple period, one must reckon that a city coming down (i.e. to the renewed earth) from heaven must be an actual entity. Gundry strongly draws attention to the exaggerated mythical features and dimensions of the new Jerusalem in Revelation. He concludes that it is all a symbol for the reality of the people of God living in his unmediated presence.[56] It is true that John is stretching language to an extremity in his description of the glory of the full emergence of the kingdom of God. But, in the end, it finally comes down to making a determination about how close John stays within the parameters of his exegesis of the scriptures. In Jewish exegesis, even Qumran, when God's new world fully comes there is always the restored Jerusalem as a place. It is hard for us to see the city as not being a place. We consider that John's language is multivalent. The new Jerusalem is both people and place.

Why then does the new Jerusalem play such a prominent role in the closing chapters of Revelation? First, and foremost, it is the counterpoint woman-city to Babylon. As Babylon seduced the nations, so the new Jerusalem will be their fount of holiness. The old Jerusalem of history is the place where their Lord was crucified. The new city will be filled with the divine presence. But, in addition, the new Jerusalem is more than metaphor. For an exegete who viewed himself as describing the consummation of Israel in the new creation, the new Jerusalem opening its gates to the nations was the appropriate image, *par excellence*, for elaborating that God's purposes had come to completion.

The Nations Come to Zion

Our overall mode of operation in this chapter was to place ourselves sensitively within the exegetical framework utilized by John as he constructed his visionary picture of the end-times. We have noted that in Revelation 21.3-7 John has given special attention to the restoration of the people-covenant in the new creation. Emerging in the exile and the post-exilic prophets the people-covenant was considered a product of the legacy of the servant of Isaiah 53 (Isa. 53.10; cf. 54.17). For John, this heritage is claimed by Jesus and his followers. In their faith com-

---

56   Gundry, 'The New Jerusalem', pp.254–64. He responds plausibly to several of the arguments of E. S. Fiorenza, *Priester für Gott*, who takes the position that the new Jerusalem is an actual place in which the direct presence of God rests. But in the end his argument is strained. In order to account for the kings of the earth entering through the gates into the city (Rev. 21.24-26), Gundry has the nations become Christian converts. If so, what is the difference between these and the residents of the city? This seems to be a distinction without a difference.

munities they now claim to be Israel (2.9; 3.9; 7.4-8; 14.1-5). Unlike traditional definitions of Israel they are not constituted by ethnic identity since membership in the people-covenant is drawn from every tribe and nation (7.9-17).

Being a careful reader of the prophets, however, John drew an additional conclusion from these texts. He inferred from texts such as Isaiah 56.1-8; 60.1-22; 66.18-23 and Zechariah 14.1-21 that there were prophecies about the conversion of the nations that were yet to be fulfilled in the last days. They could only be fulfilled when the nations were released from the sway of Babylon (Rome) and came to a full appreciation of the glory of God's presence in the new Jerusalem. For if Yahweh is One there could be no other ultimate outcome than the entire created order coming to a recognition of his universal sovereignty.

This is what stands behind John's decision to include the nations in his description of the new Jerusalem. This claim can be substantiated by an observation about the text. In Revelation 21.27, immediately following the major reference to the nations entering the new Jerusalem in Revelation 21.24-26, are these words:

> But under no circumstances anything common shall enter it (the new Jerusalem); for example, one doing abominable things and practising falsehood. Only those written in the Lamb's book of life ([will enter] cf. Rev. 21.8).

Presuming the existence of Jerusalem as a 'temple-city', nothing ritually or morally impure is allowable within its gates.[57] Although, usually for John the terminology of 'names written in the book of life' refers to the faithful who endure the coming time of crisis (3.5; 13.8), here it probably stands as a counterpoint to Revelation 20.12. Coming directly after Revelation 21.24-26 the context suggests strongly that the reference in 21.27 is to the kinds of practices among the nations that were considered by the Jews as morally abominable. The point is rhetorical. In the new creation these things are not allowable. To enter the new Jerusalem and participate in its benefits those within the nations must have a lifestyle in conformity with the values of the city. John invokes imagery of the restoration of the people-covenant in Revelation 21.7. This is immediately followed by a word of warning in 21.8. In 21.24-27 the focus shifts to the restoration of the covenant with the nations.[58]

---

57   Celia Deutsch, 'Transformation of Symbols', p.122.

58   Alan F. Segal, *Paul the Convert: The Apostolate and Apostasy of Saul the Pharisee* (New Haven: Yale University Press, 1990), pp.194–201, calls this 'a covenant with all humanity'. Traced back to the Noahide covenant in Gen. 9.8-17 God promises never again to destroy the world by water. He seals the promise by hanging up his war bow (i.e. an aetiology for the rainbow). In rabbinic exegesis the presumed stipulations of the 'Noahide commandments' (echoing the rules for accepting strangers in Lev. 17–18) are formulated and expanded. They eventually function as a set of norms for behaviour acceptable within a just human community. Segal notes that although this is primarily a rabbinic discussion, evidence for the existence of the 'Noahide commandments' can be found as early as Jub. 7.20-21. This along with something similar in the echoing of Lev. 17–18 in the issue of accepting Gentiles in Acts 15.19-21, 28-29, is sufficient evidence to indicate that a similiar tradition is operative in Rev. 21.27 and especially 21.8.

Thus, John allows for the participation of the nations in the kingdom of God. Anything less would mean that the prophets would not be fulfilled. But, entrance to the new Jerusalem is not unconditional. The covenant with the nations is now firmly in place. It presumes that all who pass through the gates of the new Jerusalem have sublimated themselves to the ways of the Lord and live a life worthy to take their place in the holy city.

Summary

Our study in this chapter has found substantial evidence that John finds embedded in the prophets, a model for the end-times analogous to what we find in Revelation 21.1–22.9. For God to be all in all entails the full realization of the people-covenant and the covenant with the nations.

What directly precipitated the change in the allegiance of the nations? When one reads the Old Testament texts the evidence is almost as fragmentary and unclear as is Revelation. There are elements in Isaiah 60 that would indicate to the reader that the nations will be compelled to come to Zion (Isa. 60.10-22). On the other hand, in Zechariah 14.16, 20-21 they come once a year at the Feast of Tabernacles to participate fully in the cultic activities freely acknowledging the kingship of Yahweh. Most texts indicate that the change is instituted after the Lord comes in theophanic power to destroy his enemies (Isa. 65.15-16; Zech. 14.5b, 9). The prophet John repeats this pattern (cf. Rev. 19.11-21; 1.7). John is content to structure his narrative as a fulfilment of the prophets.

But what is provoking this concern for the destiny of the nations? As we have noted, this, in itself, could hardly be a matter of intense interest to the average person in a Christian assembly in first-century Asia. Given the sectarian ethos of the day most would probably harbour little sympathy for the eternal destiny of many of their neighbours. The prophet John writes out of a deep pastoral interest for these churches. The theme of the conversion of the nations, important as it is, to express the full sovereignty of Yahweh, is only a small part of a wider portrait which he is in the process of producing. His overall portrait is a comprehensive vision of the Day of the Lord. This eschatological vision (as perceived by the prophet) is designed to preserve the integrity of the churches through remaining faithful to the moral vision of the Christian story. It is to this wider vision that we now give attention in the next chapter.

CHAPTER 5

THE CONVERSION OF THE NATIONS AND THE CENTRAL MESSAGE OF THE APOCALYPSE

The Setting

Albert Schweitzer is famous for his comment relegating justification by faith to a subsidiary role in Paul's theology. He referred to it as a small crater within a larger one. We would make a similar point with reference to our topic. As important as the conversion of the nations is in Revelation it does not constitute the central concern of the book. The larger crater is John's Christian-Jewish appeal in the form of a visionary account; he exhorts the people in the churches of Asia not to accommodate to the civic and cultural life of the Empire. In his view, to do so will eventuate in the same outcome that awaits the wider pagan society because of its idolatrous practices.

Thus the crucial concern for John was to maintain the integrity of what he perceives to be the true Israel. Based on the events involving the death and exaltation of Jesus of Nazareth, Israel has become reconstituted. It now consists of people of every nation brought into a people-covenant. Members of the people-covenant can be found in small assemblies, mainly in the east but scattered across the empire. Maintaining the integrity of Israel was an old story among the people of God. The stories about Balaam and Jezebel came easily to mind. John envisioned that the congregations in Asia were about to encounter a major crisis. They would be called to accommodate with ever more stringent imperial policies set in place by the authorities. This propels the central thrust of John's message. Churches must maintain their foundational faith in order to claim their inheritance. It would not be easy.

As a word of encouragement he reminds them that as participants in the people-covenant they are already able to view themselves (*proleptically*) as priests and members of the kingdom of God (1.6; 5.9-10). But they are not immune from testing and persecution. In fact they are subject to being seduced into other allegiances that are doomed to fail. These allegiances will lead to a dead end. In John's world those who pursue this course will have a surprise at the Last Judgment. They will not be found in the book of life and will not reign with Jesus Christ in the new creation. Therefore they should mark the forces opposed to the Lamb. They should not enter into any allegiance with them.

A characteristic of an interesting narrative is conflict. The counterpoint to the faithfulness of the people of God (restored Israel) in the Apocalypse is Rome and her allies. Throughout the Apocalypse the prophet John gives a very negative assessment of Rome and its vaunted power. In many ways it is the exact opposite of its glorification in Virgil's great poem the *Aeneid*. Instead of *Pax Romana*, the Empire produces chaos. This is generally reckoned to be the point of the vision of the Four Horsemen (Rev. 6.1-8); the conquest of Rome produces chaos rather than order. Throughout the Apocalypse, Rome and her allies resist a call to repent (9.20-21; 16.9, 11, 21). She shamelessly persecutes the people of God (11.3-14). Ultimately Rome will suffer destruction led by nations from the East (17.12-18). In turn, through a theophany with the Divine Warrior (Christ) coming in a final climactic battle, all the rebellious nations will be defeated (19.11-21). Corresponding to the visions of the biblical prophets the nations subjugated to the Risen Lord in the new creation will become proselytes to the way of Yahweh. The ultimate pastoral point is very clear. It would be unbelievably foolish for those who are part of the people of God to surrender their legacy in favour of entering allegiances, real or virtual, with Rome. The churches are heirs to a mighty inheritance which will culminate in receiving the benefits of the new Jerusalem. The subjugated nations through the renewal of God's ancient covenant with them will eventually be brought to this recognition. But only after they pass through the crucible of judgment.

In this chapter I will attempt to make the case that the conversion of the nations is a subsidiary part of a wider argument that the churches of Asia must remain faithful to their covenant commitments or suffer the danger of losing their salvation. It is necessary to put into proper perspective the function of the conversion of nations passages in relation to the larger theological artifact that the author of the Apocalypse is creating. Only then will we be able to determine the appropriate parameters and implications concerning what he is saying about the nations. This is what I mean by my use of the metaphor of a smaller crater within a larger one.

I will adopt the following procedures in this chapter: first, I will assess in some detail what it is that makes John uncomfortable with the way the churches of Asia are interacting with the wider culture that they regularly encounter. Second, through an analysis of relevant features of the structure of the Apocalypse, I will show how this concern shapes repeatedly the development of the narrative. Finally, I will briefly state my conclusion on how the passages on the sublimation of the nations fit into this pastoral goal of encouraging the churches to unfeigned faithfulness.

The Crisis Facing the Churches

Throughout his literary work John strategically placed seven macarisms (1.3; 14.15; 16.15; 19.9; 20.6; 22.7, 14). They enjoin readers in the churches to adhere to the message of the book and continue to maintain the faith. If one wishes to determine the point of this book one would not go far wrong by distilling the essence of the seven macarisms. Any true assessment of the Apocalypse should start with this foundation. The fact that they are primarily pastoral exhortations should always be remembered.

What did John consider as troublesome in the churches of Asia? In reading the text it seems that lurking under the overlay of a growing sense of complacency and accommodation to the dominant culture that he saw as becoming rampant in the Christian assemblies (2.4, 14-15, 20; 3.1-2, 16) two deep concerns were emerging.[1] First, there were tensions between John and other leaders and factions in the assemblies. To put it mildly, they did not endorse his views. John labels them with three names that function as pseudonyms: (1) Jezebel (2.20); (2) 'Those who hold the teaching of Balaam' (2.14); (3) the Nicolaitans (2.6, 15). Second, he mentions two congregations facing severe hostility from the synagogue (2.9; 3.9). Although there are diverse factors behind these problems I contend that they spring from a common seedbed: a growing sense of unhappiness with existing as marginalized communities. It is not difficult to see that many in the churches were seeking to accommodate to some sort of common alliance with the wider culture, whatever that may be.

The Prophetess Jezebel
Perhaps we can view this problem in its purest form by looking at Revelation 2.20. There John issues a strong warning against the church at Thyatira for accepting the teaching of a prophetess. Crucially, the woman is branded with the inflammatory name of Jezebel, one of the most notorious syncretists in the history of Israel. Her mixing of multiple religions and cults is referred to as πορνεῖαι 'flagrant acts of prostitution' and φάρμακα 'multiple sorceries' in the LXX (4 Kgs. 9.22 [MT 2 Kings]; cf. Nahum 3.4).[2] Translated in the world of the prophet John similar terminology πορνεῦσαι καὶ φαγεῖν εἰδωλόθυτα 'to commit fornication, that is to say eating meat dedicated to gods represented by idols' is used (2.20).[3] It is claimed that this is the teaching that deceives God's

---

1　Ian Boxall, *The Revelation of Saint John*, BNTC (London & New York: Continuum/ Hendrickson, 2006), p.12.

2　Similar terminology is used to describe Babylon (Rome) and those in league with her in Revelation (9.21; 17.1-6; 18.23; 21.8; 22.13). With Jezebel's delving into the deep things of Satan (2.24), perhaps even seeking accommodation with the emperor cult, she is answerable to the same powers as the earth beast (13.11-18). The latter is usually thought to represent well connected civic authorities who actively facilitated emperor worship.

3　Whether John is referring to meat sacrificed under pagan auspices and purchased in the meat markets or participation in events in temple facilities under pagan auspices is unclear. More than likely it involves all of the above. Boxall, '"For Paul" or "For Cephas"', pp.213–15, raises the intriguing point that the prophetess may well have been a Gentile who was informed by a version of Pauline openness to the wider provincial life of the empire. Coming from this background she may not have appreciated what a Christian-Jewish believer would see as its inherent dangers. Ironically, her conflict with some in the church appears to be an anticipation of the later battle between the rider on the White Horse and the nations (Rev. 19.11-18). The gruesome fate of Jezebel parallels in intensity the account of the fate of the nations (2 Kgs. 9.33-35; Rev. 19.17-18).

servants in the churches (2.20).[4] Instead of resisting the incipient syncretism emerging in the church at Thyatira, in John's view, a prominent prophetess is encouraging it. This represents a grave danger. A concern to resist it surfaces throughout the entire Apocalypse.

The Teaching of Balaam and the Nicolaitans

This incipient syncretism was not only a local phenomenon in Thyatira. In the letter to the church at Pergamum a similar issue arises (2.12-17).[5] Here the deviant teaching is attributed to Balaam. This is especially significant because it draws upon a long Jewish exegetical tradition based in scripture that has its own definite shape and concerns. By observing closely John's decision to use these traditions, and the way he shapes them, one is able to determine with some precision where his allegiances rest.

In Numbers 25.1-3 an incident is related where the Israelite women committed fornication with the Moabite men and participated in sacrifices to pagan gods. This text follows a lengthy account where Balak seeks to persuade Balaam (an Israelite discerner) to place a curse upon Israel (Num. 22.1-24.25). Later in the book (Num. 31.16) the account draws an inference that Balaam provoked the incident of the fornication with the Moabites in Numbers 25.1-3. Thus, it begins to develop in later exegetical tradition that Balaam is associated with occasions when it is considered by Hebrew prophets that the Israelite people are seduced into immorality and idolatry. Later this is especially true in Hellenistic Jewish circles where the Jews understandably confront directly the problems of accommodation with other cultures.[6] John would surely be aware of these traditions. He perceives that there is a grave danger of undue collaboration between the people of God and those engaged in idolatrous practices in such a place as Pergamum. It is also easy to see a close connection was made between this traditional exegesis and the similar social situation involving the activities of the prophetess Jezebel at Thyatira.

Besides these conflicts John also opposes a mysterious group called the Nicolaitans.[7] Various theories have been set forth about the name.[8] Most likely it represents some form of a linguistic play on the founder or the local leader of the group who had the Greek name 'Nicolaus'? The word νικᾶν 'to conquer' has

---

4   The use of πλανᾶν (eight times) is a literary characteristic of John in Revelation. It usually refers to the deceit of Satan or Babylon (18.23).

5   The same terminology that is used in 2.20 to describe the deception of Jezebel (in reverse order in the Greek text) appears in 2.14.

6   Peder Borgen, 'Polemic in the Book of Revelation', pp.202-205, has a lengthy list of references and secondary materials surveying this tradition. Especially noteworthy is Philo, Spec. Leg. 1.54-57; Vit. Mos. 1.53-55; Also Josephus, Ant. 4.126-30.

7   They clearly have a foothold in the church at Pergamum (Rev. 2.14) and, at least, have a core of supporters at Ephesus (Rev. 2.6).

8   Paul Trebilco, *The Early Christians in Ephesus*, p.318, gives a convenient summary of the main ones.

a close euphonic ring and is on John's mind since it serves as part of the promissory exhortation at the end of each of the messages to the seven churches. As a linguistic play it may well suggest that while the Nicolaitans seek to overcome through accommodation with the current cultural regime John is advocating a much different way to finish the course.

As far as I can see John does not make a clear distinction between the teaching of Balaam (2.14) and what is advocated by the Nicolaitans (2.15).[9] No doubt there were some differences. But, apparently, unlike John they were not opposed to believers participating in civic activities. Thus, overall, this seems to be the point of convergence of the entire body of teaching that John finds incompatible with what he claims to be the faith of the people of God. As the Apocalypse unfolds John equates the impact and influence of imperial culture with the work of Satan. He urges that there be a clear distinction between the people of God and the civic society of his time.

The Struggle with the Synagogue

For different reasons, John also advocates that a different stance be directed toward the synagogue. For John the issue is: where are the true Jews – in the synagogue or the ecclesia?[10] His answer is obvious. Since John is opposed to an accommodation with the civic society of his day the same thing applies with respect to relations with the synagogue. It is not a stretch to say that this sectarian position lies at the root of John's problem with some of the other churches. Several of these churches are either not manifesting their earlier enthusiasm to do good works or are plagued with those who wish to pursue wealth (Rev. 2.4; 3.2, 15-16). For John this has the sound of accommodation with the wider civic culture. Thus on all fronts the series of indictments against the churches (as well as the words of encouragement) cluster around a common theme: do not capitulate to the mainstream culture of the time.

Warning the Accommodationists

Paul Trebilco has made the claim that while John addresses other matters besides the dissident teachings in Revelation 2-3, 'the whole of Revelation' represents his response to the accommodationists.[11] If we interpret this as a way of saying that John wrote out of deep concern that the marginalized churches of Asia were listening increasingly to teachers who advocated accommodation with the civic culture I am inclined to agree. Most of the heavenly vision of Revelation 4.1–22.9 circles around this issue. We will confront these matters from

---

9   Leonard L. Thompson, *The Book of Revelation: An Apocalypse and Empire*, p.122.

10   Peder Borgen, 'Polemic in the Book of Revelation', p.204.

11   Paul Trebilco, *The Early Christians in Ephesus*, p.325.

a structural perspective in the next section. At this point I will draw attention to two places in the Apocalypse where John alludes to the influence of the dissident teachers.

First, I believe a defensible reading of Revelation 11.1-14 can interpret this text as having undercurrents of a polemic against John's opponents in the Asian churches. In my analysis in Chapter 2 I attempted to make the case that in 11.1-2 a clear demarcation is made within the people of God (v. 2, the holy city). I argued that the passage echoes directly Ezekiel 8.1–9.11 where the prophet encounters idolatrous worshippers in the temple courtyard. With their backs to the sanctuary housing the glory of God they face the east worship- ping the sun (Ezek. 8.16). Stunned with the idolatry the prophet then witnesses the appearance of a man clothed in linen along with six executioners (Ezek. 9.1-2). The man in linen puts a mark on the foreheads of the faithful (Ezek. 9.4). The executioners summarily destroy the apostates in the city (Ezek. 9.5-8). This reading identifies 'the measured ones' in the holy place as those who do not accommodate with the idolatrous culture (Rev. 11.1a). In the impending judging actions of God they will survive because they have the divine seal on their foreheads (7.3; 9.4; 14.1; 22.4).[12] On the other hand, those in the outer court will suffer judgment by being overrun by the nations with whom they sought to accommodate (11.1b-2). Since all of this involves people in God's temple in the holy city (the church) this would appear to refer to matters within the people of God. We believe the most obvious analogue to Ezekiel's vision of the false worshippers would be that, with respect to those in the outer court, John is addressing the destiny of the accommodationists. These Christian ac- commodationists to the civic culture of Rome are the central focus of John's polemic in Revelation 2–3 against what he perceives to be several apostate churches. In John's universe there would be those who follow the teaching of Jezebel and Balaam (2.14, 20-23) and the Nicolaitans (2.6, 15). As Jerusalem the holy city was overrun, both centuries earlier and recently by the new Babylon, John is suggesting that the time is near when the executioners will come among the accommodationists in the church: the new holy city will be trampled in judgment. God's seal of protection from judgment rests upon those who live in the wake of Moses and Elijah (11.3-13). But for those who go the way of the ac- commodationists (Jezebel and Balaam) there is no promise of protection from judgment or vindication in the resurrection.[13]

A second complex of echoes indicating that John remains concerned about the influence of the dissident prophets can be found in Revelation 21.8, 27.

12   Of course the earth beast (the supporters of imperial culture) and the prostitute (Rome) have similar marks among their followers (13.16-17; 14.9, 11; 16.2; 17.5; 19.20; cf 20.4). For some reason in popular interpretation it is the latter who have caught the imagination of the public with wild speculations about 'the mark of the beast' rather than the former.

13   Stephen Pattemore, *The People of God*, p.163. Pattemore argues strongly that the shaping of Revelation 11.3-13 represents a strong polemic against the positions advocated by what he calls the 'heresiarchs'.

Both of these texts constitute primarily a listing of a table-of-vices.[14] Those who pursue these vices are to have no part in the new Jerusalem. The point of placement of these texts within the narrative is important. Revelation 21.8 follows the beautiful description in 21.5-7 of promises of the wiping away of all tears and drinking at the fountain of life. The stunning announcement is made that death will be no more. The beneficiaries of these promises are members of the people-covenant. Similarly, Revelation 21.27 is immediately preceded by the description of the nations bringing glory and honour into the new Jerusalem through the gates that never close. Here it is the covenant with the nations that is renewed. The point is clear. In both situations, those who are guilty of these vices ought not to count on receiving the benefits of the restoration of covenant.

The key text that allows us to connect these polemics directly with the dissident prophets is Revelation 21.27a. It is widely recognized that the wording of this text echoes Isaiah 35.8 (MT) and 52.1 (MT). A conflation of these two texts leads to a simple conclusion that the text is saying that nothing unclean will be allowed to enter the new Jerusalem.[15] A key question is what is the force of πᾶν κοινόν 'anything unclean'? The κοινός word form carries considerable freight in Hellenistic Judaism. It functions as a general description for ritual impurity under Jewish law.[16] Here it is appropriate to use this word with reference to the kind of people not allowed into the new Jerusalem because, even though it has no temple, it has the functional form of the holy of holies. John's preference for the word for 'unclean' or 'common' and his omission of 'uncircumcised' from Isaiah 52.1 is telling. As with the Christian-Jew Matthew, the people of God are still Israel. Of the commands of Jesus (Matt. 28.20) circumcision is not among them. Israel is reconstituted out of Jews and Gentiles who accept Jesus as messiah. As with practically the whole of the early Christian movement, Gentiles were welcomed into this community without having to undergo the rite of circumcision. But this does not mean that John has abandoned major reservations about generic Gentile culture. Thus, in the closing chapters of the Apocalypse three times he launches a polemical tirade against their characteristic vices which he links with contemporary civic culture (21.8, 27; 22.15). These are but thinly veiled allusions to what he perceives that the dissident prophets are countenancing in the church.

The considerable linguistic overlap between the vice lists and the description of the teaching of the dissidents is evidence in favour of the conclusion that John is incorporating them to make sure that his readers know who are banned from the new Jerusalem. Thus, for example, in Revelation 2.14, 20 the dissidents are charged with πορνεῦσαι 'practising immorality'. While, on the other hand, the πόρνοι (21.8; 22.15) are featured in the vice list. Likewise, Rev-

---

14 A supplementary list occurs in the epilogue in 22.15.

15 Fekkes, Isaiah and the Prophet's Traditions, pp.273–4; Beale, Revelation, p.1102.

16 Deutsch, 'Transformation of Symbols', p.121. She refers to a number of key texts including 1 Macc. 1.47, 62; 4 Macc. 7.6; Matt. 15.11, 18, 20; Acts 10.15; 11.9.

elation 2.2 brands some calling themselves apostles as ψεῦδεις 'liars'. The same terminology is found in the vice list in 21.8 while the ὁ ποιῶν ψεῦδος 'the doer of falsehood' appears in 21.27 and 22.15. Especially striking is another parallel. In Revelation 2.14, 20 John accuses the prophets of accommodating to the civic culture in the 'eating of foods dedicated to idols'. It is notable that John strongly condemns εἰδωλολάτραι 'the worship of idols' in 21.8; 22.15. It is hard to see anything here less than a strong reservation on John's part for the kind of activities endorsed by the dissidents in Revelation 2. This is the central concern around which the whole of the visionary structure of Revelation is designed to address.

Of course the overlap in terminology between the descriptions of Babylon and these three vice lists is even more striking.[17] But this is precisely the point. In John's view the same satanic spirit animating the dissident teachers was also behind Babylon.[18]

Thus the vice lists not only function as a stark counterpoint to Babylon and her allies. They constitute a clear rhetorical warning to the church not to be involved in the process of assimilation with the civic culture they encounter day by day. If they do there will be consequences. Such a reading does not take us far from the big crater of the central message of Revelation.

To Express the Message: The Structure of John's Enabling Story

In the process of developing his pastoral argument that the churches of Asia constitute an alternative community to the civic and cultural life of Rome John forcefully makes the case that the church as God's covenantal community of the last days has an assured future. This is in keeping with a widespread perspective of early Christianity that the church is the community of the end-times which began with the exaltation of Jesus. With respect to the future itself, as I have argued, John shapes his understanding on these matters within the broader context of his reading of the great Hebrew prophets. As with many others of the time his essential presupposition is that embedded in the accounts in scripture are, as yet, unfulfilled events of the end-days. Especially noteworthy is the coming of a major final crisis for the people of God, a new Jerusalem to replace devastated Zion, the fulfilment of his covenant with his people, and a renewal of God's covenant with the nations. In the context of a struggle to preserve the

---

17   Roland M. Royalty, *The Streets of Heaven*, pp.223–4, gives the details.

18   Ian Boxall, 'The Many Faces of Babylon the Great: *Wirkungsgeschichte* and the Interpre-tation of Revelation 17' in *Studies in the Book of Revelation*, ed. Steve Moyise (Edinburgh/New York: T&T Clark, 2001), pp.66–7, assesses the connections between Jezebel and the Great Harlot in Revelation 17. He traces 'an interesting "triangle" within the text, linking Thyatira's "Jezebel", the Jezebel of the Old Testament, and the figure of the Great Harlot'. It has the net effect of placing some members of the churches in Asia in the same camp as the aggressive regime as Revelation 17. We believe that this is compatible with the *Tendenz* in Revelation.

integrity of his covenantal faith community in the interest of a pastoral appeal, John fashions his visions of the last times based on these scriptural motifs.

How this plays itself out structurally may be observed by studying the display which gives a concise précis of what John is attempting to accomplish in his literary work.

A Display of the Structure of Revelation

Prologue 1.1-3

A. Vision on Earth: Mission to the Seven Churches 1.4–3.22
Opening Salutations; Eulogy; Vision of the Son of Man and Message to the Seven Churches 1.4–3.22

B. Vision in Heaven: The Crisis with Idolatry and Vindication of the People of God
I Vision of God and the Lamb of Heaven 4.1–5.14
II Seven Seals: Preview of the Crisis 6.1–8.1

III The Seven Trumpets The Crisis Deepens 8.2–11.18	IV The Seven Bowls of Wrath Climax and Resolution of the Crisis 11.19–16.21

V The Fate of the Apostate Woman City An Appendix 17.1–19.10

VI The Vindication of the Righteous Covenant Community 19.11–21.8

VII The Appearance of the Pure Woman City An Appendix 21.9–22.9

Epilogue 22.10-21

Explanation of the display
As we can see from the display the Apocalypse consists of two major divisions: a vision on earth directing Christ's message to the seven churches and a vision

where the seer is taken into the heavenly places to perceive the critical features of the last days. The outcome highlighted by the vindication of the church and the restoration of the covenant with the nations underscores the perceived need for the followers of the Lamb not to compromise their commitments. Our focus in this overview is on how the structure facilitates the overall argument of the book. I intend to show the structural features of the second major vision are placed in the service of these pastoral concerns.

Discussion about the formulation of the structural outline of the Apocalypse has become an industry in itself.[19] Broadly speaking, my position parallels the major elements of Lambrecht's 'principle of encompassing'.[20] In making my case I intend to develop the positions set forth in the display.

I would ask the reader to visualize a set of Russian dolls of the same kind. But instead of following the ordinary process of unpacking the next one placed inside another in decreasing size each successive doll gives increasing and additional detail about the original model. With reference to the structure of Revelation the analogy is applicable to the key elements of the three central units of the seven seals, trumpets and bowls of wrath (6.1–16.21). The basic story that John wishes to narrate is encompassed in the vision of the seven seals. The seven trumpets and seven bowls of wrath simply increase details of the story. These visions advance both the linear progression and give additional details encompassed in the vision of the seven seals. As with any challenging artistic arrangement the visions do not follow a precise chronological order or geometric pattern. Yet the basic model remains true. Revelation 6.1–8.1 is a comprehensive overview of what John envisions will take place in the last days prior to a culminating appearance of the Divine Warrior (Christ). The successive visions deepen and bring to fulfilment in greater detail what is outlined in the opening sequence.

Revelation 4–5 sets up the opening sequence of action passages in 6.1–8.1. There is some internal evidence in the text indicating literary connections between chapters 4–5 and 6.1–8.1, but it is sufficiently distinct in form and content from the vision of the seven seals to be separated from it. Echoing strongly major theophanic passages in scripture such as Isaiah 6.1-4 and Ezekiel 1.4-28 John is ushered into the heavenly sanctuary to witness the majesty of the Divine Throne (4.1-11). In God's right hand (a necessary anthropomorphism) is a scroll reminiscent of the *libellus* used by the Roman emperor (5.1). Sealed

19   U. Vanni, *La struttura letteraria dell' Apocalisse* (2nd ed.; Brescia: Morcelliana, 1980) is the fount of recent discussion on the structure of the Apocalypse. Other influential contributions are E. S. Fiorenza, 'The Composition and Structure of Revelation', *Justice and Judgment*, pp.159-80; Bauckham, *Climax of Prophecy*, pp.1-37; and J. Lambrecht, 'A Structuration of Revelation', pp.77-104.

20   J. Lambrecht, 'A Structuration of Revelation', pp.85-95. In its simplest form the principle of 'encompassing' claims that the seven-series (seals, trumpets, bowls of wrath) contain all that follows. Only with each successive repetition of the series the action and details of the story become more complex and are expounded with greater detail.

with seven seals it contains God's decisions about the future. In a fascinating scene echoing Abraham's visit to Moriah (Gen. 22.1-19) a heavenly search is inaugurated for the one who is worthy to open the scroll (5.2-5). The Lion of the tribe of Judah/the Root of David (Christ) is the one found worthy. In the heavenly sanctuary Christ is praised (5.6-12). Only he has had the capacity to ransom God's people from every tribe and nation and make them into a kingdom and priests ready to reign on earth. The sequence ends with both Christ and God the objects of praise (5.13-14). Subsequently, the Lamb begins to break the seals to open the scroll. Here the action sequence of John's story essentially begins. As I have noted the contents of the scroll are designed to constitute a broad overview of what will take place during the last days. Ordinary reality that a scroll cannot be read until all of its seals are broken is suspended in this symbolic world. The four horsemen gallop forth into view (6.1-8). They represent the essence of Roman imperial policy which does not bring peace but a sword.[21] They signal that all will not be well in the coming days. The crucial fifth seal also speaks of judgment (6.9-11). Before true justice is done on earth there will be some who will suffer and die on behalf of the cause of the Lamb. However significantly they must wait χρόνον μικρόν 'a little while' before God's just judgments will take place.

It is here that we get a strong hint of a coming crisis – brief but brutal. In biblical thought crisis is usually followed by judgment. God's wrath falls on a rebellious creation in the sixth seal (6.12-17). Revelation 6.17 clearly encompasses 19.15-16 although we are not there in the linear development of the story! Yet this does feature a foundational point of John's theology. A broad swath of humankind become fearful, a result of God's medicinal and ecological judgmental visitations upon the creation. They live in times of crisis, but for some mysterious reason they remain unrepentant. But what about the people of faith? In the interlude between the sixth and seventh seal a different situation for God's servants is outlined (7.1–8.1). The one hundred and forty-four thousand, God's covenantal people, are sealed against the harsh outcome of the final judgment (7.2). And in the climactic vision that follows (7.9-17) we are transported proleptically forward to the time of the new Jerusalem (21.1-8). There the righteous of all ages from every place will enjoy the benefits of God's new world.[22] Thus, with this word of hope, the pastoral dimension remains central.

Having given the basic outline of his story, a new series of encompassing visions emerges. John now deepens the impact of his narrative with further

21   Marko Jauhiainen, 'Recapitulation and Chronological Progression', p.548.
22   J. Lambrecht, 'The Opening of the Seals (Revelation 6.1–8.6)' in *Collected Studies on Pauline Literature and on the Book of Revelation AnBib 147* (Roma: Pontifico Instituto Biblico, 2001), p.369, notes at least five items that parallel Rev. 7.9-17 and 21.1-8; the only use of λατρεύω 'to worship' in 7.15 and 21.3; the sheltering motif of σκηνεῖν in 7.15 and 21.3; the theme of removal of all evil; the themes of thirst solved by the water of life; and the theme of God wiping away all tears.

details. At the same time he creatively moves it forward in a gradual linear progression so that the reader gains the impression that the story is progressing and will have a discernible conclusion.[23] After a brief period of silence wherein the martyrs' prayers ascend into the heavenly sanctuary the unit on the seven trumpets unfolds (8.2–11.18). John sets forth a series of ecological and medicinal punishments that the Holy One visits on a rebellious creation (8.2–9.19). Again, the punishments do not result in repentance. The net effect is that humankind becomes even more hardened in acceptance of idolatry and its accompanying perversions (9.20-21).

In the meanwhile, it is asserted once more that the people of God are sealed to protect them from these punishments (9.4; cf. 3.10; 7.2). They are measured for protection at the last judgment (11.1a). And although they must face ridicule and the prospect of martyrdom, through the resurrection of the two witnesses there is assurance of vindication at the end (11.3-12). We are now in the time of crisis or tribulation. But following the linear progression inherent in the story John learns that there is a major development. Announced initially in Revelation 6.11 as ἔτι χρόνον μικρόν 'yet a little while', by the time of the interlude in 10.6, John learns that this era of trial is about to end. God is ready to rectify his creation (11.15-18). The kingdom of the world is about to become the kingdom of the Lord.

Embedded in the interlude of the unit on the seven trumpets are several structural features that invite special attention. They appear to be placed strategically in the text to facilitate understanding of the movement of the story. First and foremost is the reference to the open scroll (10.1-11). The appearance of a 'second' scroll obviously invites attention. Is it the same scroll (now open after the seals have been broken) as the one that appeared in Revelation 5.2? The textual tradition is difficult. The Greek diminutive βιβλαρίδιον 'little scroll' appears most frequently, but in some manuscripts (viz. 10.2, 8) βιβλίον 'scroll' or 'book', the word used in 5.2, occurs. Even if it is the same scroll as 5.2 the shift in terminology probably indicates a focus on certain particularities of the context. Revelation 10.7 echoes Daniel 12.4, 6-8. The Danielic text raises questions about the nature of a period of crisis of 42 months or 1260 days after which the righteous will be vindicated. In Revelation 10.8-11 John takes and eats the scroll thus internalizing its message. It is both sweet and sour. It is sweet because the elect will be preserved through the crisis and will come to enjoy the benefits of the new age (11.15-19). It will be sour because it will only come after a terrible ordeal.[24] The particularities of the message of the open scroll will then unfold in the chapters that focus on the crisis of 1260 days wherein the people of God are in conflict with the imperial powers (11.2; 12.6, 14; 13.5).

---

23   To emphasise a sense of growing intensity of the punishments we are told that they now cover one third of the earth as opposed to the figure of one quarter in the vision of the seven seals.
24   Mounce, *The Book of Revelation*, p.210.

This analysis is in keeping with the other major structural feature of this section which features the woes. In Revelation 8.13, probably a counterpoint to the Trisagion of 4.8, a vulture announces that three woes will fall on earth (8.13). This literary feature is additional support for the idea of linear progression of the action. The first two woes initiate a series of ecological and medicinal judgments (9.12; 11.14). The third woe (never directly specified) climaxes the linear progression. Almost certainly it incorporates the destruction of Babylon and defeat of the nations (11.19–19.21). It not only stresses the certainty of judgment for Babylon and her allies but functions as a partial warning to the church not to accommodate to their idolatrous power.

A third structural element placed in the text features a series of stormy upheavals (lightning, thunder and earthquakes) that give the appearance of a theophany (4.5; 8.5; 11.19; 16.18-21).[25] These upheavals gradually intensify. They portend the coming judgment of God in answer to the prayers of the saints. Thus they also climax in the destruction of Babylon.

If the seven trumpets unit represents the onslaught of the conflict of the final crisis the seven bowls of wrath represents its full-blown fury and resolution. What is most striking about the latter unit is that when the bowls are poured out on earth as an expression of the full wrath of God they come with methodical precision (16.2-21). There are no interludes. After a few short verses, Babylon is in ruins. Until the very end, the alliance of imperial powers, in imitation of the Exodus plague sequence, accepts punishment rather than turn in genuine repentance to the God of Israel (16.9, 11, 20). All they can do is shake their fist at God.

These are not just misguided humans. Structurally, what is most striking about this unit on the seven bowls of wrath is that the type of material usually featured in the interludes is moved forward to the first part of the unit (11.19–15.4). The function of this move is to give a full literary explanation for both the crisis described as present in chapter 10 and its final outcome in chapter 16. Babylon and its allies among the nations are not merely misguided. They come under the sway of the unseen demonic power of Satan and his allies – the sea and earth beasts (12.1–13.18). The latter, symbolizing both the rebirth of the Flavian dynasty and its support by the wealthy elites who furnish the priesthood and take the important positions of power, paint pictures of Rome in horrific terms.[26] Any who accommodate to its operation will pay a terrible price. Yet, even here John's spiritual concern for the followers of the Lamb surfaces. In the midst of the full fury of God's wrath on Babylon there is a brief aside to the reader in the covenant community:

Blessed is he who is awake keeping his garments that he may not go naked and be seen exposed (16.15).

25   Bauckham, *The Climax of Prophecy*, pp.199–209.
26   Steven J. Friesen, *Imperial Cults and the Apocalypse of John: Reading Revelation in the Ruins* (New York: Oxford University Press, 2001), pp.202–203.

Once again we glimpse a pastoral concern: the bottom line for John.

Upon the defeat of Babylon in Revelation 16.21, through the literary device of the two contrasting cities John brings his story to a resounding conclusion. This is confirmed by observation of a striking editorial delineation he makes between the two cities: Babylon and Jerusalem. The delineation can be clearly detected by the literary seams in the text at 17.1 and 21.9. In 17.1 John narrates that one of the seven angels who had the seven bowls (of wrath) invites him to see the prostitute (Rome) who commits fornication with the kings of the earth.[27] Then there follows a description of the demise of Rome, the dirge over her fate by her allies and the praise for her defeat by the people of God. The unit ends in 19.10 with a charge not to worship the angel but to worship God. On the other hand, almost the same Greek wording is used in 21.9 to introduce the description of the new Jerusalem. The unit then ends in 22.8-9 with a charge not to worship the angel but to worship God. It would be difficult to find a clearer set of literary seams anywhere in ancient literature. Thus the major feature of the closing chapters of Revelation is a strong comparison between the fate of the two cities. Babylon is described in 17.1–19.10. Jerusalem is described in 21.8–22.9. Of course, John indulges in intricate literary interplay making numerous comparisons and contrasts between the two cities.[28] But the overall thrust is clear; those allied with Babylon will suffer a terrible fate. The covenant community which comprises the new Jerusalem will enter a state of blessedness.

This brings us to the action unit of Revelation 19.11–21.8. In my display I refer to this as 'the Vindication of the Righteous Covenant Community'. The unit is structured by a series of καὶ εἶδον 'I saw' statements (19.11, 17, 19; 20.1, 4; 11, 12; 21.1, 2). Of these seven, 19.11, 17, 19; 20.1, 4, 11 and 21.1 can be considered as legitimate use of the formula to open a thought unit.[29] If so, this unit which takes us from the theophanic appearance of Christ in his parousia to the coming of the new Jerusalem in 21.1-8 also represents a clear editorial literary arrangement. This unit contains some of the most obscure and differently interpreted pericopes in all of scripture. It includes the famous 'millennium passage' (20.4-6) where the righteous ones (6.9-11; 7.1-8; 14.1-5) now reign as judges and priests. But what is usually overlooked is the net of effect of the entire unit. When put together, the pericopes function as a very strong pastoral appeal for faithfulness among the covenant community. The parousia of the Divine Warrior (Christ) defeats the enemies of the Word of God (19.11-18). The sea beast, false prophet (earth beast) and the dragon, the powers that energize evil Babylon, are consigned to the lake of fire. Joining them there are those who have strong allegiance to this evil trinity. Their names are not found in the Lamb's book of life. On the other hand, the people of God, as judges and priests, set up thrones (20.4-6). They assist the Lamb

---

27   The exact words Δεῦρο δείξω σοι 'Come, I will show to you...' is the same as that occurs in 21.9. In 17.1 John is shown the prostitute. In 21.9 he is shown the bride of the Lamb.

28   C. Deutsch, 'Transformation of Symbols', p.123.

29   Cf. There is a possible parallel in the seven references to the Lamb, husband of the Bride in the new Jerusalem unit (Rev. 21.9, 14, 22, 23, 27; 22.1, 3).

in ruling in God's kingdom in his new world. In the new Jerusalem they have full access to the water of life. Eden has returned. What stronger pastoral appeal to faithfulness could there be? Those in the churches who hear this message are left in no doubt. The faithful are encouraged by the blessings which are promised. Those accommodating to the imperial powers are dutifully warned of impending dangers.

At the end of the book, structurally, John ends with an epilogue. The major feature of this epilogue is a series of moralistic exhortations highlighted by frequent reminders that the time is near or Christ is coming soon (22.10, 12, 20).[30]

Broadly speaking these references to the nearness of Christ's parousia seem to have a close connection to the working out of the events promised to be revealed in Revelation 1.1. More specifically, it can refer to the contents of the scroll that the Lamb receives directly from God (5.1-5). There have been further attempts at precision. One is to show that when the seer claims 'What must take place soon' he is referring directly to the judgment of Babylon and the coming of the new Jerusalem.[31] But even if this interpretation is accepted, it does not make any sense unless the overarching message is embraced. This would include the parousia and the arrival of the new Jerusalem. At its core the promise asserts that Christ will defeat the nations and vindicate the covenant people.

Finally, a noteworthy reference is found in Revelation 22.14 in the last of the seven beatitudes that, for our purposes, should not be overlooked. We learn that the blessed (for John the faithful in the seven churches) are those who are engaged in washing τὰς στολὰς αὐτῶν 'their robes'. They have the right to gain entry into the city with the restored tree of life.[32] The text echoes Exodus 19.10, 14.[33] There, in preparation for the theophany at the Mount the Israelites are to 'wash their garments' in preparation for the divine visitation at Sinai. It is noticeable that this passage is close to Exodus 19.5-6 where Israel is promised that if they keep covenant they will become a kingdom of priests. This language is picked up in Judaism after the exile. For many interpreters Israel functions as a priestly nation on behalf of the human community. In later Judaism the act of washing is transferred to a key rite demanded of proselytes as a condition for joining the priestly community to carry out a similar mission.[34]

Returning to Revelation one sees that, in turn, these traditions in Israel are transformed even more. In 5.9 and 7.14 Christ is praised because his atoning

---

30   This completes another collection of seven references to either the coming of Christ as ταχύ / τάχει 'quickly' or that the time is ἐγγύς 'near' (Rev. 1.1, 3; 22.6, 7, 10, 12, 20).

31   Marko Jauhiainen, 'ΑΠΟΚΑΛΥΨΙΣ ΙΗΣΟΥ ΧΡΙΣΤΟΥ (Rev. 1.1): The Climax of John's Prophecy?', *Tyn Bul* 54/1 (2003) p. 117. There are many other positions.

32   The variant οἱ ποιοῦντες τάς ἐντολὰς αὐτοῦ 'those who keep his commandments' scattered in some ancient texts, probably represents an early interpretation. Beale, *The Book of Revelation*, p.1140; cf. Aune, Revelation, pp.1197–8.

33   Håkan Ulfgard, *Feast and Future*, p.83. cf. Gen. 49.11.

34   Peder Borgen, 'Polemic in the Book of Revelation', pp.206–209.

death has ransomed the people of God. One becomes a priest of God by being part of this community (1.5). Following the earlier model of proselyte traditions in Judaism, people of every tribe, tongue, people and nation are added through conversion into the community (5.10; 7.9, 14). They have (white) robes as symbols of worthiness to dwell in heaven (6.11).[35] The conversion theme is driven home when we compare 22.14 with Revelation 7.14. In the latter text John adds that those whose robes are washed 'are made white in the blood of the Lamb'.[36] It should be stressed that, most likely, this is a reference to conversion and not to martyrdom.[37]

We conclude that the macarism of Revelation 22.14 that features a blessing refers to all peoples who choose to appropriate the power of Jesus' redemptive death as the basis for their lives. The surrounding references to access to the tree of life (22.2) and the right to enter the city through its gates (21.25) suggest an editorial intention to incorporate into the synthesis all those involved in the covenant communities. This represents a daring and innovative reinterpretation of Second-Temple analysis of Exodus 19. It gives added meaning to Revelation 7.9-14. The great multitude includes the entire covenant peoples.

Revelation 22.15 adds an additional thrust to the paraenetic function of 22.14. It is clear that those who are committed to the alliance with Babylon ('fornicators, murderers, idolaters') are not eligible to participate in God's new world. Yet, at the same time, as I have shown in this chapter, the references to φάρμακοι 'sorcerers' and the one ποιῶν ψεῦδος 'doing falsehood' are sufficiently close to the descriptions of the teachings of Babylon and the activities of the prophetess Jezebel to cause discomfort even in the ranks of the churches. In short this paraenetic warning is aimed as much at the accommodationists in John's churches as it is toward those who give full allegiance to the Roman regime. Until the concluding moments of the book the centre of the fundamental message remains clear. Do not accommodate to the civic and cultural life of the Roman Empire!

The Significance of the Sublimation of the Nations

Throughout this chapter our argument has hovered around a central theme; the conversion of the nations is a small crater within a larger one. The larger

---

35   Håkan Ulfgard, 'Feast and Future', pp.85–6, describes John's vision of heaven as God's temple or place of dominion while human beings, allowed into it, are given the priestly dignity of serving the Holy One in his immediate presence.

36   In Rev. 7.14 the subjects are identified as all those among the people of God who came through the great crisis or tribulation. In 22.14 the subjects are John's immediate readers. The Greek present in 22.14 functions as a paraenetic usage. See also Rev. 3.4-5, 17-18.

37   G. R. Beasley-Murray, *The Book of Revelation NLB* (Grand Rapids, William B. Eerdmans, 1981), p.147. cf. Ulfgard, 'Feast and Future', p.83.

crater serves as the foundation of John's message. Its pastoral focus (non-accommodation by the small Christian assemblies in Asia to the Roman Empire) is integrally related to the smaller crater of the destiny of the nations.

John was a Christian-Jewish prophet whose identity was shaped in the core of the faith of Israel and Jewish community life. He carried no particular brief for the Gentiles. Evidence abounds throughout the Apocalypse that he was well schooled in the prevailing moralisms with respect to Gentile ways. Yet by a reading of the prophets through the eyes of identification with the faith of the Christian community he gained new insights. His heavenly vision is congruent with these insights. The nations with their idolatrous ways are presently in subjection to evil unseen powers that work themselves out in the habitual practices of the current empire. A revitalized people of God has arisen in the last days. These are people from different tribes and nations who have sublimated themselves to the way of the Christ (1.6; 5.9; 7.9). They are now an established part of his kingdom. But most people in Rome have not. Despite God's ecological and medicinal judgments against their rebellion they continue to refuse to repent. From the elites to the slaves they choose to suffer divine wrath rather than honour the Creator in worship. To the discerning reader the Exodus motif has re-emerged with even stronger force.

But it is not only with respect to the plagues. In Exodus 19.10 only those who appropriately 'wash their garment' may attain access into the glory of divine presence as at Sinai. The prophet has sought to underscore what is involved in this process. Much of this is congruent with early Christian faith. What is surprising is what takes place in the new creation following the parousia. There, in keeping with the word of the Hebrew prophets, not only are the people of God vindicated, but God's covenant with the nations is renewed. From their destitute state of being vanquished they have now come to a remarkable state of elevation. Sublimated by recognition of the lordship of Christ they have now become part of the great multitude (Rev. 7.9). Of course this small crater is only part of the web of the great pastoral message of the Apocalypse. One should already shape one's life in view of the dawning reality that the present dominance of the empire will be reversed. Yet, for pastoral purposes, it maintained an amazing delicate balance. The nations would be punished severely for their perfidy. Yet, in the terminology of Paul, echoing Isaiah 45.23, there will come a time when the knee will bow and the tongue confess that Jesus is Lord (Philipp. 2.10-11).

CHAPTER 6

THE ABIDING VALUE OF JOHN'S APOCALYPSE

Some Alternative Readings

The prophet John was deeply indebted to certain texts in the Hebrew prophets out of which he formulated the basic structure of his view of the end-times. Nourished in the bosom of early Christian eschatological thinking John viewed himself as living in the last days. As a response to perceived pastoral needs he writes to encourage the churches in Asia. He envisions the fulfilment of the ancient prophetic word concerning the end-times which he conceives are soon to take place.

An integral part of the eschatology of the biblical prophets centred on reflection about the destiny of the nations. Texts in such works as Ezekiel, Second and Third Isaiah and Zechariah all referred to a coming crisis when Jerusalem would be surrounded by hostile nations and could only be saved by divine intervention often in the form of a theophany.[1] On the one hand Jerusalem is to be purged and vindicated. On the other, through the sheer power of the theophany the rebellious nations are defeated and judged. As a result of the theophany the nations are compelled to acknowledge the new order in Jerusalem by giving it full recognition in regular pilgrimages.

The prophet John stamps this eschatological vision on the historical situation of the eastern part of the Roman Empire which he encounters directly in the first century of our era. In its simplest form the book of Revelation is about the transfer of power. Power no longer will be the province of the nations. It will be taken from them and given to the people of God. God is the king of the nations (15.3). Christ is 'King of Kings and Lord of Lords' (19.16). He is ruler of the kings on earth (1.5). With the restoration of the people-covenant God's people will sit on thrones and assist their Lord in the reign of the kingdom (20.4-6). Then the kings of earth, incorporated into the renewed covenant with the nations, will bring the glory and honour of the nations into the new Jerusalem (21.24-26).[2] To describe the role of the nations in the new Jerusalem I have settled on the term 'eschatological covenantal restitution'. Through the renewal of the covenant with the nations, the allegiance of the peoples and tribes has shifted from Babylon to

---

1   Of course there are earlier precedents as in the Assyrian crisis.
2   Nils Dahl, 'Nations in the New Testament', p.68.

the new Jerusalem. They now constitute a mighty moral order. This interpretation of the Apocalypse differs from the two major alternatives. First, there is the view most prominently held by Richard Bauckham, who advocated that the nations will be converted in ordinary history through the suffering witness of a vibrant martyr-church.[3] Thus, the book of Revelation is viewed primarily as a call for suffering service for the people of God. This will have the effect of winning the nations over to the way of the Lamb.[4] A second alternative view is also noteworthy. This view takes the position that those seduced by the beast (the nations) do not survive the parousia of Christ the Divine Warrior and the judgment he visits upon them (19.11–20.15). The coming of the nations into the new Jerusalem accompanied by their kings is reckoned to be evidence that regular followers of the Lamb in ordinary history have been raised in the new creation and now have become 'the nations'. Revelation 21.24-26 is an expression of the exercise of their royal and priestly dignity in the fully realized kingdom of God.[5]

In this chapter we wish to assess succinctly these major alternative readings. As much as possible we will compare and contrast these views with our position of eschatological covenantal restitution. Since the Apocalypse of John was first circulated in the churches of Asia a countless number of interpretations have been canvassed.[6] Yet, as a canonical book which brings closure to the current English New Testament, Revelation continues to be seminal for Christian reflections about the end. We will close the chapter with consideration of the abiding theological viability of the particular reading which we advocate.

Conversion Through Suffering Witness: A Selective Critique

The arguments of Richard Bauckham in his classic essay on the Conversion of the Nations have already undergone several extensive critiques.[7] Bauckham's

3   Richard Bauckham, *Climax of the Covenant*, 238–337; *idem.*, *The Theology of the Book of Revelation*, pp.98–104.

4   Richard Bauckham, *Theology of the Book of Revelation*, p.101.

5   David Mathewson, *A New Heaven and a New Earth*, pp.169–72, outlines several other alternative positions besides the ones mentioned. We assume that the position of Rissi, *The Future of the World*, pp.71–4, 78, that the former enemies will return from the lake of fire into the new Jerusalem has been adequately evaluated and rejected by other commentators. A variation of this view that sometimes appears in the literature is Jeffrey Marshall Vogelgesang, 'The Interpretation of Ezekiel in the Book of Revelation', unpublished doctoral dissertation, Harvard University (Ann Arbor, Michigan: University Microfilms International, 1985). The views of Sweet, *Revelation*, pp.308–309, were addressed in Chapter 1. What Mathewson refers to 'the *survivors* of the judgment constituting the people of God in the new Jerusalem' is unclear but does overlap, to some degree, my own position.

6   A. W. Wainwright, *Mysterious Apocalypse: Interpreting the Book of Revelation* (Nashville: Abingdon Press, 1993) is a good beginning to review the main contours of their interpretation.

7   Ronald Herms, *An Apocalypse for the Church and the World*, pp.37–44, 138–45; David Mathewson, *A New Heaven and a New Earth*, pp.171–85; *idem.* 'The Destiny of the Nations',

argument is that the open scroll reveals how the suffering witness of a martyr-church will initiate the conversion of the nations. But, as Marco Jauhiainen points out, the textual evidence is somewhat meagre.[8] It is arguable that only Revelation 11.3-13 (especially verse 13) openly raises the issue. The scope and content of the message of the open scroll is a subject of debate, especially if it be taken to be 11.1–19.21. Wide-ranging subject matter such as a growing conflict between the people of God and the empire, the defeat of the nations and the climactic account of the coming of the Divine Warrior are dominant in these chapters. Noticeably absent are clear indicators that a rebellious world, in ordinary history, will come to repentance. In fact, a perusal of Revelation 16 leads to the opposite conclusion.

Nevertheless, the very intriguing text of Revelation 11.13 is worthy of further attention. Aside from the fact that it serves as linchpin of Bauckham's argument in its own right, it is a crucial text.

Revelation 11.13 is housed in the wider account of the two witnesses about which Bauckham has much to say.[9] As we assess Bauckham's interpretation we will occasionally note that there are many insights that promote agreement with his analysis. However, our goal is to point out why his final conclusion is not substantiated.

The account of the mission and destiny of the two witnesses can be considered to be a parable of the church in its role as witness to divine truth as it passes through the tribulation thought to be close at hand.[10] However, just as with the interpretation of Jesus' parables, the readings of this 'parable' vary widely. As we argued in an earlier chapter, major Hebrew prophets in the Second-Temple period did anticipate the repentant subjugation of the nations inherent in their pilgrimage to honour Yahweh in Jerusalem. With the partial exception of the Jonah story (the one example which proved the rule), such a result did not come to pass. According to Bauckham Revelation 11.13 is John's vision of how this will take place. It will come as a result of the faithful suffering witness of the church through this difficult time. The two witnesses through their proclamation, martyrdom, resurrection and ascension are the continuing symbolic embodiments of the power of the redemptive death of Christ, the Lamb of God. This power is now housed in the people of God. The full expression of this witness in the life of the martyr-church leads to repentance.[11]

At this point a simple observation may be significant. In the 'parable' itself the martyrdom and vindication of the two witnesses do not lead to the repentance

pp.121–42; Eckhard J. Schnabel, 'John and the Future of the Nations', *BBR* 12/2 (2002), pp.243–71; Marco Jauhiainen, 'Climax of John's Prophecy', pp.99–117 are the ones with which I am most familiar.

8   Marco Jauhiainen, 'Climax of John's Prophecy', p.108.
9   Bauckham, *Climax of Prophecy*, pp.273–83, is the place where Bauckham offers his main analysis.
10   Bauckham, *Climax of Prophecy*, p.274.
11   Bauckham, *Climax of Prophecy*, pp.272–83.

of the nations. Besides the controversial text in 11.13, the closest one comes is Revelation 11.11 when, after the martyrdom of the witnesses, the people of the great city are filled with fear when they see the two prophets raised to life.[12] By and large the death of the witnesses is treated as a celebration. The earth dwellers exchange gifts and rejoice over their demise (11.10). It is only after the occurrence of the earthquake (a sign of theophany?) that we see things begin to change. This seems to be a major difficulty for Bauckham's proposal. The people flatly reject the witnesses. There are only indications of change after direct heavenly intervention.

The occurrence of the earthquake echoes Revelation 6.12 and 8.5, two earlier references to an earthquake. In both instances these texts are expressions of the punishing wrath of God. In Revelation 6.12 this comes at the opening of the sixth seal which is the initial description of God's wrath on the Day of the Lord. Revelation 8.5 describes the activity of God in initiating the judgmental plagues of the vision of the seven trumpets. Of course, what is striking in 11.13 is that, although a tenth of the city died, the greater number, οἱ λοιποί 'the rest', become filled with fear and give glory to God. This text appears to be saying that the day of the wrath of God is a day of destruction (6.17; 11.13; 16.18). But through it also shines a glimpse of hope. Despite the recalcitrance of those who refuse to turn to God as a result of the ecological and medicinal plagues (9.20-21) and the signs and prophetic proclamation of the two witnesses, there is still hope. The source of this hope is the activity of the Lord on his Day. In the text it is represented by an awe-inspiring theophany that results in the people of the city giving him honour.[13]

---

12   The connection between Revelation 11.8 'the great city' and 11.13 'city' suggests that the referent in both texts is to the same place. This is confirmed by the reference to the nations trampling τὴν πόλιν τὴν ἁγίαν 'the holy city' in 11.2. Jean-Pierre Ruiz, *Ezekiel in the Apocalypse*, pp.281-9, has an extensive excursus on this issue. I differ in my interpretation of 'the great city' in 16.19. Ruiz believes it refers to Jerusalem. I accept the majority position that it refers to Rome. However, on the issue of the identification of the city in 11.13 he has no doubt, 'Consequently, the πόλις in 11.13 is also Jerusalem.' We agree. In 11.8 the 'great city' is referred to as Sodom and Egypt. The reference to Sodom echoes Isa. 1.9-10 and Ezek. 16.46-49. Egypt was the traditional place of bondage from which the people of God found deliverance.

13   The phraseology to describe the people of the city giving honour to God in 11.13b has been the subject of much comment. Schnabel, *John and the Future of the Nations*, pp.253-4, understands ἔμφοβοι ἐγένετο 'they became full of fear' along with 'they gave δόξαν (glory) to the God of heaven' as a case of terror of anxious apprehension and not a genuine expression of repentance. His main argument is that ἔμφοβοι with a form of γίνομαι 'to become' always in the New Testament means 'terrified' or 'frightened' in a sense of the absence of faith (Lk. 24.5, 37; Acts 10.4; 24.25). He also points out that to give glory to God, although mostly a positive term for worship in Revelation, does function frequently as a *Gerichtsdoxologie* in Hebrew scripture. What this is supposed to lead one to infer is that God may be praised on account of his awesome power and absolute will rather than freely offered allegiance (Dan. 4.34 cf.; 1 Kgs. 18.39; Dan. 2.46-49; 3.28-30). However, Bauckham, *Climax of the Covenant*, pp.278-9, is able to show that in Rev. 14.7 φοβήθητε τὸν θεόν καὶ δότε αὐτῷ δόξαν 'fear God and give him glory', which clearly is meant to elicit genuine

We understand the account of the two witnesses as a parable of the days preceding the full onslaught of the Day of the Lord. The witnesses clothed in sackcloth (11.3), the traditional garb of repentance, call the nations to turn from idolatry to honour God (cf. 10.11; 11.18). They have the capacity to do signs of judgment as part of their prophetic mission but these alone will not produce repentance.[14] The two witnesses have the characteristic of Moses, who later confronted Balak (predecessor of Balaam), and Elijah, who dueled with Jezebel and the prophets of Baal.[15] Sealed by the Lord for security from the effects of divine wrath and assured of vindication in the final judgment they are not protected against martyrdom. Ironically, although they bear the characteristics of Elijah and Moses (both in Jewish tradition taken to heaven), they die. Throughout this era the church will face martyrdom. Notably, it takes a beast from the pit (evil powers) to facilitate their death (11.7).

The witnesses' death takes place in the city where their Lord was crucified (11.8). This is, of course, Jerusalem. What is striking is that the narrative account of Revelation climaxes with the coming of the new Jerusalem.[16] Before that day comes, old Jerusalem and Babylon (the two great cities of the east known to the prophet) must undergo a grim assessment that finally will result in their destruction.[17] In Revelation 11.8, 13 it is Jerusalem. The echoes of its known destruction in John's day emerge in 11.2 and are probably behind 11.13. Its successor, Babylon (Rome), as a source of power gone awry, will suffer a similar fate (16.19; 18.2-24). As with the Jerusalem of Ezekiel's day the fundamental problem is idolatry. The reference to the death of the seven thousand in the earthquake is a case in point (11.13). Elijah found seven thousand faithful in all Israel after his contest with the prophets of Baal (1 Kgs. 19.18). It is a striking expression of the *lex talionis* that the same number is destroyed when the Lord visits the 'great city' in 11.13.

---

repentance, is linguistically very similar to 15.4 and 11.13 (cf. 16.9). Also he notes that in Revelation 'to give glory to God' in a positive sense is the normative usage (4.9; 14.7; 16.9; 19.7). Perhaps this interpretive problem is more apparent than real. In short, as pointed out by Schnabel, this is a judgment doxology. It anticipates parabolically, in the account of the resurrection and ascension of the two witnesses, the coming of the Lord on the last day. This will involve a response of awesome terror when the nations (11.9) will be ushered into the presence of the Lord. Some will be judged harshly (9.20-21; 16.19). But in 11.13 this text is an anticipation that many, finding themselves in the presence of the sheer grandeur of the Lord (1.7), in repentance, will sublimate themselves to him and become participants in the renewed covenant with the nations. Beale, *The Book of Revelation*, 603–604, acknowledges this is a possibility although he is reluctant to say there may be such a thing as 'a second chance'. We doubt such an issue is in focus. Beale presumes the world-view operative within modern revivalism. We would stress what is primarily important for John is that his account correlates with the Hebrew prophets' emphasis on the pilgrimage of the nations on the Day of the Lord.

14   Bauckham, *Climax of the Covenant*, p.277.

15   This clearly serves as a not too subtle warning to the prophets and prophetesses in the churches of Asia that their alliances with the civic activities of the empire will have severe consequences.

16   Jean-Pierre Ruiz, *Ezekiel in the Apocalypse*, p.289.

17   Jean-Pierre Ruiz, *Ezekiel in the Apocalypse*, pp.288–9.

This blistering evaluation of the 'great city' may ultimately be a metaphor for the corrupt civic culture of the empire. John may be referring to developments not only within the empire but also in a church that collaborates with the teaching of Jezebel and Balaam. Those who make strong alliances with the earth dwellers, people and nations, at the same time dismissing the perceived purity of the faith that John advocates, may well be the ones directly addressed in this verse.

Bauckham does draw attention to an interesting feature of the text. Unlike most of the accounts of this type in the Bible, it is not the faithful remnant that is preserved but 'the faithless majority'.[18] Bauckham draws the conclusion that this is an anticipation of the large-scale conversion of nations as a result of the faithful witness of a martyr church.[19] But this particular conclusion cannot be substantiated from the text in other places. Rather it does appear that this is an anticipation of the eventual outcome of John's story with the coming of the new Jerusalem. The tenth of the city destroyed represents the punishment of the nations imbedded in idolatry (again echoing Elijah's confrontation with the false prophets of Baal). When the Divine Warrior appears at his parousia they will be judged (19.15-18, 21; 20.11-15). On the other hand, at the great theophany many will change. The 'faithless majority' will repent and turn toward God. They will be welcomed by the Divine Warrior into the renewed covenant with the nations (cf. 21.24-26; 22.2).

Such a position is confirmed by analysis of Revelation 1.7. This is also a much discussed text in the Apocalypse. This text follows a short prologue and is part of the initial greetings and salutations of the book (1.4-8).[20] The importance of this text is underscored by its strategic placement at the beginning of the book.

The opening words of the text in 1.7a consists of a paraphrase of a portion of Daniel 7.13: 'Behold he comes with the clouds.' In Daniel 'one like a son of man' comes on the clouds to a throne to judge the nations (7.13-14).[21] For John the one

---

18   Bauckham, *Climax of the Covenant*, pp.282–3.

19   Bauckham, *Climax of the Covenant*, pp.282–3.

20   Although as noted by Leonard L. Thompson, 'Lamentation for Christ as a Hero: Revelation 1:7', *JBL* 119/4 (2000), p.685, 1.7 exists as a separate literary unit. Thompson thinks it is distinct from the initial extended greeting in 1.4-6 and the first person divine acclamation in 1.8. He thus concludes that the context is of limited assistance in allowing us to interpret the verse.

21   It is noteworthy that a form of ἔρχομαι 'I come' appears both in Rev. 1.7a and Dan. 7.13 (LXX). But there is also an interesting web of parallels with major features in Revelation starting in Zech. 2.14 LXX (MT and English text 2.10). Zech. 2.14 (LXX) opens with the wording ἰδοὺ ἐγὼ ἔρχομαι 'behold I come'. This refers to the coming of Yahweh. Immediately following is the promise of the Lord 'to dwell' with his people which in Greek is an intensive form of σκηνοῦν (cf. Rev. 7.15; 21.3). In turn, the text in Zech. 2.15 (LXX) then goes on to assert that many nations on that day will take refuge in the Lord and will be his people. In this text the basic features of the template of John's vision for the coming of the Lord is found. We would conclude that Zechariah 2 was an important text for him. An additional observation is made by Marko Jauhiainen, *The Use of Zechariah*, 74–5. He notes that the formula 'I come' is used by Christ seven times as a way of highlighting the importance of the coming Day of the Lord (2.5, 16; 3.11; 16.15; 22.7, 12, 20).

who is coming is Christ, who, later in chapter one, is identified as 'one like a son of man' (1.12-20). Either John has linked Daniel 7.13 with Zechariah 12.9-14 (the other major scriptural text behind 1.7), or has drawn on an early Christian collection of proof texts (*testamonia* tradition).[22] This is because there follow three successive clauses explaining the coming of Christ to complete the verse. All of these verses open with the coordinating conjunction καί 'and', and all echo directly material in Zechariah 12.10, 12. The reference in the first of these clauses, 'every eye will see him' echoes a reference to the inhabitant of Jerusalem looking on one pierced. The phrase has been universalized to account for the all-encompassing future rule of Christ over the whole creation.[23] The second and third clauses also are drawn from Zechariah 12.10, 12 as well. We are told that those who pierced him ('treated me shamefully' LXX) and all of the tribes of the earth will wail over him.[24]

Through a process of *gezērâ sāwâ* Bauckham connects the phraseology of 'all the tribes of the earth' in Zechariah 12.12-14 to the Abrahamic promises. This helps him move in a direction of understanding the wailing of the tribes of the earth in a positive sense.[25] The nations, to be won over by the martyr witness of the church, will be the inheritors of the blessings promised to the children of Abraham. They greet the Lord's coming in repentant acknowledgment.[26] But if we understand the text more in the sense of a ritual wailing of honour at the appearance of a hero/martyr who has defeated death, the response of the nations is much more ambiguous. The latter seems to be more in keeping with both the message of Zechariah 12 (many perish but some are saved) and Revelation. Ultimately, at the parousia, the Divine Warrior will receive appropriate recog-

---

22   The use of Zech. 12.10, 12 in Matt. 24.30 and Jn. 19.27 is well known. We are inclined to agree with Leonard Thompson, 'Lamentation for Christ', pp.687–8, that the reconstruction of the text or tradition that John used is a very risky enterprise given his literary tendencies and our lack of knowledge of the particular text he used. Thompson gives adequate evidence that most likely (as we have noticed in other places) John used a text closer to the present MT (but not quite the same) than the LXX. But we cannot be certain.

23   Beale, *Book of Revelation*, pp.196–7. It is no longer the citizens of Jerusalem who will behold him but all the earth will be subject to him.

24   Our translation of κόψονται ἐπ᾽ αὐτόν 'will wail over him' follows that of the same construction in Rev. 18.9, 'the kings of the earth…will wail over her' (i.e. the kings will wail over Babylon upon her destruction). Leonard Thompson, 'Lamentation for Christ', pp.683, 688–90, argues that in Rev. 1.7 the prepositional phrase ἐπ᾽ αὐτόν should be translated with a view toward the direction and object of the lamentation. He associates it with a ritual funeral lamentation and gives evidence that this is overwhelmingly its usage in ancient Greek literature. This is opposed to most other translations that take the subjects as wailing ('on his account'), that is, the subjects engage in wailing because of fear and the terror concerning the actual fact he is there. This opens up the speculative question as to whether the subjects, 'Those who pierced him and all the tribes of the earth', all are greeting him with repentance, or sheer terror at the prospect of their future judgment. Like most speculative questions if one goes in this direction it is difficult to see whether it could ever be resolved.

25   Bauckham, *Climax of Prophecy*, pp.320–22.

26   Bauckham, *Climax of Prophecy*, p.322.

nition from the created order. Whether this will be for the particular benefit or detriment of those doing the wailing will be revealed at the last day. Although the immediate context in both Zechariah and Revelation is not all that clear, this reading does comport with our conclusions about Revelation 10:13.

The argument that, on the basis of the witness of the martyr-church, there will be a massive conversion of the nations who triumphantly greet Christ at his parousia above and beyond the regular constituency of the church cannot be substantiated from the text of Revelation. As Jauhiainen concisely points out, for John, before the parousia, there are only two groups that matter; those who have been deceived into committing themselves to the ways of the beast or those from every nation and tribe (true Israel) who, as the people of God, serve the Lamb in Christian assemblies.[27] After the defeat of the beasts that deceive it will be different. Many of the nations, freed from this deception, in repentance, will seek entrance into the new Jerusalem. But until then John lives in a binary world.

The Redeemed Become the Nations

I will now give attention to the second major alternative to our position on the conversion of the nations. This is the view that members of the early Christian assemblies, already perceived as priests and kings in God's kingdom, in actuality become the nations and their rulers in the new creation.[28] Earlier Martin Kiddle developed this interpretation. He even suggested that the complement of believers drawn from various peoples (5.9-10; 7.9) would be the nations; the actual martyrs (20.4-6) would be the kings.[29] However, in general, the core of this view is that at the time of the parousia the rebellious nations would be destroyed. They would be replaced in the new creation by followers of the Lamb who would function as the future nations. Only those written in the Lamb's book of life (21.27) would be eligible for access to the city. This is understood to be the chosen elect of the Lamb who were faithful to him in the churches prior to the parousia (3.5; 13.8; 17.8).

A recent defence of this position is that of Eckhard Schnabel.[30] Schnabel develops his position in conversation with the work of Richard Bauckham. At the heart of Schnabel's argument is the presupposition that the ordinary reader of Revelation 19-20 would conclude that the only survivors of the parousia are the resurrected saints. Thus the references to the ἄνθρωποι 'humankind'

---

27   Marco Jauhiainen, 'Climax of John's Prophecy', 107–108.
28   Cf. David Mathewson, *A New Heaven and A New Earth*, 170.
29   Martin Kiddle, *The Revelation of St. John*, p.439; cf. Beale, *The Book of Revelation*, pp.1097–100.
30   Eckhard J. Schnabel, 'John and the Future of the Nations', pp.265–70.

and λαοί 'peoples' in Revelation 21.3 must be to followers of the Lamb.[31] This is buttressed with references to Revelation 5.9-10 and 7.9 which is read as a statement of the multi-ethnic composition of the church. Within the people-covenant community of the new creation the future vindication of the redemptive community is fully realized. These people become the nations and kings (21.24-26).[32] The reference to the healing of the nations in Revelation 22.2-3 is both an announcement of the realization of the benefits of the new age coming to the followers of the Lamb and the final curing of the wounds of martyrdom. As converts who 'washed their robes' with faithful service (22.14) they have access to the tree of life (22.2) and the right to enter the city of the new Jerusalem (21.24-26).[33]

Yet, exegetically, this demands a considerable stretch. To make this analysis work creates some difficulty. The main problem centres on the need to make a massive change of references to the nations in the text. In Revelation 12–20 the nations are clearly allied with the regnant forces and power structures of the age (Rome). Often deceived, they are strongly opposed to the ways of the Lamb. The kingdom of the Lamb consists of those who once belonged to these nations but have now ἐκ 'come out' or separated themselves from the nations to become part of the people of God (5.9; 7.9). Indeed, at the core of the pastoral problem John is facing is a tendency of some in the churches to integrate their faith with the ways of the nations. John is concerned to remind his readers that, in his view, in the present order of things, the ways of the nations and the ways of the people of God are incompatible. The nations are destined to be defeated at the parousia of Christ when his people will share in his victory (2.26-27; 11.15-18; 19.15). Upon the subjugation of these vast peoples, the remnants which survive will enter into a renewed covenant with the nations. The King of Kings who defeated the nations will now shepherd them (15.4; 21.24-26; cf. 19.15). This is the basic framework of the narrative-story of Revelation. As it unfolds it involves a major shift of power. In keeping with the hopes of earlier prophets the nations and their kings now come to Jerusalem – the home of the vindicated covenant people of God – to give honour to Israel's God and the Lamb.[34]

On this reading the role of the nations is consistent throughout. There is no need to have the people of God who have come out of the nations suddenly metastasize into the nations to compensate for their earlier presumed obliteration. Moreover, this reading is fully consistent with John's strong tendency to construct his literary work as a fulfilment of the expectation of the biblical prophets. Schnabel's reading does not take this important factor fully into account. The idea that only Israel would survive the judgment of the Day of the

---

31   Eckhard Schnabel, 'John and the Future of the Nations', pp.266–7.

32   Eckhard Schnabel, 'John and the Future of the Nations', p.267.

33   Eckhard Schnabel, 'John and the Future of the Nations', pp.267–70. Also noteworthy is the tying together of several references to the nations having access to the water of life (21.6; 22.1, 2; 22.17).

34   David Mathewson, *A New Heaven and A New Earth*, p.175.

Lord and all the nations would be obliterated was outside of their purview. The auxiliary conclusion of Schnabel that the only survivors of the parousia are the resurrected saints, at least for John, is thus questionable. The references in Revelation 21.3, 24-26 (cf. 15.4) echo a version of the *Völkerwallfahrt* motif. True, the resurrected saints, the vindicated people-covenant, now inherit the new Jerusalem. But under the renewed covenant with the nations they also have access to the city which houses the tree of life. They have sublimated themselves to the way of Christ. The vindicated people of God and the converted nations now participate in the benefits of the new creation. Much of the terminology to describe these benefits, of course, is metaphorical. But it is anchored in a very real vision of the prophets: the people of God secure in Jerusalem and the nations coming up to the holy city honouring its king and the one God. John has simply given it a Christian overlay.

In the epilogue John gives his final word to the churches. Revelation 22.14 is typical of this appeal. Those in a present covenant relationship with Christ are given pastoral guidance about the coming future blessings they will enjoy. But, in the next verse (22.15), those who structure alliances with the idolatrous civic culture of the day, whether inside or outside of the Christian assemblies, will not share in these benefits. This binary perspective of the separation of the apostates from vindication of the present faithful and suppliant nations constitutes the core of eschatological covenantal restitution.[35]

A Hermeneutic for Today

Having lived through the momentous time of calendrical change into the third millennium one can appreciate that a renewal of interest in things apocalyptic would be in the air.[36] But, surprisingly, a decade later, interest continues unabated in such works as the book of Revelation. This book remains the most accessible expression of ancient apocalyptic fervour to a Western readership and still generates intense conflicts over matters of interpretation.

The scope of this monograph is limited to questions of interpretation of one area of the book: the conversion of the nations. But even in this area I have had to limit our discussion. There is no doubt that the first-century description of the rise and fall of Babylon (the Roman Empire) and shift of allegiance of the nations from it to the sovereignty of the Lamb have made a tremendous impact

---

35   David Mathewson, *A New Heaven and A New Earth*, p.172 refers cryptically to 'the survivors of the *judgment* scenes in chapters 19–20 who constitute the people of God in the new Jerusalem' (Zech. 14.12-16; 1 Enoch 90.20-27, 30-36). This comes close to my position. But Mathewson does not develop or evaluate it. Also note Mounce, *Revelation*, p.397, who seems to be sympathetic to the position.

36   Allan J. McNicol, 'The Lure of Millennium 2000: What is at Stake for the Christian Believer', *Christian Studies* 17 (1999), pp.5–15.

on art, liturgy and literature.[37] *Wirkungsgeschichte* in these areas would make a very interesting study. That is not our question. Rather, we seek to approach the Apocalypse on its own terms. In keeping with our analysis in this book we are constrained to ask what is the abiding value of its conclusions about the conversion of the nations?

To begin it is wise to recall Nils Dahl's insightful comments concerning the social world out of which the Apocalypse emerged. As we have noted, Dahl viewed it as a minority report on the value of the empire. It exposed the concealed hatred latent in many of the oppressed minority groups throughout this vast realm.[38]

> The nations are engaged on both sides in the final, cosmic conflict. They are associated and allied with the power of antichrist; but they are also suppressed and exploited, and they will take their revenge.[39]

John, probably an exiled Jew from his own land in Greater Syria, and now a member of a small counter-cultural community in Asia, could well understand these sentiments. Anticipating the collapse of Rome he relishes giving delicious details of its defeat. In his description of the punishment of its leaders and chief adherents surely these sentiments come to the surface. But this is not the dominant focus. One other massive feature imposes itself. As a Christian Jew, steeped in the worldview of the prophets, he had a deep appreciation for the power of the wrath of Yahweh exercising judgment upon evil doers on the Day of the Lord. This would be linked with an equally resolute commitment to the belief that on that day Yahweh would reverse the structures of the age and vindicate his faithful remnant. Raised upon stories ranging from Pharaoh's daughter touchingly snatching the Hebrew child Moses from a basket perched precariously among the reeds, to the exploits of Esther, John cherished the belief that Yahweh preserved a faithful remnant. Centuries later that remnant persisted in the life of a series of small assemblies stretched across the empire gathering in the name of Jesus Christ. In John's time they were under assault. Leaders from within, as a matter of strategy, were enticing them to incorporate themselves into the civic life of the empire. Horrified, he perceives the purity of the remnant community to be at stake. He resists with fierce intensity. Yahweh will reverse the status of the nations. In the coming Day of the Lord they will no longer exercise their power unopposed over the remnant. There will be an astonishing reversal. The nations will be suppliant to the vindicated pure remnant. This is what fuels the deep pastoral appeal implicit throughout the book.

---

37   See *The Apocalypse and the Shape of Things to Come*, ed. Frances Carey (Toronto/Buffalo: University of Toronto Press, 1999).

38   Nils A. Dahl, 'Nations in the New Testament', p.68.

39   Nils A. Dahl, 'Nations in the New Testament', p.67.

Contemporary readings of the Apocalypse on its own terms offer a number of possibilities. It is not late-breaking news to note the spectacular growth of interest in matters biblical in many Asian countries and major parts of the Southern Hemisphere. Peoples who have broken with an earlier colonial presence still find themselves under considerable oppression from their own civic authorities. In this context the burgeoning faith communities in these places could well hear a word from this text. They could appreciate John's insistence that a radical transfer of power is coming. Some day the idolatrous gods of the age will be dethroned.[40]

In a different context Revelation also speaks to thoughtful people in the West who, increasingly, are dismayed at the decadent trends within key power structures of our culture. Just as John sought to fortify the Christian assemblies as a contrast society that sought to embody a different value system to that inherent in the civic culture of his time, so there are many today who hear the call to confront contemporary syndromes of power. These expressions of idolatrous power may well be in big business, government, scientism, or even areas as diverse as professional sports and higher education. From all these sources there are frequent blatant enticing calls to submit to their idolatrous claims of ultimacy. What is astonishing is that although John envisions that these powers will ultimately be crushed by a greater force (a divine event such as the theophany of the parousia) it will ultimately be the way of suffering love that will replace them and prove triumphant in the new creation. This is the ethical model which John calls his readers to implement in the contemporary era as a sign of what will ultimately prevail (1.5-6; 11.3-13; 13.10; 20.4-6). With this I am in agreement with Richard Bauckham. For the present, in the face of the massive power structures presently in place, it appears futile. There is no doubt that John is saying that until the end of the age the present power structures will survive. But as a lighthouse points the way to the safety of a harbour so the alternative way of suffering love points to a more holistic way of structuring life that always will attract a remnant and ultimately will abide in the coming new order of creation, when God will be God. It is to be modelled today as a sign of what will be.

In addition, what is striking about the Apocalypse is that despite the call to be an alternative community to the idolatries of the time, John never advocates that the remnant retreat into sectarian isolation. Instead the communities that confess to follow the Lamb are to stand firm in non-violent resistance to the gods and power structures of the age. They may pay a price for a while; but they are not to give up on the peoples, tribes and nations who are a vital part of the created order. Even worship, as Richard Bauckham points out, so prominent in the Apocalypse, is not conceived as a pietistic retreat.[41] It is the source of energy

---

40   See especially Christopher Rowland, *Revelation, Epworth Commentaries* (London: Epworth Press, 1993), pp.31–53.

41   Richard Bauckham, *The Theology of the Book of Revelation*, p.161.

to resist the idolatries of the civic culture. In a time when Christendom is in a rapid process of disestablishment, the message of the Apocalypse warning the early Christian assemblies not to retreat from *critical* engagement and critiques of the current power structures can be a fruitful model for the faith community today. The call to a counter-cultural witness is a constant testimony to the reality that God's purposes are not complete until evil is abolished and the nations are gathered into his kingdom.[42] But it is lonely witness. Until the parousia there will not be substantive change. This is not a call to triumphalism.

For the past two decades in the institution where I teach, every second year I have taught a course on the Apocalypse. In most instances, after the first few weeks, there are students who are disappointed that I am unable to assure them that we are living in the final days before the parousia. Setting aside the observation that most humans are self-centred enough to believe that they live in the most important time in human history, the question of the truth of the prophecy of the book cannot be avoided. We have noted in this chapter that the prophet John has Christ state seven times that he is coming soon.[43] Even if the reference in Revelation 1.1 to 'what must take place soon' is to the defeat of Babylon and the exaltation of the bride of Christ (the new Jerusalem),[44] a clear expectation that the end is near is evident to any reader. Yet, the final evaluation of any literary work must be carried out in an appropriate context. Within the parameters of Judaism the prophetic word is always to a community urging it to make an immediate appropriate response to the crisis at hand, as well as providing a wider framework with respect to who is ultimately in charge in the future. John's visions of the end are imaginative construals of how God will finally exercise his rule over the creation.[45] Needless to say such an understanding of the portrayals of the final Day of the Lord explodes any suggestion that the Apocalypse is a code or time clock of how future events in history will unfold. Rather, as it was for the original readers, it is a reminder to the readers concerning who will be the defeated and who will be the victors. Good and evil is sometimes difficult to sort out. But ultimately evil is self-destructive and will destroy those who enter into a Faustian bargain with it. Deep down John was warning his first-century readers that structures of power that appear relatively benign may be pervaded with evil. Things can change very quickly. We need to see reality from a different perspective. In the much larger theatre – that of the divine perspective – it is only a brief period before the powers of this age will become ashes and dust and will be replaced by a vastly different order.

42   Richard Bauckham, *The Theology of the Book of Revelation*, p.162.
43   See Chapter 6, footnote 21.
44   Marko Jauhiainen, 'The Climax of John's Prophecy', p.117.
45   Richard Bauckham, *God Will Be All in All: The Eschatology of Jürgen Moltmann* (Minneapolis: Fortress Press, 2001), p.147.

Universal Sovereignty Not Universal Salvation

Our conclusion that in the new creation, for John, God's sovereignty will be universal may raise the question in some minds that this is a version of universal salvation. In some sense John's vision can be construed as a version of the ancient idea of ἀποκατάστασις 'restoration of all things' (cf. Acts 3:21 and some of the fathers of the church). We have designated it as 'eschatological covenantal restitution'. In it the writer presents his understanding of the final reconciliation between God and all things found in other places in the New Testament.[46] But this is a far cry of claiming this is a divine pronouncement of what is actually going to happen. As Jürgen Moltmann has noted, such things are quickly dismissed and even believers come to think that we need not be serious about the implications since we cannot alter them anyway![47]

John's firmly held belief, anchored in the prophetic texts of Hebrew scripture, was that God would visit his punishing wrath against the nations. He had no brief for their deviant idolatries so evident in his lifetime. They will receive their just deserts at the Day of the Lord (14.9-12, 17-20; 19.20-21; 20.11-15). There would be no escape. The haunting account of the vast judgment in Revelation 20.11-15 is entirely given over to the punishment of those who did not acknowledge the enthronement of the Lamb. This does not sound like universal salvation. In his imaginative construal of the new creation the emphasis is on the radical renovation of the old order. We are given a glimpse of what it will be when God is fully recognized as sovereign. The old nations will be no more. Those remainder of the nations not subject to the Last Judgment will be sublimated into the renewed covenant with the nations. They will join the faithful remnant in having access to the new Jerusalem. There are paraenetic references as to who will and will not be in the holy city (21.8, 27; 22.15). But as far as we can determine, these function as a present warning that apostates to the faith will have no place in the renewed order. The prophet John is no universalist in the sense it is generally understood today. His emphasis is that when the kingdom comes God is all in all and his sovereignty is complete. But there are many in this age who will not inherit its benefits. Even more significant, a presence in that new world is contingent on present actions.

Perhaps it is not far from the truth if we describe the prophet John as a Christian-Jewish teacher who views reality in a strong binary fashion. As one whose literary work rests at the end of the canon of the New Testament, theologically, he is also very close to the centre of Matthew, the first book of the Christian canon. Among the many well-travelled passages in Matthew is his famous parable on the Great Judgment (25.31-46). Those who are welcomed and commended on the last day are those who behaved compassionately

---

46   Cf. Eph. 1.19-23; 3.9-12.
47   Jürgen Moltmann, *The Coming of God: Christian Eschatology* (trans. Margaret Kohl, Minneapolis: Fortress Press, 1996), p.239.

toward those who brought the good news of the gospel and saw the Christ in 'the little ones' in their community. But the ones rejected are those who failed to receive the emissaries of the Messiah or showed the mercy to their needy fellow disciples. This is exactly the theological position that John takes with respect to the problems he encounters in the seven churches of Asia. As with the church at Ephesus (Rev. 2:4) John perceives that many of his readers have lost their first love by becoming infatuated with the debased civic culture of the time. That is an old story. In the wider biblical context it began very early in Genesis 2–3. As a devout prophet of the people of God of 'these last days', John argues strongly that his readers recover their strong allegiance to the way of Christ's suffering love that they once demonstrated (Rev. 2:5). The people of God must always be a contrast-society. The prophet John is remembered for many things. But his call for the people of God to mediate the face of Christ in the life of their local assemblies will be his abiding legacy.

CONCLUSION

Our study began with recognizing that a major problem in the interpretation of Revelation continues to exist. It centres on the strong tension between contrasting accounts of the destruction and ingathering of the nations at the end of the age. What did the prophet John believe was about to take place? After all the plagues and carnage appearing in full view throughout the narrative, does the return of paradise and the tree of life at the end signal a coming restitution of a full relationship between the Creator and the total created order? Will the destruction of the nations, save the faithful people of God, be the necessary precursor to the ultimate expression of the triumph of the Kingdom of God? Or will the nations ultimately recognize the futility of their rebellion against the Creator and come to acknowledge his sovereign power?

Much is at stake with reference to the resolution of this theological question. Christianity is a global religion. Yet, especially in the West, we are living in an increasingly pluralistic society where there are massive interactions between peoples of all nations. A central theme of the canonical writings cherished in Christianity is that the people of God are the inheritors of the promises first given to Abraham and his offspring. Mediated through Christ these promises nourish the conviction that the nations will find their true fulfilment in the triumph of the Kingdom of God. Since the Apocalypse is the text which concludes the biblical story, it is vital that some clarity emerge among interpreters on what it has to say on the destiny of the nations. Will only the faithful people of God of this age gain the blessings of the new creation? Or will God's kingdom ultimately encompass a wider constituency?

In this monograph I have not attempted to address in detail the current cultural ramifications of this issue. I have worked on the more restrictive task of assessing what the key writing in question (Revelation) has to say on the matter of the destiny of the nations. I have concluded that on this issue Revelation does have a coherent message. The narrative does assert that all nations will finally come to acknowledge the sovereignty of the God of Abraham, Moses and Jesus. Moreover the narrative has its own special way of setting out this position. This can be stated succinctly. The gospel of the kingdom will continue to be proclaimed to a rebellious creation that, by and large, refuses to change its self-serving goals. Indeed, aside from the contrast-society of the people of God, the leaders of the nations will steer a course of increasing opposition to the kingdom. The Apocalypse claims that at some point a divine theophany, featuring the parousia of Christ, will occur. Emerging after the ensuing judgment will be a new order. It will feature a renewal of covenantal commitments. The vindicated people of God will be the centre of the restored creation (the new Jerusalem) as the appropriate inheritors of God's covenantal blessings. The people and tribes who sublimated themselves to Christ at the parousia will become participants in a renewed covenant with the nations.

I have labelled this theological position embedded in the Apocalypse as 'eschatological covenantal restitution'. A surprising and pleasing outcome of this project is that the eschatology of Revelation represents a strong continuity (albeit clothed in Christian-Jewish concepts) with the eschatological vision of the exilic and early post-exilic prophets. On its terms this brings the biblical story to fulfilment.

An additional significant conclusion is that, with reference to the destiny of the nations, this is only a small crater within the larger crater of the total argument of the Apocalypse. The central purpose of the Apocalypse was to alert the accommodationists in the churches of Asia to the dangers of close involvement with Roman civic culture. They were in grave danger of forfeiting their places in the kingdom. Through the death, burial and resurrection of Christ the kingdom was inaugurated. Through the power of the suffering love of Christ in their community-witness, the churches were supposed to continue to engage in kingdom work as they waited for God to bring it to completion with the coming of the new Jerusalem. The author perceives that many in this circuit of small assemblies have gone off course. As well as a word of encouragement, this is a stern tract urging them to get back on the right track.

This reading of Revelation raises several issues for contemporary students of the book. First, it presumes that the ideal reader knows what it means to be part of a contrast-society wherein the dominant culture regards many of his or her basic values as illegitimate. This reader, like those in the Apocalypse, may well cry out 'O Sovereign Lord, how long?' (6:10). Second, as with many scored in the churches of Asia there is a tendency to turn one's eyes away from the task at hand and accommodate to the fleeting cultural concerns of the day. N. T. Wright speaks of a situation of children innocently splashing each other in a sheltered pool by the shore while, unnoticed, a tidal wave gathers nearby.[1] That is precisely how John views his role as a spokesperson to the churches. The series of divine warnings culminating in the parousia is under way. The people of God are to harness the energy gained from this esoteric knowledge for appropriate preparation for what is coming. The alternative is to be drowned through accommodation with the banalities of contemporary civic culture.

Finally, it would be a mistake to leave this reading of Revelation with the impression that the book is steeped in pessimism. On the contrary, the prophet maintains a positive attitude toward the created order. What existed in the beginning will return in the fully redeemed new creation. It will be different, but it will be better than before. The divine order present in heaven will be on

---

1   Nicholas Thomas Wright, 'A Scripture-formed Communion? Possibilities and Prophets after Lambeth, ACC, and General Convention', *Journal of Anglican Studies* 7(2), p.167.

earth. Properly construed, our daily labour in the present is not in vain. It only awaits its fulfilment in the new order. Perhaps this is why this most esoteric of writings within the canon continues to fascinate as well as arouse fear.

BIBLIOGRAPHY

Aune, D. E., *Revelation 1-5* (Word Biblical Commentary, 52a; Dallas: Word Books, 1997).

—— *Revelation 6-16* (Word Biblical Commentary, 52b; Nashville: T. Nelson, 1998).

—— *Revelation 17-22* (Word Biblical Commentary, 52c; Nashville: T. Nelson, 1998).

Aus, R., 'The Relevance of Isaiah 66:7 to Revelation 12 and 2 Thessalonians 1', *Zeitschrift für die neutestamentliche Wissenschaft und die Kunde der älteren Kirche* 67 (1976), pp.252-68.

—— 'God's Plan and God's Power: Isaiah 66 and the Restraining Factors of 2 Thessalonians 2:6-7', *Journal of Biblical Literature* 96 (1977), pp.537-53.

—— 'Paul's Travel Plans to Spain and the "Full Number of the Gentiles" of Romans 11: 25', *Novum Testamentum* 21 (1979), pp.232-62.

Barker, M., *The Revelation of Jesus Christ: Which God Gave to Him to Show to His Servants What Must Soon Take Place (Revelation 1.1)* (Edinburgh: T&T Clark, 2000).

Barr, D. L., 'Waiting for the End that Never Comes', in Moyise, S. (ed.), *Studies in the Book of Revelation* (Edinburgh: T&T Clark, 2001), pp.101-12.

—— 'The Story John Told: Reading Revelation for Its Plot', in Barr, D. (ed.), *Reading the Book of Revelation: A Resource for Students* (Resources for Biblical Study, 44; Atlanta: Society of Biblical Literature, 2003), pp.11-24.

—— *The Reality of Apocalypse: Rhetoric and Politics in the Book of Revelation* (Atlanta: Society of Biblical Literature, 2006).

Bauckham, R., *Jude, 2 Peter* (Word Biblical Commentary, 50; Waco: Word Books, 1983).

—— *The Climax of Prophecy: Studies on the Book of Revelation* (Edinburgh: T&T Clark, 1993).

—— *The Theology of the Book of Revelation* (New Testament Theology; New York: Cambridge University Press, 1993).

Bauckham, R. (ed.), *God Will be All in All: The Eschatology of Jürgen Moltmann* (Minneapolis: Fortress Press, 2001).

Bauckham, R., and T. Hart, *Hope against Hope: Christian Eschatology at the Turn of the Millennium* (Grand Rapids: Eerdmans, 1999).

Bauer, W., Arndt, W. F., Gingrich, F. W., and Danker, F. W., *Greek-English Lexicon of the New Testament and Other Early Christian Literature* (Chicago: University of Chicago Press, 3rd edn, 2001).

Beagley, A. J., *The 'Sitz im Leben' of the Apocalypse with Particular Reference to the Role of the Church's Enemies* (New York: De Gruyter, 1987).

Beale, G. K., *The Book of Revelation* (New International Greek Testament Commentary; Grand Rapids: Eerdmans, 1999).

——— *The Temple and the Church's Mission: A Biblical Theology of the Indwelling Place of God* (New Studies in Biblical Theology, 17; Downer's Grove: Apollos, 2004).

——— 'Review Article: J. W. Mealy, After the Thousand Years', *Evangelical Quarterly* 66 (1994), pp.229–49.

Beasley-Murray, G. R., *The Book of Revelation* (New Century Bible Commentary; Grand Rapids: Eerdmans, rev. edn, 1981).

Begg, C. T., 'The Peoples and the Worship of Yahweh in the Book of Isaiah', in Graham, Marrs, and McKenzie (eds.), *Worship and the Hebrew Bible: Essays in Honour of John T. Willis* (Festchrift John T. Willis; Sheffield: Sheffield Academic Press, 1999), pp.35–55.

Biguzzi, G., 'Ephesus, Its Artemision, Its Temple to the Flavian Emperors, and Idolatry in Revelation', *Novum Testamentum* 40 (1998), pp.276–90.

——— 'Is the Babylon of Revelation Rome or Jerusalem?', *Biblica* 87 (2006), pp.371–86.

Blenkinsopp, J., *Isaiah 56–66: A New Translation with Introduction and Commentary* (The Anchor Bible, 19B; New York: Doubleday, 2003).

Bøe, S., *Gog and Magog: Ezekiel 38–39 as Pre-Text for Revelation 19,17–21 and 20,7–10* (Tübingen: Mohr Siebeck, 2001).

Boismard, M. É., 'Notes sur l'apocalypse', *Revue Biblique* 59 (1952), pp.161–72.

Borgen, P., 'Polemic in the Book of Revelation', in Evans and Hagner (ed.), *Anti-Semitism and Early Christianity: Issues of Polemic and Faith* (Minneapolis: Fortress, 1993), pp.199–211.

Boring, M. E., 'Revelation 19-21: End Without Closure', *Princeton Seminary Bulletin*, 15 suppl. (1994), pp.56–84.

——— *Revelation* (Interpretation; Louisville: John Knox Press, 1989).

——— 'The Theology of Revelation: The Lord Our God the Almighty Reigns', *Interpretation* 40 (1986), pp.257–69.

Boxall, I., '"For Paul" or "For Cephas?": The Book of Revelation and Early Asian Christianity', in Rowland and Fletcher-Lewis (eds.), *Understanding, Studying, and Reading: New Testament Essays in Honour of John Ashton* (Festchrift John Ashton; Journal for the Study of the New Testament Suppl., 153; Sheffield: Sheffield Academic Press, 1998), pp.198–218.

——— 'The Many Faces of Babylon the Great: *Wirkungsgeschichte* and the Interpretation of Revelation', in Moyise (ed.), *Studies in the Book of Revelation* 17 (Edinburgh: T&T Clark, 2001), pp.51–68.

——— *The Revelation of Saint John* (Black's New Testament Commentaries, 18; New York: Continuum, 2006).

Brown, S., 'The Hour of Trial (Rev 3:10)', *Journal of Biblical Literature* 85 (1966), pp.308–14.

Buchanan, G. W., *The Book of Revelation: Its Introduction and Prophecy* (Eugene, Oregon: Wipf and Stock, 2005).

Caird, G. B., *A Commentary on the Revelation of St. John the Divine* (Harper's New Testament Commentaries; New York: Harper and Row, 1966).

Carey, F. (ed.), *The Apocalypse and Shape of Things to Come* (Toronto: University of Toronto Press, 1999).

Charlesworth, J. H. (ed.), *The Old Testament Pseudepigrapha* (2 vols; Garden City: Doubleday & Co., 1985).

Childs, B., *Isaiah* (Old Testament Library; Louisville: Westminster John Knox Press, 2001).

Collins, J. J., 'Sibylline Oracles', in Charlesworth, J. H. (ed.), *The Old Testament Pseudepigrapha*, vol. 1 (Garden City: Doubleday, 1983), pp.317–472.

Corsini, E., *The Apocalypse: The Perennial Revelation of Jesus Christ* (trans. and ed. F. J. Maloney; Good News Studies, 5; Wilmington: 1983).

Court, J. M., *The Book of Revelation and The Johannine Apocalyptic Tradition* (Journal for the Study of the New Testament, Suppl, 190; Sheffield: Sheffield Academic Press, 2000).

Dahl, N. A., 'Nations in the New Testament', in Glasswell, M. E. and Fasholé-Luke, E. W. (eds.), *New Testament Christianity for Africa and the world: Essays in Honour of Harry Sawyerr* (Festschrift H. Sawyerr; London: SPCK, 1974), pp.54–68.

Daniélou, J., *A History of Early Christian Doctrine Before the Council of Nicaea, Vol. 1: The Theology of Jewish Christianity* (Baker, J. A., ed. and trans.; London: Darton, Longman and Todd, 1964).

Davies, G., 'The Destiny of the Nations in the Book of Isaiah', in Vermeylen, J. (ed.), *The Book of Isaiah – Le livre d'Isaïe: les oracles et leurs relecteures: Unité et complexité de l'ouvrage* (Bibliotheca Ephemeridum Theologicarum Lovaniensium, 81; Louvain: Leuven University Press, 1989), pp.93–120.

Day, J., 'The Origin of *Armageddon*: Revelation 16:16 An Interpretation of Zechariah 12:11', in Porter, S. E., Joyce, P., Orton, D. E. (eds.), *Crossing the Boundaries: Essays in Biblical Interpretation in Honour of Michael D. Goulder* (Festschrift M. D. Goulder; Biblical Interpretation, 8; Leiden: Brill, 1994), pp.315–26.

Decock, P. B., 'The Scriptures in the Book of Revelation', *Neotestamentica* 33 (1999), pp.373–410.

Deutsch, C., 'Transformation of Symbols: The New Jerusalem in Rev 21:1–22:5', *Zeitschrift für die neutestamentliche Wissenschaft und die Kunde der älteren Kirche* 78 (1987), pp.106–26.

Donaldson, T. L., 'Proselytes or "Righteous Gentiles?" The Status of Gentiles in Eschatological Pilgrimage Patterns of Thought', *Journal for the Study of the Pseudepigrapha* 7 (1990), pp.3–27.

Draper J. A., 'The Heavenly Feast of Tabernacles: Revelation 7.1-17', *Journal for the Study of the New Testament* 19 (1983), pp.133–47.

Duff, P. B., *Who Rides the Beast? Prophetic Rivalry and the Rhetoric of Crisis in the Churches of the Apocalypse* (Oxford: Oxford University Press, 2001).

Eliot, T. S., 'East Coker 4', in Eliot, T.S., *Four Quartets*

Eller, V., 'How the Kings of the Earth Land in the New Jerusalem: "The World" in the Book of Revelation', *Katallagete* 5 (1975), pp.21–7.

Ellis, E., *The Old Testament in Early Christianity: Canon and Interpretation in the Light of Modern Research* (Wissenschaftliche Untersuchungen zum Neuen Testament, 2; Grand Rapids: Baker, 1991).

Farrer, A., *The Revelation of St. John the Divine* (Oxford: Clarendon, 1964).

Fekkes, J., '"His Bride Has Prepared Herself": Revelation 19–21 and Isaian Nuptial Imagery', *Journal of Biblical Literature* 109 (1990), pp.269–87.

———— *Isaiah and Prophetic Traditions in the Book of Revelation: Visionary Antecedents and Their Develoments* (Journal for the Study of the Old Testament, Suppl, 93; Sheffield: JSOT Press, 1994).

Feuillet, A., *The Apocalypse* (trans. T. E. Crane; Staten Island: Alba House, 1965).

Fiorenza, E. S., *Priester für Gott: Studien zum Herrschafts- und Priestermotiv in der Apokalypse* (Neutestamentliche Abhandlungen, 7; Münster: Aschendorff, 1972).

———— 'Redemption as Liberation: Rev 1:5f and 5:9f', *Catholic Biblical Quarterly* 36 (1974), pp.220–32.

———— 'The Composition and Structure of the Book of Revelation', *Catholic Biblical Quarterly* 39 (1977), pp.344–66.

———— *The Book of Revelation: Justice and Judgment* (Philadelphia: Fortress, 1985).

———— *Revelation: Vision of a Just World* (Proclamation Commentaries; Minneapolis: Augsburg Fortress, 1991).

Friesen, S. J., *Imperial Cults and the Apocalypse of John: Reading Revelation in the Ruins* (New York: Oxford University Press, 2001).

Garrow, A. J. P., *Revelation* (New Testament Readings; New York: Routledge, 1997).

Giblin, C. H., 'Structural and Thematic Correlations in the Theology of Revelation 16–22', *Biblica* 55 (1974), pp.487–504.

———— 'Recapitulation and the Literary Coherence of John's Apocalypse', *Catholic Biblical Quarterly* 56 (1994), pp.81–95.

———— 'The Millennium (Rev 20:4-6) as Heaven', *New Testament Studies* 45 (1999), pp.553–70.

Giesen, H., *Die Offenbarung des Johannes* (Regensburger Neues Testament; Regensburg: F. Pustet, 1997).

Goulder, M. D., 'The Phasing of the Future', in Hartman, L., *et al.* (eds.), *Texts and Contexts: Biblical Texts in Their Textual and Situational Contexts: Essays in Honor of Lars Hartman* (Festschrift L. Hartman; Oslo: Boston: Scandinavian University Press, 1995), pp.391–408.

Gundry, R. H., 'The New Jerusalem: People as Place, Not Place for People', *Novum Testamentum* 29 (1987), pp.254–64.

Hanson, P. D., *The Dawn of Apocalyptic: The Historical and Sociological Roots of Jewish Apocalyptic Eschatology* (Philadelphia: Fortress, rev. edn, 1979).

Harland, P. A., 'Honouring the Emperor or Assailing the Beast: Participation in Civic Life Among Associations (Jewish, Christian, and Others) in Asia Minor and the Apocalypse of John', *Journal for the Study of the New Testament* 77 (2000), pp.99–121.

Harrelson, W., 'The Celebration of the Feast of Booths According to Zech XIV 16–21', in Neusner, J. (ed.), *Religions in Antiquity: Essays in Memory of Erwin Ramsdell Goodenough* (Studies in the History of Religions, 14; Leiden: Brill, 1968), pp.88–96.

Harrington, W. J., 'Positive Eschaton Only: Revelation and Universal Salvation', *Proceedings of the Irish Biblical Association* 15 (1992), pp.42–59.

————— *Revelation* (Sacra Pagina, 16; Collegeville: Liturgical Press, 1993).

Harrisville, R. A., *The Concept of Newness in the New Testament* (Minneapolis: Augsburg, 1960).

Hartman, L., *Prophecy Interpreted: The Formation of Some Jewish Apocalyptic Texts and of the Eschatological Discourse Mark 13 par.* (Coniectanea biblica New Testament Series, 1; Lund: Gleerup, 1966).

Heil, J. P., 'The Fifth Seal (Rev 6,9-11) as a Key to the Book of Revelation', *Biblica* 74 (1993), pp.220–43.

Hemer, C. J., *The Letters to the Seven Churches of Asia in Their Local Setting* (Journal for the Study of the New Testament Suppl. Series, 11; Sheffield: JSOT, 1986).

Herms, R., *An Apocalypse For the Church and For the World: The Narrative Function of Universal Language in the Book of Revelation* (Beihefte zur Zeitschrift für die neutestamentliche Wissenschaft und die Kunde älteren Kirche, 143; New York: De Gruyter, 2006).

Hill, C. E., 'Paul's Understanding of Christ's Kingdom in 1 Corinthians 15:20-28', *Novum Testamentum* 30 (1988), pp.297–320.

Hirschberg, P., *Das eschatologische Israel: Untersuchungen zum Gottesvolksverständnis der Johannesoffenbarung* (Wissenschaftliche Monographien zum Alten und Neuen Testament, 84; Neukirchen-Vluyn: Neukirchener, 1999).

Janse, S., *'You are my son:' The Reception History of Psalm 2 in Early Judaism and the Early Church* (Contributions to Biblical Exegesis and Theology; Leuven: Peeters, 2009).

Jauhiainen, M., 'The Measuring of the Sanctuary Reconsidered (Rev 11,1-2)', *Biblica* 83 (2002), pp.507–26.

————— 'ΑΠΟΚΑΛΥΨΙΣ ΙΗΣΟΥ ΧΡΙΣΤΟΥ (Rev 1:1): The Climax of John's Prophecy', *Tyndale Bulletin* 54 (2003), pp.99–117.

————— 'Recapitulation and Chronological Progression in John's Apocalypse: Towards a New Testament Perspective', *New Testament Studies* 49 (2003), pp.543–59.

————— 'The OT Background to Armageddon (Rev 16:16) Revisited', *Novum Testamentum* 47 (2005), pp.380–93.

————— *The Use of Zechariah in Revelation* (Wissenschaftliche Untersuchungen zum Neuen Testament, 199; Tübingen: Mohr Siebeck, 2005).

Kiddle, M., *The Revelation of St. John* (The Moffatt New Testament
        Commentary; repr., London: Hodder and Stoughton, 1963).
Klauck, H. J., "'Do They Never Come Back?" Nero Redivivus and the
        Apocalypse of John', *Catholic Biblical Quarterly* 63 (2001), pp.683–98.
Kraft, H., *Die Offenbarung des Johannes* (Handbuch zum Neuen Testament,
        16a; Tübingen: Mohr, 1974).
Kraybill, J. N., *Imperial Cult and Commerce in John's Apocalypse* (Journal for the
        Study of the New Testament Suppl., 132; Sheffield: Sheffield Academic
        Press, 1996).
Lambrecht, J., 'A Structuration of Revelation 4,1–22,5', in Lambrecht, J. (ed.),
        L'Apocalypse johannique et l'apocalyptique dans le Nouveau Testament
        (Bibliotheca Ephemeridum Theologicarum Lovaniensium, 53;
        Leuven: Leuven University Press, 1980), pp.77–104.
———— 'The People of God in the Book of Revelation', in *Collected Studies on
        Pauline Literature and on the Book of Revelation* (Analecta biblica,
        147; Rome: Editrice Pontificio Istituto biblico, 2001), pp.379–94.
———— 'Final Judgments and Ultimate Blessings: The Climactic Visions of
        Revelation 20,11–21,8', *Biblica* 81 (2000), pp.362–85.
Lawrence, D. H., *Apocalypse* (New York: Viking, 1932).
Lee, P., *The New Jerusalem in the Book of Revelation: A Study of Revelation 21–
        22 in Light of Its Background in Jewish Tradition* (Wissenschaftliche
        Untersuchungen zum Neuen Testament, 129; Tübingen: Mohr
        Siebeck, 2001).
Leske, A. M., 'The Influence of Isaiah on Christology in Matthew and Luke', in
        Farmer, W. R. (ed.), *Crisis in Christology: Essays in Quest of Resolution*
        (Great Modern Debates, 3; Livonia: Dove, 1995), pp.241–70.
Lindars, B., *New Testament Apologetic: The Doctrinal Significance of the Old
        Testament Quotations* (London: SCM Press, 1961).
Lohmeyer, E., *Die Offenbarung des Johannes* (Handbuch zum Neuen
        Testament, 16; Tübingen: Mohr, 2nd edn, 1953).
Lohse, E., *Die Offenbarung des Johannes* (Das Neue Testament Deutsch, 11;
        Göttingen: Vandenhoeck & Ruprecht, 15 edn, 1993).
Lust, J., 'The Order of the Final Events in Revelation and Ezekiel', in
        Lambrecht, J. (ed.), *L'Apocalypse johannique et l'apocalyptique dans
        le Nouveau Testament* (Bibliotheca Ephemeridum Theologicarum
        Lovaniensium, 53; Louvain: Leuven University Press, 1980), pp.179–
        83.
Mathewson, D., 'The Destiny of the Nations in Revelation 21:1–22:5: A
        Reconsideration', *Tyndale Bulletin*, 53 (2002), pp.121–42.
———— 'A New Heaven and A New Earth: The Meaning and Function of the
        Old Testament in Revelation 21.1–22.5', *Journal for the Study of the
        New Testament* 238 (2003).
Mayo, P. L., *Those Who Call Themselves Jews: The Church and Judaism in the
        Apocalypse in John* (Princeton Theological Monograph Series, 60;
        Eugene: Pickwick Publications, 2006).

McKelvey, R. J., *The New Temple: The Church in the New Testament* (Oxford Theological Monographs; London: Oxford University Press, 1969).

—— *The Millennium and the Book of Revelation* (Cambridge: Lutterworth, 1999).

McNicol, A. J., 'Revelation 11:1-14 and the Structure of the Apocalypse', *Restoration Quarterly* 22 (1979), pp.193–202.

—— *Jesus' Directions for the Future: A Source and Redaction-History Study of the Use of the Eschatological Traditions in Paul and the Synoptic Accounts of Jesus' Last Eschatological Discourse* (Macon, GA: Mercer, 1996).

—— 'Rebuilding the House of David: The Function of the Benedictus in Luke-Acts', *Restoration Quarterly* 40 (1998), pp.25–38

—— 'The Lure of Millennium 2000: What Is at Stake for the Christian Believer?', *Christian Studies* 17 (1999), pp.5–15

—— 'All Things New', *Christian Studies* 21 (2005–2006), pp.39–55.

Mealy, J. Webb, *After the Thousand Years: Resurrection and Judgment in Revelation 20* (Journal for the Study of the New Testament Suppl., 70; Sheffield: Sheffield Academic Press, 1992).

Miller, K. E., 'The Nuptial Eschatology of Revelation 19–22', *Catholic Biblical Quarterly* 60 (1998), pp.301–18.

Moltmann, J., *The Coming of God: Christian Eschatology* (trans. M. Kohl; Minneapolis: Fortress Press, 1996).

Montefiore, C. G., and H. Loewe, *A Rabbinic Anthology: Selected and Arranged with Comments and Introductions* (New York: Schocken Books, 1974).

Moyise, S., 'The Old Testament in the Book of Revelation' (Journal for the Study of the New Testament Suppl., 115; Sheffield: Sheffield Academic Press, 1995).

—— 'Does the Lion Lie Down With the Lamb', in Moyise, S., *Studies in the Book of Revelation* (Edinburgh: T&T Clark, 2001), pp.181–94.

Müller, U. B., *Die Offenbarung des Johannes* (Ökumenischer Taschenbuchkommentar zum Neuen Testament, 19; Gütersloh: Gerd Mohn, 1984).

Nickelsburg, G. W. E., *1 Enoch 1: A Commentary on the Book of 1 Enoch: Chapters 1–36; 81–108* (Hermeneia; Minneapolis: Fortress Press, 2001).

Nock, A. D., *Conversion: The Old and The New in Religion from Alexander the Great to Augustine of Hippo* (New York: Oxford University Press, 1963 (paper)).

Oberweis, M., 'Erwägungen zur apokalyptischen Ortsbezeichnung "Harmagedon"', *Biblica* 76 (1995), pp.305–24.

Osborne, C. D., 'Alexander Campbell and the Text of Revelation 19:13', *Restoration Quarterly* 25 (1982), pp.129–38.

Osborne, G. R., *Revelation* (Baker Exegetical Commentary on the New Testament; Grand Rapids: Baker Academic, 2002).

Pattemore, S., *The People of God in the Apocalypse: Discourse, Structure, and Exegesis* (Society for New Testament Studies monograph series, 128; New York: Cambridge University Press, 2004).

Pilgrim, W. E., 'Universalism in the Apocalypse', *Word & World* 9 (1989), pp.235–43.

Prigent, P., *Commentary on the Apocalypse of St. John* (trans. W. Pradels; Tübingen: Mohr Siebeck, 2004).

Puthussery, J., *Days of Man and God's Day: An Exegitico-Theological Study of* ἡμέρα *[hemera] in the Book of Revelation* (Rome: Pontificia Università Gregoriana, 2002).

Rahlfs, A., Alfred, O. G., and Hanhart, R. (ed.), *Septuaginta* (New York: American Bible Society, rev. edn., 2006).

Resseguie, J. L., *The Revelation of John: A Narrative Commentary* (Grand Rapids: Baker Academic, 2009).

Rissi, M., *The Future of the World: An Exegetical Study of Revelation 19.11–22.15* (*Studies in Biblical Theology*, 23; Naperville: A.R. Allenson, 1972).

Roloff, J., *The Revelation of John: A Continental Commentary* (Minneapolis: Fortress Press, 1st Fortress Press ed., 1993).

Rowland, C., *The Open Heaven: A Study of Apocalyptic in Judaism and Early Christianity* (London: SPCK, 1982).

——— *Revelation* (London: Epworth Press, 1993).

——— 'The Lamb and the Beast, the Sheep and the Goats: "The Mystery of Salvation" in Revelation', in Bockmuehl, M. N. A., and M. B. Thompson, *Vision for the Church: Studies in Early Christian Ecclesiology in Honor of J. P. M. Sweet* (Festschrift J. P. M. Sweet; Edinburgh: T&T Clark, 1997), pp.181–91.

——— 'The Apocalypse in History: The Place of the Book of Revelation in Christian Theology and Life', in Rowland, C. and Barton, J., *Apocalyptic in History and Tradition* (Journal for the Study of the Pseudepigrapha Suppl., 43; New York: Sheffield Academic Press, 2002), pp.151–71.

Royalty, R. M., *The Streets of Heaven: The Ideology of Wealth in the Apocalypse of John* (Macon: Mercer University Press, 1998).

Ruiz, J.-P., *Ezekiel in the Apocalypse: The Transformation of Prophetic Language in Revelation 16,17–19,10* (European University Studies; Frankfurt: Peter Lang, 1989).

Schnabel, E. J., 'Die Nationen in der Johannesoffenbarung', in Holthaus, H. S., and Müller, K. W. (eds), *Die Mission der Theologie: Festschrift für Hans Kasdorf zum 70* (Festschrift for Hans Kasdorf, Bonn: Verlag für Kultur und Wissenschaft, 1998), pp.59–76.

——— 'John and the Future of the Nations', *Bulletin for Biblical Research* 12 (2002), pp.243–71.

——— 'Israel, The People of God, and The Nations', *Journal of the Evangelical Theological Society* 45 (2002), pp.35–57.

Scott, J. M., 'Paul's *Imago Mundi* and Scripture', in Ådna, J., *et al.* (eds.), *Evangelium, Schriftauslesung, Kirche: Festschrift für Peter Stuhlmacher zum 65* (Festschrift Peter Stuhlmacher; Göttingen: Vandenhoeck & Ruprecht, 1997), pp.366–81.

Segal, A. F., *Paul the Convert: The Apostolate and Apostasy of Saul the Pharisee* (New Haven: Yale University Press, 1990).

Smalley, S. S., *The Revelation of John: A Commentary on the Greek Text of the Apocalypse* (Downers Grove: InterVarsity Press, 2005).

Smith, D., 'The Millennial Reign of Jesus Christ: Some Observations on Rev 20:1-10', *Restoration Quarterly* 16 (1973), pp.219–30.

Sparks, H. F. D. (ed.), *The Apocryphal Old Testament* (New York: Oxford University Press, 1984).

Stuhlmacher, P., 'Eschatology and Hope in Paul', *Evangelical Quarterly* 72 (2000), pp.315–33.

Sweet, J. P. M., *Revelation* (Westminster Commentaries; Philadelphia: Westminster Press, 1979).

———— 'Maintaining the Testimony of Jesus: The Suffering of Christians in the Revelation of John', in Styler, G. M., Horbury, W., and McNeil, B., *Suffering and Martyrdom in the New Testament: Studies Presented to G. M. Styler by the Cambridge New Testament Seminar* (London: Cambridge University Press, 1981), pp.101–17.

———— 'Revelation', in Hooker, M. D., Barclay, J. M. G., and Sweet, J. P. M., *Early Christian Thought in its Jewish Context* (New York: Cambridge University Press, 1996), pp.160–73.

Thompson, L. L., *The Book of Revelation: Apocalypse and Empire* (New York, Oxford University Press, 1990).

———— 'Lamentation for Christ as a Hero: Revelation 1:7', *Journal of Biblical Literature* 119 (2000), pp.683–703.

Trebilco, P., *The Early Christians in Ephesus from Paul to Ignatius* (Grand Rapids: Eerdmans, 2007).

———— *Jewish Communities in Asia Minor* (Monograph Series/Society for New Testament Studies, 65; New York: Cambridge University Press, 1991).

Trudinger, P., 'Some Observations Concerning the Text of the Old Testament in the Book of Revelation', *Journal of Theological Studies* 17 (1966), pp.82–8.

Ulfgard, H., *Feast and Future: Revelation 7:9-17 and the Feast of Tabernacles* (Coniectanea biblica; New Testament Series 22; Stockholm: Almqvist & Wiksell, 1989).

Vanhoye, A., 'L'utilisation du Livre d'Ézéchiel dans l'Apocalypse', *Biblica* 43 (1962), pp.436–76.

Vanni, U., *La struttura letteraria dell' Apocalisse* (Aloisiana, 8a; Brescia: Morcelliana, 2nd edn, 1980).

———— 'L'Apocalypse johannique: état de la question', in Lambrecht, J. (ed.), *L'Apocalypse johannique et l'apocalyptique dans le Nouveau Testament* (Bibliotheca Ephemeridum Theologicarum Lovaniensium, 53; Louvain: Leuven University Press, 1980), pp.21–46.

Vogelgesang, J. M., 'The Interpretation of Ezekiel in the Book of Revelation' (Unpublished doctoral dissertation, Harvard University, 1985).

Wainwright, A. W., *Mysterious Apocalypse: Interpreting the Book of Revelation* (Nashville: Abingdon Press, 1993).

Walker, P. W. E., *Jesus and the Holy City: New Testament Perspectives on Jerusalem* (Grand Rapids: Eerdmans, 1996).

Westermann, C., *Isaiah 40–66: A Commentary* (Old Testament Library; Philadelphia, Westminster Press, 1969).

Whybray, R. N., *Isaiah 40–66* (New Century Bible Commentary; repr., Grand Rapids: Eerdmans, 1981).

Van Winkle, D. W., 'The Relationship of the Nations to Yahweh and to Israel in Isaiah XL–LV', *Vetus Testamentum* 35 (1985), pp.446–58.

Wise, M., Abegg, M. Jr., and Cook, E., *The Dead Sea Scrolls: A New Translation* (San Francisco: HarperSanFrancisco, rev. edn, 2005).

Witherington, B., *Revelation* (New Cambridge Bible Commentary; New York; Cambridge University Press, 2003).

Wright, C. J. H., *The Mission of God: Unlocking the Bible's Grand Narrative* (Downers Grove: InterVarsity Press, 2006).

Wright, N. T., 'A Scripture Formed Communion? Possibilities and Prospects After Lambeth, ACC, and General Convention', *Journal of Anglican Studies* 7 (2009), pp.163–82.

Yarbro Collins, A., *The Combat Myth in The Book of Revelation* (Harvard Dissertations in Religion, 9; Missoula: Scholar's Press, 1976).

———— 'The Political Perspective of the Revelation to John', *Journal of Biblical Literature* 96 (1977), pp.241–56.

———— *Crisis and Catharsis: The Power of the Apocalypse* (Philadelphia: Westminster Press, 1984).

———— 'Insiders and Outsiders in the Book of Revelation and Its Social Context', in Neusner J., Ernest, S. F., and McCracken-Flesher, C., *'To See Ourselves As Others See Us': Christians, Jews, and 'Others' in Late Antiquity* (Chico: Scholars Press, 1985), pp.187–218.

———— 'Vilification and Self-Definition in the Book of Revelation', *Harvard Theological Review* 79 (1986), pp.308–20.

———— 'Eschatology in the Book of Revelation', *Ex Auditu* 6 (1990), pp.63–72.

———— 'The "Son of Man" Tradition and The Book of Revelation', in Charlesworth, J. H., *Messiah* (Minneapolis: Fortress Press, 1992), pp.536–68.

INDEX OF PRIMARY SOURCES

INDEX OF AUTHORS AND CHARACTERS

9 780567 026088